FROM
VINES
TO
WINES

A Garden Way Publishing Book

Storey Communications, Inc.
Pownal, Vermont 05261

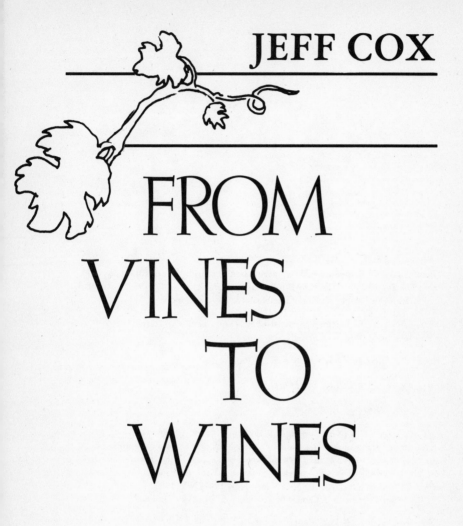

JEFF COX

FROM
VINES
TO
WINES

*The Complete Guide
to Growing Grapes
and Making
Your Own Wine*

with illustrations by the author

Grateful acknowledgment is made for permission to reprint the excerpt on page 125 from *The Supper of the Lamb*, by Robert Capon. Copyright © 1967, 1969 by Robert F. Capon, Reprinted by permission of Doubleday & Company, Inc.

This quality paperback edition is published by arrangement with Harper & Row, Publishers, Inc. All rights reserved.

Printed in the United States by R.R. Donnelley

First paperback printing, December 1988.

Cover illustration by Joyce Kitchell

Designed by Ruth Bornschlegel

Library of Congress Cataloging in Publication Data
Cox, Jeff, 1940-
  From vines to wines.

  Originally published: New York: Harper & Row, 1985.
  "Garden Way Publishing book."
  Bibliography: p.
  Includes index.
  1. Viticulture. 2. Wine and wine making.
3. Viticulture - United States. I. Title.
SB389.C69 1989   641.8'72   88-44898 ISBN 0-88266-528-6 (pbk.)

For Marilyn, with whom I've shared the wine

CONTENTS

ACKNOWLEDGMENTS *xiv*
INTRODUCTION *xv*
MAKING WINE *xix*
   Glossary xix

PART 1—SELECTING THE VINES

THE CONTEXT OF WINEMAKING *2*
   The Purpose of This Book 2
   The Secrets of Good Wine 2
THE ORIGIN OF CLASSIC WINE
GRAPES *5*
   The Spirit of Grape Growers 7
A SELF-EDUCATION IN WINE *8*
   Recognizing Wine Quality 8
   Courses on Wine Appreciation 11
CLIMATE AND GEOGRAPHY AFFECT
CHOICE OF WINES *12*
   Vinifera on the Eastern Seaboard 12
   Problems in the South 13
   *Vinifera Finds a Real Home on the West
   Coast 14*
   Vinifera in Mid-America 14
   Breeding Resistant Vinifera 14
IDENTIFYING WINE-GROWING AREAS *15*
   The Value of Regional Designations 16
   BATF Viticultural Areas 16
   Your Single Most Important Decision 17

vii

PART 2—GROWING THE GRAPES

CHOOSING A VINEYARD SIZE AND SITE *30*
  How Much Wine to Make 30
  Spacing the Vines 33
FINDING A FAVORABLE SITE *34*
  Sloping Land Is Best 35
  Spacing Vines on Level Land 36
VINEYARD SOIL AND GRAPE
QUALITY *38*
  Types of Soil 38
  Direct Soil Effects on Grapes 38
  Testing Soil pH 39
  Determining Your Soil Type 40
  Problem Soils 40
  Effects of Soil and Stone Color 41
  Soil Depth Should Be at Least 30 Inches 41
  Vineyard Drainage 42
  Rootstocks for Problem Soils 42
  Preparing the Soil for Grapes 43
  Prepare Soil in the Autumn 44
OTHER SITE CONSIDERATIONS *45*
  Consider the Prevailing Winds 45
GRAPE TRELLISES *45*
  Types of Trellis Systems 46
  Choosing the Trellis System 50
HARDWARE FOR CONSTRUCTING A
TRELLIS *50*
CONSTRUCTION DIRECTIONS *54*
ORDERING AND PLANTING
GRAPESTOCK *55*
  Handling Bare-Rooted Stock 56
  Trimming the Roots 56
  Planting the Grapevines 56

Cutting Back Tops of Newly Planted Vines
58
Watering and Protecting Young Vines 59
Nick Off First Flower Clusters 60
MANAGING VINEYARD ROWS AND
AISLES 60
Cover Crops for the Beds 60
To Mulch or Not to Mulch 60
Handling Weeds in the Beds 62
Techniques for Managing Aisles 62
Stone Mulches 63
Irrigation 64
HOW TO PRUNE GRAPES 65
How a Vine Grows 65
Relationship of Training System to
Pruning 69
Pruning in the First Two Years 69
Multiple Trunks 72
Allow No Fruit in First Years 72
Recognizing Winterkill 73
When to Prune 75
Recognizing Fruitful Buds 75
Pruning Prevents Overcropping 77
Leaving Spurs or Canes 77
GRAPEVINE PRUNING ILLUSTRATED 78
BALANCED PRUNING 78
Pruning Muscadines 79
Bleeding 87
Delayed and Double Pruning 88
Managing Vine Vigor 91
CLUSTER THINNING 91
Timing of Cluster Thinning 92
Positioning Cluster-Thinned Shoots 93
Other Benefits of Cluster Thinning 93
TRELLIS SYSTEMS ILLUSTRATED 95
Which Clusters to Remove 104

PEST CONTROL STRATEGIES *104*
   Naturally Occurring Controls 104
   Applied Biological Controls 105
   Feeding Repellents 105
   Traps 106
   Dormant Sprays 106
   Botanical Insecticides 107
   Chemical Insecticides 107
FERTILIZATION *108*
   Making Compost 109
HANDLING GRAPE CROPS *111*
DETERMINING RIPENESS *112*
   Brix 113
   Titratable Acidity 116
   pH 119
   Brix:TA Ratio Measures Ripeness 120
   A Better Measure of Ripeness 120
HARVESTING BOTRYTIZED GRAPES *121*
WEATHER AS A HARVEST FACTOR *122*
HARVESTING *123*

PART 3—MAKING THE WINE

MAKING CONSISTENTLY FINE WINE *126*
   Crush Immediately After Picking 127
   Decisions of the First Few Days 128
   The First Day's Procedures 130
   Cleanliness 133
   Primary Fermentation Vats 134
   Adding Sulfite to the Must 136
   Adding Sugar to Musts 142
   Adjusting Acidity 145
   Acid Adjustment and pH 147
   Harvest Day Summary 149
   Pressing Whites for Fermentation 150

Adding the Yeast 152
Types of Wine Yeast 154
A Stuck Fermentation 156
THE PRIMARY FERMENTATION *156*
Punching Down the Cap 156
Fermentation Temperature 157
Skin Contact Time 158
Malolactic Fermentation 160
Pressing the Must 161
THE SECONDARY FERMENTATION *162*
New Wine 163
Using Airlocks 163
Cleaning the Carboys 166
The First Racking 167
Cold Stabilization 168
Using Barrels 169
Preparing New Barrels 173
Reusing Barrels 174
Oak Chips in Glass Containers 175
The Importance of Oak 178
FURTHER RACKING AND AGING *178*
How Much Aging? 179
Storage Conditions for Aging 180
WINE DISORDERS *181*
FILTERING *182*
FINING *182*
BLENDING *183*
FINAL MEASUREMENTS BEFORE
BOTTLING *185*
Alcohol Content of Finished Wine 185
Testing Residual Sugar 186
BOTTLING *187*
Pre-cleaning Bottles 188
Cleaning Again at Bottling 188
Filling the Bottles 189
CORKING *190*

LABELING *192*
  Attaching the Labels 193
  Foil Capsules 194
CELLARING THE WINE *195*
  Cellar Temperature 195
  An Insulated Storage Area 196
WINE ACCOUTERMENTS *197*
  Corkscrews 198
  Wineglasses 199
SENSORY EVALUATION OF WINE *200*
  Clarity and Color 200
  Looking at the Rim 201
  Legs 202
  The "Nose" of the Wine 202
  Retronasal Aroma 203
  Educating the Nose 204
  The Taste of Wine 204
  Body 205

APPENDIX 1. The Home Winemaker's
Record Book *206*

APPENDIX 2. For More Information *208*

APPENDIX 3. Sources of Supplies *212*

APPENDIX 4. Sources for Grapevines *215*

APPENDIX 5. Grape Pests and Their Controls *217*

INDEX *241*

TABLES

1. An Overview xxv

2. Recommended Wine Grapes for U.S. Regions 20

3. Heat Summations at Various Towns and Cities in California by Climatic Regions 24

4. Vinifera in California—Habits and Regional Suitability 26

5. Superior Wine Grapes for California's Hot Regions 27

6. Index of Sunlight Received by Various Slopes (45° North Latitude) 37

7. Index of Sunlight Received at Various Latitudes (15° Slope) 37

8. Soil Types in Wine Regions of France 39

9. Growing Seasons (Number of days of average daily temperature over 50°) 48

10. Trellising Systems 51

11. Balanced Pruning for Mature Vines in Eastern and Northern Regions 81

12. Leaf Deficiency Symptoms of Four Trace Elements Important to Quality Grape Production 110

13. Hydrometer Readings/Brix Equivalents 115

14. Correcting Hydrometer Readings Based on Temperature 116

15. pH Effect on Sulfite Additions 141

16. Figuring Sugar Adjustment 144

17. Optimum Serving Temperatures 204

ACKNOWLEDGMENTS

The role of the author of a book like this one is to be a synthesizer and coordinator of knowledge—most of it developed or discovered by other people. I would like to thank the following people personally. Thanks to:

Jack Hudders for getting me interested in wine. Bob Teufel and Mike Michaelson for fomenting that interest over the years. Tom Jacobsen and Tim White who kindly offered to read the manuscript with their experts' eyes.

Friends in the Napa Valley who took me in: Gary Wu of Beaulieu Vineyards; the Kresge family; Peter Forni; the Triglia family; Arnold Tudal; Theo Rosenbrand of Sterling Vineyards; Mike Grgich; Michaela Rodena of Domaine Chandon; Alan Tobey of Wine & The People in Berkeley; Tom Cottrell and Bob Pool of the New York State Agricultural Experiment Station in Geneva; Dr. Konstantin Frank; all the folks at Sakonnet Vineyards in Rhode Island; Dr. John McGrew of the USDA.

And most special thanks to Marilyn, Shane, and Chandra Cox for their support through this project.

J.C.

INTRODUCTION

Fresh grapes and wine are perhaps the most luscious foods we mortals encounter during our sojourn here. That's a big part of the unique affinity between grapevines and men. That's how the vine has tempted us to take it down from the wild trees, to protect it and work with it, so we can have its fruit at will.

The vine repays our care with lavish benefits. For three days after drinking a bottle of 1969 Chambertin, the sun and blood of Burgundy drenched my aura. The memory of the taste lingered.

Vines splurge on flavor in those very climates that are most hospitable to man—northern California and southern France, for two outstanding examples. They seem to be luring us, coaxing us to stay and care for them, suggesting how good life can be in those places.

Not every climate ripens the most flavorful grape varieties so slowly and perfectly. But every place has its potential: in the colder regions east of Paris, the vignerons take their high-acid, low-sugar underripe grapes and transform them into Champagne. In Austria, where hard freezes hit clusters still hanging on the vine, they make *Eiswein.*

In the United States, we've hardly begun to explore our viticultural potential. Who knows what vinous treasures could flow from the south-facing shale and slate hills of eastern Pennsylvania or the fertile, stony soils of the Ozarks? Our Lafites and Romanée-Contis lie undiscovered beneath forests and fences. Or, possibly, they're waiting for us in our backyards.

In wine-growing areas, you see the vines stretched on their trellises, their arms wide open in welcome, or, in a different light, resembling rows of crucified men. In winter, there are the bones: black and dead-looking trunks waiting to be reborn in new green flesh. The new growth creates the grapes, develops them over a summer, and finishes its work with sugar and perfume. The ripe grapes can be transformed into wine (a totally transcendent change that couldn't be predicted from knowledge of grape juice alone), but only with the intervention of man or woman to perform the practical rituals of winemaking. Wine is truly a collaboration of vine and man, and the consummation of their affinity.

Winemaking meshes a person into some of the cycles of the vine. But to also grow the vines and control all aspects of the process that leads to wine enmeshes one completely. And once so enmeshed, reattaches the grower to the earth. Thank goodness one doesn't have to sit in za-zen on Mount Shasta to achieve this state. It can be as simple as having a relationship with a bunch of grapes.

The relationship, however, requires the sensitivity and affection that characterize a human affair. Whether man or woman, you are the husband of the grapes. You have to understand your partner's needs and fulfill them. If you've chosen a variety suited to your soil and climate, taste and temperament, the result can express both your property and yourself in subtly telling ways for those who can appreciate the expression. A bottle of homemade wine speaks of your industry before it's opened and the quality of your taste after it's opened.

I'm writing this introduction on a hillside overlooking the Napa Valley above St. Helena. Below me are thousands of acres of vines, just showing the new shoots of spring. Here's a whole valley exploring this relationship, a whole society devoted to perfecting the wine.

Good wine flows freely here. The people are friendly and open. Is it possible to be this close to nature in its grandest forms, both cultivated and natural, and not be that way?

Flowers, especially roses, go with wine, and as I walked the neighborhood streets in St. Helena this morning, roses toppled in bushels from treetops and hedges. Before lunch, I hiked a trail into the mountains. This is Napa at its most verdant. Columbine, iris, wild geranium, and so many other flowers cultivated with such care at home grow wild here, in little patches in the woods, or showing among the wild oats. A single iris by the trail, delft-blue and bone white. A group of carmine columbines scattered down a slope of lichen-covered dead wood.

Because of the quality of the wines made here, people pay attention to their food. I know of no other small town in America that has as many world-class restaurants as St. Helena.

There's something wonderfully human and concise about this town's dedication to flowers, wine, and food. The community makes its own wines and profits from it. There's a *reason* for this place. It's where the good stuff comes from.

I'm in the Napa Valley looking for correspondences to my vineyard at home in Berks County, Pennsylvania, and for clues to the attitude the best growers and home winemakers in this wine-drenched culture carry to their task. The attitude, I'm finding, is one of love for the grapevine: one must really care for them as well as take care of them.

"Handle the vine like a man; the wine like a woman," Ed Lino told me. Ed, now eighty-one, retired from the sea to grow grapes in Calistoga in the northernmost part of the valley over thirty-five years ago. He talks to his vines. "Now little feller," he says to a spindly Chardonnay, "you'll have to do better than this." He pours another glass of Portagee Pete, as he calls the pink wine he makes from lightly crushed Cabernet Sauvignon, and declares, "The best wine to drink in the whole world is homemade wine." He should know. And I agree with him.

I'm writing this book to express my enthusiasm for the backyard vineyard and basement bodega. It's ritual: doing the same things year after year at their prescribed times. It's myth: some spirit of the wine definitely joins the party if the door's not closed. It's sacrament: the miraculous transformation of rainwater into grape juice into wine gets my blessing.

The way is open for anyone with the proper conditions to discover this great plant-man collaboration. Wine is the child of the marriage of man and grapevine. So go forth, be fruitful, make wine from your own grapes. You may have as good a time as I did the night Marilyn was in the barrel, crushing grapes with her feet, and I was on the outside, encouraging her with wine and kisses.

St. Helena, California
April 23, 1983

MAKING WINE

Before we strike off into grape-growing and winemaking territory, an orientation will be helpful. First, I've included a glossary of all terms you will encounter. Second, Table 1 (page xxv) shows the major steps in the process, describes their purpose, and lists special equipment you may need to carry them out. All these steps are explained in detail in the text.

GLOSSARY

AGING Storing wine to allow it to mature.

AIRLOCK A device that allows gas to escape from a vessel containing wine, but allows no air to enter.

AISLE The vineyard floor between the rows of grapes.

ANTHER The male structure of the grape flower. It produces pollen.

ARM Permanent wood on a grapevine from which fruiting wood is grown. The french term is *cordon*.

AROMA The smell of the grape variety used in a given wine. If there's no varietal smell but there is a grapey smell, the aroma is termed *vinous*.

BASAL Toward the base, or older wood on a grapevine.

BED The prepared soil in which the grapevines are planted.

BERRY An individual grape.

BLEEDING Sap that runs from a cut-off cane, arm, or trunk.

BLENDING Mixing two or more wines together for adjustment of flavor, acid, or aromas in the finished wine.

BODY A certain fullness of feel in the mouth imparted by a well-made wine; a full structure in the taste of a wine.

BOTRYTIS A mold that attacks grapes. Under special climatic conditions, it can concentrate the flavors and sugars and produce superior wine.

BOUQUET The smells in wine that develop in the bottle and are especially detectable when a wine is well aged.

BRIX A measure of the percentage of sugar in the grape juice or must.

CALCAREOUS A soil with a lot of calcium compounds in it, such as limestone or chalk soils. Preferred in Europe for fine wine grapes.

CALYPTRA The covering of the emerging grape flower.

CANE One-year-old grape wood.

CAP Residue of skins and grape particles that float on the must during primary fermentation.

CAPSULE A foil covering for the top of a wine bottle.

CARBOY Five-gallon bottles, such as used for bottled-water coolers. Used extensively in the home winemaking process.

CHAPTALIZING Adding sugar to crushed grapes of deficient natural sugar.

CLUSTER Flowering and, subsequently, fruiting organ of the grapevine.

CLUSTER THINNING Technique whereby some clusters are removed early in the year from emerging shoots. Used to control the size of the eventual crop and to hasten ripening.

COLD STABILIZATION Chilling wine to about 30° F so that potassium bitartrate crystals precipitate out.

COMPOST Partially rotted vegetable matter used as a fertilizer and soil conditioner under the vines.

CORDON See ARM.

COROLLA Individual grape flower before it blossoms.

COVER CROP Plants grown to cover the soil.

CRUSHING Crushing and smashing fresh grapes to a pulp to release the juice prior to fermentation.

CULTIVAR Horticultural shorthand for "cultivated variety." Same meaning as *variety;* i.e., a kind or type of grape vine, such as Cabernet Sauvignon.

CULTIVATION Weeding, fertilizing, and otherwise caring for a plant. Usually means only weeding.

DRY WINE A wine in which almost all the sugar, or all the sugar, has been fermented to alcohol. Any wine with less than a half percent sugar.

ENOLOGY The science of winemaking.

FERTILIZATION Adding plant nutrients to the soil.

FILTERING Running wine through a filter to remove sediment or yeast.

FINING The process of adding a substance to a wine to clear it of cloudiness.

FRUITFUL BUD A bud that will grow into a shoot with flowers and fruit on it.

FRUITING CANE A cane of one-year-old wood that has fruitful buds.

GRAFT To splice together two different grape woods.

HERBACEOUSNESS In wine tasting, a vegetable taste. In grape growing, herbaceous growth is green and succulent.

HUMUS Fully decayed organic matter that adds structure and nutrients to a soil.

HYDROMETER An instrument for measuring the specific gravity of liquid.

INTERNODE The portion of a shoot or cane between the nodes.

LATERAL SHOOT A shoot that develops from another shoot during the growing season. Usually trimmed off.

LEES Sediment in the fermenting or finished wine.

LEGS Rills of wine that form on the sides of a wineglass.

MALOLACTIC FERMENTATION A beneficial fermentation in wine caused by *Leuconostoc* bacteria. It changes malic acid to lactic acid, softening the taste. It may happen naturally, but is usually induced by the winemaker.

MULCH Any covering for bare soil, from black plastic to grass clippings or spoiled hay.

MUST A mixture of crushed grapes, juice, stems, skins. The term refers to this mixture from the time the grapes are crushed until the mixture is pressed.

NODE The lumpy, regularly spaced places on a cane or shoot from which leaves and fruit clusters form. Where the buds are.

OAKING Adding oak flavors to a wine by aging the wine in an oak barrel or soaking chips of oak in the wine.

OVERCROPPING Allowing too many fruit clusters to form, which will weaken the vine.

OXIDATION The combination of air with components of fresh juice or wine. Some oxidation is desirable in the early part of the fermentation, but oxidation is not desirable at all later in the process, as it causes browning and reduces wine quality.

PEDICEL The stem that attaches the grape berries to a cluster.

PEDUNCLE The stem that attaches the grape cluster to the shoot.

pH A measure of the *intensity* of acidity in a liquid, such as wine. It measures the concentration of hydrogen ions.

POMACE The solid waste left after the juice is pressed out of the must.

PRESSING Squeezing the juice or wine from a must with a grape press.

PRIMARY FERMENTATION The initial, rapid fermentation during which about the first two-thirds of the sugar in the must is converted by yeast to alcohol.

PRUNING Cutting off any portion of a grapevine. Usually refers to the cutting back of aerial parts in the late winter to control vine size, vigor, or crop.

PUNCHING DOWN Mixing the cap on a must down into the juice or fermenting wine. Done at least twice a day during the primary fermentation.

RACKING Siphoning wine from one container to another to separate the wine from the lees.

RESIDUAL SUGAR Sugar left in a wine after fermentation is finished.

RETRONASAL AROMA The smells of a wine that are detected when they enter the nasal cavity from the back; that is, they waft into the nose from behind the palate.

RIM The thin edge of wine in a tilted glass. The rim color is a measure of quality.

ROOTSTOCK Roots of a grape variety to which fruiting wood is grafted. Rootstocks are usually chosen for resistance to soil-borne diseases or pests, or because they grow well in certain soil types.

ROW A length of grapevines lined up in a row.

SCION Wood that's grafted to a rootstock, or to aerial parts of a growing vine.

SECONDARY FERMENTATION The slower fermentation, accomplished away from air, that reduces the sugar left after the primary fermentation to alcohol.

SHOOT The growing structure that emerges from buds on a grapevine. This summer's shoot will be next year's fruiting cane. Shoots are herbaceous and carry leaves, fruit clusters, and tendrils.

SPUR Fruiting canes pruned to five buds or less.

STEMMER-CRUSHER A machine that removes stems from clusters of grapes and crushes them to make a must.

STEMMING Removing stems from clusters of grapes before or after crushing.

STICKING A stoppage of fermentation before sugar is entirely converted to alcohol, usually due to yeast dying off from lack of nutrients or to chilling. Stuck fermentations can often be restarted.

STIGMA The female portion of a grape flower that accepts a pollen grain from the anther.

STOCK Vegetable material for planting, such as grape stock for planting in a vineyard.

SULFITING Adding potassium metabisulfite to a must to kill or stun unwanted yeasts. Wine yeasts are tolerant of the amounts of sulfite added to a must.

TANNIN A bitter substance contained primarily in grape stems. Tannin preserves long-lived wines, eventually decomposing when the wine reaches maturity.

TEINTURIER A grape variety used to add color to a wine.

TENDRIL A grape vine's anchoring growths. They arise from shoots and wind around trellis wires.

TITRATABLE ACIDITY A measure of the amount of total acid in a must or wine, expressed as its tartaric acid content.

TOPPING UP Adding a sound and similar wine to a vessel to fill it up, when the wine you have doesn't reach the top.

TRACE ELEMENTS Plant nutrients needed in very small amounts, but crucial to plant health nevertheless. Zinc, manganese, iron, and magnesium are examples.

TRAINING Tying and pruning vines to achieve a desired shape on a trellis.

TRELLIS A support for grape vines that maximizes the amount of sunlight the vines receive.

TRUNK The aerial part of the grapevine that emerges from the soil and gives rise to arms and their fruiting canes.

VARIETY Same as CULTIVAR.

VÉRAISON The point in a grape berry's development when it first begins to turn color during ripening.

VIGOR Intensity of a vine's growth.

VINIFY To ferment; i.e., to charge a solution containing sugar with yeast. The yeast then converts the sugar to alcohol and carbon dioxide gas.

VINTAGE There are several meanings. Vintage refers to the crop of any given year. It is sometimes used to refer to the crops of years of exceptionally fine quality, such as with Vintage Port or Vintage Champagne. Also refers in general to the harvest of grapes from a vineyard.

VITICULTURE The science of growing grapes.

YEAST One-celled plants that grow naturally on grape skins and convert sugar to alcohol. Yeast is the catalyst that changes grape juice to wine. Special strains of yeast are used in fine winemaking, and are available commercially.

Table 1 AN OVERVIEW

MAJOR STEPS	PRIMARY OBJECTIVE	SPECIAL EQUIPMENT
Selecting the grape variety	To find a grape that will produce wine to your taste, and that will ripen properly in your climate and on your soils	
Choosing a vineyard site	To find the place on your property that will get the optimum sun to the vines while minimizing frost dangers	
Preparing the soil	To prepare soil for grapes in advance. It should be dug deeply, and fertilized, if necessary, in order for young vines to make their best growth	The digging can be done by hand, but a backhoe will save your back
Constructing a trellis	To give grapes proper trellising to achieve maximum berry quality. Trellis type will depend on grape variety	Stakes, end posts, wire, and wire anchors

The above should be done prior to planting and is best completed the fall before new vines are planted.

Planting the vines	To give bare-rooted planting stock the best possible start	Pruning shears

MAJOR STEPS	PRIMARY OBJECTIVE	SPECIAL EQUIPMENT
Training to trellis	To develop a strong trunk and arms that support fruiting canes, and train them for optimum sun exposure on the trellis	

Training can take from two to four years, although three years is most common. There is little grape production during this time.

MAJOR STEPS	PRIMARY OBJECTIVE	SPECIAL EQUIPMENT
Cluster thinning*	To prevent overcropping and subsequent weakening of the vines, and to hasten ripening	
Controlling pests	To prevent diseases and pest damage	A sprayer
Harvesting ripe grapes	To pick the wine grapes at optimum levels of sugar, acid, and pH	A hydrometer, an acid test kit, and access to a pH meter
Crushing the grapes	To release juice, color, and flavor components in preparation for fermentation	A grape crusher is useful for large batches (over 50 gallons), but the crushing can be done by hand (or foot)
Adding sulfite	To stun or kill wild and unwanted yeasts in the crushed grape must	Potassium metabisulfite as powder or tablets

*Cluster thinning takes place in the spring, and harvest in late summer or fall.

MAJOR STEPS	PRIMARY OBJECTIVE	SPECIAL EQUIPMENT
Adding the yeast	To add yeast suited to your grapes and winemaking goals	Special wine yeasts
Primary fermentation†	To produce a rapid fermentation of the first two-thirds of the grape sugars within a week or so	A primary fermentation vat, open topped, such as a stainless steel 55-gallon drum
Pressing the grapes	To separate the wine from the skins, seeds, stems, and sediment. Pressing of white grapes is usually done before the primary fermentation	A grape press, fine-mesh plastic pressing bag, funnel, plastic hose, and vessels for the wine (see next step for types of vessels)
Secondary fermentation	To ferment the remaining grape sugar to alcohol over the next two or three months	Five-gallon glass carboys or oak barrel; airlocks
Racking	To remove the wine from the deposits of sediment in the bottom of the secondary fermentation vessels	An extra carboy; plastic siphon hose

†The primary and secondary fermentations and the first racking or two will take place from harvest through late fall or early winter.

Aging	To allow the young wine to settle down and begin to mature	A cool, dark storage area, not subject to wide temperature fluctuations

White wines need at least six months and red wines a year of aging between the end of the secondary fermentation and bottling. Several rackings will be done during this period.

MAJOR STEPS	PRIMARY OBJECTIVE	SPECIAL EQUIPMENT
Blending	To correct color, acidity, overly tannic wines, or to adjust oak flavors. Unless the blend will be better than any component wine, don't blend.	
Bottling	To get the wine into handy bottles for further storage and drinking.	Siphon hose, corks, hand corking machine; labels and foil capsules

After bottling, the wine can age toward peak maturity in your cellar. Again, storage conditions must be cool, dark and not subject to wide temperature changes. Most white wines will reach peak maturity in two or three years. Fine, tannic reds may take five or more years. Good but ordinary reds will reach their peak anywhere from a year to three years after bottling.

A Note to the Reader

The information about winemaking contained in this book is, naturally enough, subject to differences of opinion and interpretation. The author and publisher are not engaged in rendering legal, accounting or other professional services through the sale of this book. When expert assistance is required, the reader should seek the services of a competent professional.

PART 1

SELECTING
THE VINES

The right wine-grape variety
for you is the one that ripens
well in your area.

THE CONTEXT OF WINEMAKING

Being a home winemaker is a lot like being an amateur opera singer. Both activities entertain friends. When done badly, reaction can range from disgust to token tolerance. When done competently, reaction ranges from enjoyment to admiration for the performer. When done with excellence, the audience will stare in disbelief, rise to applaud, and demand more.

The Purpose of This Book

The purpose of this book is to bring the reader swiftly and surely to the goal of excellence. As I am a longtime grower and winemaker myself, be prepared to hear me say how I did it, but don't be tempted to follow. Rather digest the information you find here and proceed as you see fit. Handling a living being such as a grapevine calls for skill and attention to detail. So does making wine. Both, to achieve excellence, must be done artfully. As all artists know, what works for one doesn't necessarily work for the other. Same materials, same physical laws, but—*Voilà!*— here a Picasso, there a Van Gogh. There's no way to teach the art: that comes from within. But if your enthusiasm waxes strong enough, art will break through. I've met many artists of the grape in my travels. All shared one common trait: they were determined, no matter what, to do their very best. It's my hope that the material in this book will help readers do their very best with this delicate task of home winemaking.

The Secrets of Good Wine

There's a maxim among traveled wine drinkers that any wine tastes best in the region (and with the regional food) it comes from. If that's true, then homemade wines must taste best when drunk at home, so if you are making exceptional wine to begin with, it doesn't get any better than that. There are not many peak experiences available to us for the dollar or so our homemade wine costs. My personal peak experience came during a lunch a few years ago on a sweet, dry, sunny summer day. I knifed a ripe cheese made from our goat's milk and slathered it on chunks of bread fresh from the oven, bread made from grain I'd ground by hand that morning. It was washed down with a thick, oaky homemade Chancellor from that sumptuous year, 1976. All three foods are the product of predigestion by yeasts or bacteria. All three involve triple partners: goat, bacteria, and man; wheat, yeast, and man; grape, yeast, and man. Lunching in the center of such a maelstrom of interspecies cooperation and pregnant numerology, I never felt more at home nor more in the right place.

Auspicious years for mankind are often years of great excellence for wine, as the destinies of man and grape do seem forever interwined. The immensely great year of 1945 springs to mind. Man and grape collectively sighed in relief at the end of the Great War and went back to celebrating life with the finest vintage of the century.

"The secret of the wine is the grapes it's made from," says Bill Wagner, a longtime New York State winemaker whose Finger Lakes Chardonnays can give any white wine a run for its money. The winemaker's role is to protect and preserve the quality of good grapes right into the bottle. Jim Mitchell of Sakonnet Vineyards in Rhode Island, who does as good a job with French-American hybrid grapes as anyone, quotes these maxims:

1. The most important elements of great wine are first, the grape; second, the climate; third, the soil, and fourth—in that order—the skill of the winemaker.
2. The best wines are made as far north as that particular grape variety will grow.
3. To produce great wines, the vines must suffer, rather like athletes.

Pondering this last, Robert Weaver, professor of Viticulture and Enology at the University of California at Davis, says,

"One viticultural theory is that a struggling vine produces better wine than one that has better growing conditions. If this is true, the reason may be that the struggling vine has smaller berries than the vine growing under more favorable conditions. Thus there is more skin (which contains more pigments, flavor and tannins) per gallon of wine than when the grapes are larger."

The elements for great wine, then, are just the same for the home winemaker as for commercial wineries: the right grape variety in the right climate and soil achieves the right balance of sugar, acid, pH, and flavor components. When all these things come together, the results can be spectacular indeed. The world's foremost example is the sauterne produced at Château d'Yquem south of Bordeaux. Speaking of this wine—an incredibly luscious, sweet, long-lasting, golden drink fit for toasting the Second Coming—Emile Peynaud, the renowned French enologist, said, "If you could measure a taste, an odor, you would find a number value for Yquem that is ten times greater than for a white wine. There is an intensity, a concentration, a richness, a complexity of odor and flavor completely unique." Most wines can be imitated: "One can always copy them elsewhere," Peynaud says. "But Yquem is absolutely inimitable. We haven't even been able to imitate it in Sauternes."

Wherever the property, there is a variety of grape that will produce the most excellent wine possible. Your task, long before the first bottles come to life in your cellar, is to identify that vine, for, as Doug Knapp, president of the American Wine Society, says, "The grape *makes* the wine." Attempts to produce a rich Napa-style Cabernet in Minnesota may be doomed to failure, but perhaps that property could be the home of the finest *Kay Gray* in the world. So what if it's not Yquem? It's probably a lot better *Kay Gray* than they can produce in Sauternes.

THE ORIGIN OF CLASSIC WINE GRAPES

In order to find the perfect variety for you, it's valuable to look for a moment at the original home of *Vitis vinifera,* the classic wine grape, to see what its habits and needs are and evaluate its potential for your place. *V. vinifera* varieties have the potential to make the greatest wines. In areas where they don't ripen well or are otherwise hard to grow, hybrids of vinifera and American grapes (French-American hybrids) are often grown. American wine grape varieties by themselves can also be used.

THE EVOLUTION OF MODERN WINE GRAPES

Winemaking as we know it began with native European vines of the species *Vitis vinifera.*

Early explorers in the Americas found native North American grapes of the species *V. labrusca,* which seldom produced good wine.

Crosses between *V. vinifera* and *V. labrusca* were made both in North America and Europe to produce hybrids. Because most of this breeding work was done in France, many of these are called French-American hybrids. They were developed to combine the wine quality of vinifera with the superior disease and cold resistance of labrusca.

Today the finest wines are still made from *V. vinifera* varieties, but there are also excellent French-American hybrids that grow well in the eastern United States.

Interestingly, vinifera is native to the same area of southwestern Russia as the original Indo-European peoples, whose prehistoric migrations carried the Indo-European language and the vinifera grape to all parts of the ancient world. Some scientists say the original home was around the Caspian Sea, while legend and tradition favor ancient Armenia. The philologists have the last word, however. The ancient Indo-Europeans most likely came from an area southeast of Poland, and north of the Caspian Sea. The word sleuths know this because as the tribes migrated east to India, west to Greece, and north into Europe, they carried with them their language. They've discovered, for example, that there is a word for beech in Sanskrit, although no beech grows in India. It was obviously carried there by a people who came from a land where beech does grow. By closely examining words for flora and fauna in the modern Indo-European languages (current in all of Europe save for Finland, Hungary, and Turkey, and through much of the Middle East to India), they've located the original home in the place where that flora and fauna grow without cultivation. And it is precisely in this area that *V. vinifera* still grows wild. According to Maynard Amerine, a foremost wine scientist in the United States, "The fruit of wild vinifera is palatable and the wine is of a quality comparable to that made from present cultivars."

The vines grew wild in the trees. Incidentally, I know a farmer near Bordeaux who grows vines on his fruit trees to this day.

There's evidence of vine cultivation 6,000 years ago in the Near East, although there's no evidence of any cultivation west of Greece until 1000 B.C. The westward movement of the vine then followed the ancient Phoenician sea routes. By the time of Christ, the first vineyards were being established along the Moselle River in Germany. The westward movement continues: it was only in 1958 that *Vitis vinifera* traveled across the Pacific from California and was first introduced to the Philippines.

As vinifera moves, local growers tend to cross it with native vines. This happened in the eastern United States in the eighteenth and nineteenth centuries, producing some excellent hybrids. In the Caribbean and Venezuela, vinifera and native *V. caribea* vines have produced vigorous races of Criollas that suit that climate, opening a potential for a true grape culture.

Physical evidence of the migration of Indo-Europeans carrying their beloved grapes is supported by the philologists. In

India, the Sanskrit word for wine is *vena*. In Italy, *vino*. It acquired an intercalary *h* as it became *vinho* in Portugal. Up north it became *vin* in France, *wein* in Germany and *wine* in English. Although the words are different, they're obviously variations of the original Indo-European word for wine. What that word was, nobody knows.

There are many biblical references to vines. One of the most well known is found in Num. 13:23–24. "They came to the valley of Eshcol; there they cut off a vine branch with a cluster of grapes, which two men carried away on a pole, as well as pomegranates and figs. This place was called the valley of Eshcol after the clusters which the sons of Israel had cut there." *Eshcol* is the Hebrew word for "cluster." According to L. H. Bailey, the horticultural taxonomist, *"Syrian* is said to be the variety that the spies found in the land of promise. Clusters of 20 to 30 pounds are common to this coarse-growing kind, but its quality is so poor that it is now rarely grown." After forty years in the desert, I suppose the Israelites thought *Syrian* was just fine.

After thousands of years of history and migration, about 6,000 varieties of grapes are now grown on 22 million acres worldwide. Despite this welter of grapestock, you *can* find the variety suited to your taste and land.

The Spirit of Grape Growers

But before looking for the perfect grape to marry, be aware that you're entering into a human endeavor with a long history and a fine tradition of good humor. "The world of wine is united by a marvelous spirit of sharing and friendliness," says Bern Ramey in his book on the great wine grapes. And I remember what a grape grower said to me as I browsed the equipment shelves in The Compleat Winemaker in St. Helena, California. Without prompting, he offered this cheerful observation: "It's wonderful here. Everybody's involved in winemaking in one way or another. Nobody's jealous. Competitors share their knowledge, and they know how to have fun." Having fun is what this is all about.

A SELF-EDUCATION IN WINE

Winemaking is an immediate, year-to-year business. Finding the right vine, on the other hand, can take years—although if the vines are selected carefully, it's possible to find the ideal vine in the first try. Then you must establish the vineyard and wait several years before it bears the kind of crops needed to make wine. When your vineyard does produce good crops, be prepared for them. Find a local source of fresh wine grapes now and start making wine as soon as it's feasible. By the time the vineyard is producing, you'll know how to treat the grapes after they ripen as well as before. The testing and waiting time will be a lot more fun if wine is flowing in this interim.

Recognizing Wine Quality

Understand from the outset that there's no possibility of making a fine red Bordeaux unless you live there. Good California Cabernet will forever come only from California. The pursuit of quality will not necessarily be furthered by imitating any existing wine. What we're doing here is looking for unique wine of the highest quality.

To do that, it's necessary to recognize the quality in your glass. And so, I'm setting you a pleasant task, which can be dispensed with only if your palate is already well educated; that is, it's familiar with the aromas and taste of a great Rheingau, a great Mosel, a great Champagne, a superb Burgundy (from Burgundy, of course), a great Médoc, a great Graves, and the best that California and New York State have to offer. There are many other fine wines from other areas, but knowing the quality that's found in the best of the above leaves one in a position to recognize quality wherever it's met and to go for it in the vineyard. The discriminating palate is the critical palate, and it's sad to see someone wrinkle up his or her nose at a fine wine, not because it's bad, but because of the lack of education of that palate. Or worse, to be served a very ordinary wine with assur-

ances that it represents high quality. Wine marketers do it all the
time, but we excuse it as hype fed to a public that doesn't know
any better in order to boost sales. I'm sure I'm not the only wine
aficionado who laughs at the so-called wine experts, usually re-
plete with ascots, who sniff at you from the TV commercials and
assure you that in all their travels they have never tasted a wine
as good as whatever-they're-paid-to-sell. A good rule of thumb
is that one should stay away from any wine mass-marketed on the

---

A GRAPE VARIETY SAMPLER

You can become familiar with the taste of the classic *Vitis
vinifera* grape varieties by trying these several categories:

Cabernet Sauvignon
Red Bordeaux (Pauillac)
Napa and Sonoma Valley
Rioja from Spain
Northern Italian Cabernet   **RED**

Pinot Noir
Red Burgundy (but not Beaujolais)
California Coast

"Cuvée du Pinot" (Napa Valley sparkling wine)
French Champagne (with Chardonnay)

Chardonnay
California Coast
Champagne (with Pinot Noir)
Chablis (from France)
White Burgundy   **WHITE**
Meursault

Riesling
Rheingau "mit Prädikat"
Mosel
California Coast "Johannisberg Riesling"
An Eastern U.S. Riesling from Finger Lakes or
Pennsylvania

tube, which is by necessity mass-produced. Cheap, drinkable jug wines are to be had, and serve their purpose. But quality bears an inverse relationship to the size of the advertising budget. The task, then, is to invest in the refinement as well as the education of your palate, especially by looking for properly aged wines from the best years. It will do no good to buy a bottle of the finest Bordeaux at high cost if it comes from a dismal year. Rather, if you're going to spend on the best, consult a vintage chart to help make sure it's the best—that is, a first-growth from a good year with enough age to be at its peak. Fulfilling this latter qualification is difficult with California wines, since well-aged North Coast Cabernets are rare. Price a bottle of Beaulieu Vineyard 1974 Private Reserve Cabernet: three figures.

And here's a little secret California vintners are loath to reveal: California reds don't seem to age like fine French reds. Perhaps it's the intensity of the sun—no one knows. Great French reds are very much like flowers in their aging process. For years they are like buds—tightly closed, filled with promise. Slowly the tannins fall away, the flower opens, spilling its perfume and fruit. And then, its moment passes; it slowly fades into unpalatability. For my parents' fiftieth anniversary, I bought two bottles of 1926 Pichon Lalande, a very high class Pauillac. I decided to keep one, and gave them the other. My bottle had faded and wasn't worth drinking. Miraculously, theirs was glorious, like their marriage, which truly was golden. Once the bottle was opened, though, it faded within a half hour. Similarly, a rather wealthy friend who lives in New York City invited me to share a bottle of 1918 Haut-Brion with him. The treasure was intact, a veritable dowager empress of a wine, with full—if short-lived—powers. Like the woman in *Lost Horizon* who leaves Shangri-La and ages several hundred years in a few minutes, the wine died within a half hour. The last quarter of the bottle had to be poured out. With great French reds, ten to fifteen years of bottle age usually bring the wine to perfection, although exceptional vintages (like the 1918—another year that, like the 1945, saw the end of a terrible war) keep going for decades. The taste and smell of a properly aged Bordeaux (cedar, woodsmoke, antebellum New York City apartments) or Côte d'Or Burgundy (fields of wildflowers, bee propolis) is core curriculum for any educated palate. While California reds don't seem to age like the French, a good five or seven years of bottle age on big Cabernets, Petit Sirahs, Zinfandels, and the like do improve them greatly, and the final word on California aging isn't in. There's such a limited stock of well-cellared wine that it's impossible to be definitive on the subject. This will change as the developmental years of the 1970s recede into history.

Courses on Wine Appreciation

The cost of a self-education will run to several hundred dollars at least, but that's what it takes. There are also excellent wine education courses given in major cities, where knowledgeable people preselect wines for their quality. This route may cost less and take less time, and you'll be assured that the wines you're tasting are first-rate. The danger is that you may be unduly influenced in your taste by the teacher or others in the class —that is, you'll be more inclined to like what the "expert" likes. Self-education has this virtue: your favorite wines will really be *your* favorites. For in this final analysis, *liking* the wine makes all the difference. The uneducated person who likes sweet Italian pop wine is every bit as entitled to his opinion as the connoisseur is to his affection for Montrachet. One would hope, though, that education means refinement, and that taste will change with experience. For someone contemplating making fine wine at home, acquiring a love and knowledge of good wine is a prerequisite for success. Otherwise, one gets stuck in the trap of the dilettante and takes the scrawl of a monkey for high art.

The vine you eventually plant for wine will be determined by taste cultivated through sampling, and by your local climatic considerations. Viniferas, unfortunately, require rather special conditions to do their best, although they can be grown most anywhere. The French-American hybrids and American types do well through great chunks of the country, but their wines don't have the potential to transform themselves into the elixirs that are top-notch viniferas. I tiptoe through the last statement because a well-made French-American hybrid wine or even American grape wine will beat an ordinary vinifera, no problem. Just because vinifera has great potential in special, favored areas doesn't mean it will make the best possible wine on a given acre of soil. When it came time to choose a variety for my Pennsylvania vineyard, for instance, I chose a red French-American hybrid.

CLIMATE AND GEOGRAPHY AFFECT CHOICE OF WINES

After tasting your way through the recommendations made earlier, you'll probably be tempted to test some vinifera grapes. To me (and many, many others), they simply make the best-tasting wine. And you can probably succeed, especially if you're willing to take great pains, even, in the far north, to taking the vines down from their trellises and burying them over winter. But all this will avail you little if the berries don't ripen properly, or succumb to disease. If you're interested in vinifera, definitely include them in your group of test vines, just to see how they do. There are only a few *commercially* successful vinifera vineyards in the East, mostly because extra handwork and costs prevent decent profits. As a home viticulturalist and winemaker, however, the bottom line is the quality of the wine, unencumbered by the necessity for profit, and vinifera varieties may be for you.

Vinifera on the Eastern Seaboard

Because of the booming interest in vinifera plantings in the East, there are some spectacular success stories, such as the recent developments with Cabernet Sauvignon on the north fork of Long Island's eastern end, or the plantings made by growers in southeastern Pennsylvania.

The area from the Virginia coast north along Delaware,

through southern New Jersey and eastern Long Island, on to the coast of Rhode Island, along Narrangansett Bay, and out to Martha's Vineyard holds the greatest chance of success for commercial or home plantings of vinifera because of the winter warming effect of the Gulf Stream offshore. Many acres of Cabernet Sauvignon and other viniferas have recently been planted. Similarly, the eastern side of Lake Michigan and the Finger Lakes have good winter snow cover and temperatures moderated by the water. Proximity to a large body of water is a definite plus for the grape grower. The old farmer's saying that "grapes like to see water" is a recognition that the water is leveling out temperature highs and lows for the delicate grapes. But one old-timer explained that it was more that "when the grapes are planted so they see water to the south, the sunlight bounces off the water and up under the leaves, and that helps ripen them, dries them, and keeps the mold away."

Problems in the South

The South, from Norfolk to Miami and west to Texas, Oklahoma, and Kansas, is home to more species of grapevines than any other similar-sized region in the world. These wild grapes are seldom known for the quality of their fruit, but they are exquisitely suited to the climate, which can give vinifera a rough time. Much of the region is subject to warm winters with occasional cold blasts from the north. Vinifera tends to go weakly into those mild winters, not really prepared for the odd night when temperatures get down to 10° or 15° F. Buds swell during warm winter days, then freeze at night. Vinifera pumps sap early, and late freezes can split canes and trunks. Pests, mildews, molds, rots, and especially Pierce's disease (caused by a Rickettsia-like organism; it destroyed large plantings of vinifera along Alabama's Tombigbee River in the 1820s) all attack vinifera in the south. Most wild grapes in the Gulf States are resistant, and some are immune, suggesting that the area is the original home of Pierce's disease. Grafting vinifera to these rootstocks can prevent soil-borne problems, but not the disease itself, which attacks the aerial parts of the vine. It is the biggest problem with vinifera in the South. Yet, vintners from Tennessee to Georgia are plunging ahead with plantings of the classic wine grapes.

Vinifera Finds a Real Home on the West Coast

Californians, with their perfect climates, tend to snicker at these eastern attempts to grow vinifera, secure that no matter what easterners do, they'll never be able to rival the soils and the weather of the Golden State and the Pacific Northwest. And they're right.

Vinifera in Mid-America

In the most northern states, vinifera can be grown only with difficulty because of the intense cold. The Southwest, on the other hand, is blooming with new plantings of vinifera in the higher elevations. The Midwest shares many of the problems of the South, and the Rocky Mountain States support plantings at the lower elevations.

Breeding Resistant Vinifera

There is a development on the horizon that, if it lives up to its potential, could make vinifera as hardy and disease resistant as any Concord. And that's genetic engineering.

With conventional cross-breeding techniques, it takes from twenty to twenty-five years to come up with a marketable new grape variety. But with gene-splicing techniques, that time could be cut to a few years, or even months. The major push is tailoring the grape to the environment, rather than finding and developing the areas in which important varieties can be grown. An advance was made in sharing gene-splicing information when the United States finally started to participate in the Office of International Vines and Wines in 1982. This organization is a kind of global think tank on enologically-important grapes.

Research into wine grapes was heretofore hampered by the lingering effects of Prohibition. To this day, the USDA's research center in Beltsville, Maryland, is enjoined from studying wine grapes. The New York State Agricultural Testing Station at Geneva and the University of California at Davis, have carried forward the bulk of the research into new wine grapes, but now gene-splicing work at many stations, and pioneer-minded owners ("Each vineyard is actually a miniresearch station," says Lucie Morton, a Virginia wine consultant) are pushing wine grape research to the front. In fact, wine grapes are fast becoming the boom crop of U.S. agriculture. "We are finding that the grape is more adaptable than the old wine makers would have us believe," says Carole Meredith, a viticulturalist at UC-Davis. "There are lots of little niches."

IDENTIFYING WINE-GROWING AREAS

The French wine laws are the strictest in the world. The term "Controlled Appellation" means that the wine was grown in a specially delimited area that alone has the right to use the regional name. Examples of controlled appellation are "Bordeaux," meaning that the grapes are from anywhere within that large region; "Haut-Médoc," which means that the grapes were from the specific upper Médoc area of Bordeaux, and "St. Julien," meaning that the grapes were from that commune in the Haut-Médoc district of Bordeaux. The appellations, then, cut the pie finer and finer. America, too, is beginning to delimit viticultural areas by law, but in a different way. The process is under the control of the Treasury Department's Bureau of Alcohol, Tobacco and Firearms (three all-time favorite American amusements).

The Value of Regional Designations

The BATF designates special regions as "viticultural areas." Its regulations became mandatory on January 1, 1983. No wine label can now carry the designation "estate bottled" unless the winery is in an official area. And no label can carry a geographical designation unless that designation is a government-approved viticultural area. For instance, if you live in Polk Valley, California, you can't use that name on your commercial label until you get the BATF to designate Polk Valley an official area. That doesn't stop us home winemakers, but a look at the official viticultural areas is interesting because it gives us, at a glance, those areas where winemaking is in full flower, where there are commercial growers seeking the government's imprimatur, and where, of necessity, grapes for wine do well. You may even live in one of these areas, in which case your task of selecting a vine is greatly simplified by the fact that there will be commercial growers nearby who can share their experiences and save you a lot of trial-and-error learning. It's a good idea to visit local vintners—commercial or home-style—whether you're in a viticultural area or not.

BATF Viticultural Areas

The list on pages 18–19 shows the approved and proposed viticultural areas to date. You'll notice there's a Shenandoah Valley, California, and a Shenandoah Valley, Virginia. Growers in these places were in a long, difficult dispute with the BATF over which area would get the right to the name. The agency gave a slight nod to the East by ruling that California's Shenandoah Valley must be accompanied by the name of the state, while Virginia's can be just plain old Shenandoah Valley.

You'll also notice there are several multistate areas. One of the most interesting of these is the Ohio River valley, comprising parts of West Virginia, Kentucky, Ohio, Illinois, and Indiana. The designation was proposed and promoted by the Indiana Wine Grower's Guild and the Ohio Wine Producers' Association.

The Ohio River valley was once known as the "Rhein of America," before Prohibition wrecked viticulture in this country. The area runs from Cairo, Illinois, to just south of Wheeling, West Virginia, near the Pennsylvania border. It includes 30,000 square miles on both sides of the Ohio River, bounded by high ridge lines. There's a 175-day frost-free growing season and the prevailing winter winds are from the southwest. A distinctive "Ohio-type" rain pattern means that the weather is changeable and moist. Gray-brown podzol soils dominate the slopes and hilltops where grapes will be most at home. The character of the valley was created by glacial erosion, which means that ground rock flours are prevalent in the soil, supplying good mineral nutrition to the vines. The slopes create good air drainage so necessary in such a moist region, and there are warm microclimates that face south on these slopes, just as they do on the Rhein.

Your Single Most Important Decision

Identifying the grape that gives wine you like and which grows well and ripens its grapes consistently in your climate is perhaps the single most important decision you'll make in your quest for fine homemade wine. My decision to forgo vinifera in favor of planting fifteen French-American hybrids—thirteen Chancellor and two Colobel *teinturier* vines (the latter for color, in which Chancellor can be deficient in poor years)—was based on the fact that the best wine I've made to date was a 1976 Chancellor, and the best commercial French-American hybrid wine I've encountered was a 1979 Château Esperanza (Finger Lakes) Chancellor. I also know that while Chancellor can have some mildew problems, it grows well in Berks County, isn't prone to winter kill, has no undue problems with pests, and gives me a good gut feeling. There is no variety of vinifera with all those advantages.

OFFICIAL AMERICAN VITICULTURAL AREAS

Approved

CALIFORNIA

Carmel Valley
Cienega Valley
Chalone
Edna Valley
Green Valley (Solano County)
Guenoc Valley
Lime Kiln Valley
Livermore Valley
McDowell Valley
Napa Valley
Paicines
San Pasqual Valley
Santa Cruz Mountains
Santa Maria Valley
Shenandoah Valley
Sonoma Valley
Suisun Valley

MICHIGAN

Leelanau Peninsula
Fennville

MISSOURI

Augusta

NEW YORK

Finger Lakes
Hudson River Region

OHIO

Isle St. George
Loramie Creek

PENNSYLVANIA

Lancaster Valley

VIRGINIA

Rocky Knob

VIRGINIA—WEST VIRGINIA

Shenandoah Valley

Petitioned For

ARKANSAS

Altus
Arkansas Mountain
Ozark Mountains

CALIFORNIA

Alexander Valley
Anderson Valley
Arroyo Seco
Central Coast
Chalk Hill
Clarksburg
Clear Lake
Cole Ranch
Dry Creek Valley
El Dorado
Fiddletown
Green Valley (Sonoma County)

CALIFORNIA (cont.)

Howell Mountain
King City
Knights Valley
Lodi
Los Carneros
Madera
Mendocino
Merritt Island
Monterey
Murrieta
North Coast
Northern Sonoma
Pacheco Pass
Paso Robles
Potter Valley
Rancho California

Petitioned For *(continued)*

CALIFORNIA *(cont.)*
Russian River valley
San Benito
San Lucas
Santa Clara
Santa Ynez Valley
Sobre Vista Vineyard
Sonoma Mountain
Temecula
Willow Creek
York Mountain

MARYLAND
Catoctin
Lingamore
Maryland Cumberland Valley

MASSACHUSETTS
Martha's Vineyard

MICHIGAN
Lake Michigan Shore

MISSISSIPPI
Mississippi Delta

MISSOURI
Hermann

OHIO
Grand River valley

OREGON
Umpqua Valley
Willamette Valley

VIRGINIA
Monticello
North Fork of the Roanoke

WASHINGTON
Yakima Valley

WEST VIRGINIA
Kanawha River Valley

Multi-state

CENTRAL DELAWARE RIVER VALLEY
New Jersey,
Pennsylvania

OHIO RIVER VALLEY
West Virginia,
Kentucky,
Ohio,
Illinois,
Indiana

LAKE ERIE
Ohio,
Pennsylvania,
New York

SOUTHEASTERN NEW ENGLAND
Rhode Island,
Massachusetts,
Connecticut

COLUMBIA VALLEY
Washington,
Oregon

WALLA WALLA VALLEY
Washington,
Oregon

Table 2 RECOMMENDED WINE GRAPES FOR U.S. REGIONS

WHITE VINIFERA	RED VINIFERA	WHITE HYBRID	RED HYBRID	AMERICAN GRAPES
New York State: Finger Lakes and the Hudson River Region				
Chardonnay Riesling		Ravat 51 Cayuga Seyval Blanc	Chancellor Foch	Delaware
Southern New Jersey, Eastern Long Island and Coastal Rhode Island				
Chardonnay Riesling Sauvignon Blanc Gewürztraminer	Pinot Noir Cabernet Sauvignon Merlot	Seyval Blanc Vidal 256 Cayuga	Chancellor	
Northwestern Pennsylvania				
Riesling		Vidal 256 Ravat 51 Seyval Blanc	Chancellor Chelois de Chaunac Foch	
Southeastern Pennsylvania				
Chardonnay Riesling Gewürztraminer		Seyval Blanc Vidal 256 Cayuga	Chancellor Foch de Chaunac	
Ohio				
Gewürztraminer Chardonnay		Vidal 256 Seyval Blanc	Chambourcin Foch de Chaunac	Delaware

Virginia

Chardonnay	Seyval Blanc	Chancellor
Riesling	Vidal 256	Foch
Sauvignon Blanc	Cayuga	Villard Noir
Gewürztraminer	Aurora	Chambourcin

Southeast and Gulf States

(Due to special conditions, varieties of Muscadinia rotundifolia are recommended for this region. They are classified as bronze, black, or white.)

BRONZE	BLACK	WHITE
Carlos	Bountiful	Dearing
Magnolia	Chief	Dixie
Scuppernong	Cowart	Higgins
	Noble	

Bunch grape varieties that will grow in the Southeast include Moored, Alwood, Delaware, Rougeon, and Rosette.

Arkansas

Verdelet Blanc	Villard Noir	Delaware
Villard Blanc	Baco Noir	Niagara
Seyval Blanc	Chancellor	
Vidal 256		
Aurora		

continued

Table 2 summarizes variety recommendations from growers and grape scientists in regions from coast to coast, excluding California, which is covered in Tables 3, 4, and 5.

	WHITE VINIFERA	RED VINIFERA	WHITE HYBRID	RED HYBRID	AMERICAN GRAPES
Oklahoma			Aurora Seyval Blanc Villard Blanc	Rougeon	Delaware

(Muscadines also do well in southern Oklahoma.)

	WHITE VINIFERA	RED VINIFERA	WHITE HYBRID	RED HYBRID	AMERICAN GRAPES
Texas Hill Country	Chenin Blanc Colombard	Barbera Carnelian	Ravat 51	Baco Noir	
Central Midwest			Vidal 256 Aurora Seyval Blanc Ravat 51	Chancellor Chelois Foch Baco Noir de Chaunac	Delaware
Northern Cold Tier			Seyval Blanc Aurora	Foch Millot	

Wine grapes that don't require winter protection include St. Croix and Swenson Red (reds) and Kay Gray and Edelweiss (whites).

Arizona—New Mexico

Chardonnay
Sylvaner
Riesling

Cabernet Sauvignon
Pinot Noir
Ruby Cabernet
Zinfandel

Oregon-Southern Washington

Chenin Blanc
Chardonnay
Semillon
Riesling
Sauvignon Blanc
Pinot Blanc

Pinot Noir
Meunier
Cabernet Sauvignon
Merlot
Malbec

Southwestern Idaho

Sylvaner
Chardonnay
Riesling
Gray Riesling
Gewürztraminer

Pinot Noir

Seyval Blanc
Chelois

British Columbia

Aurora
Okanagan Riesling
New York Muscat

Foch
Chelois

Grapes just love California, and one can grow just about anything in this state. But there are wide climatic differences within
the state, and various grapes do best in regions suited to their
culture. Tables 3, 4, and 5 will allow California readers to select
varieties suited to their region. The regions are based on heat
summations (total degrees above 50° F over the growing season). Cities and towns are listed by region and heat summation.
Then grape varieties are listed by the regions that best suit them.
Table 5 lists grapes suited to the hotter regions of California and
the hot, dry desert areas of the Southwest.

Table 3 HEAT SUMMATIONS AT VARIOUS TOWNS
AND CITIES IN CALIFORNIA BY CLIMATIC REGIONS

TOWN OR CITY	HEAT SUMMATION	TOWN OR CITY	HEAT SUMMATION
Region I (Less than 2500)			
Branscomb	1810	Santa Cruz	2320
Lompoc	1970	Gonzales	2350
Watsonville	2090	Hayward	2370
Bonny Doon	2140	Betteravia	2370
Campbell	2160	Peachland	2380
Blocksburg	2230	Ben Lomond	2390
Riverside	2240	Suyamaca	2410
Woodside	2320	Santa Maria	2490
Region II (2501–3000)			
Willits	2520	Atascadero	2870
Santa Clara	2550	Redwood City	2870
Weaverville	2550	Soledad	2880
Palo Alto	2590	Napa	2880
San Luis Obispo	2620	Santa Barbara	2880
Gilroy	2630	Los Gatos	2880
Sebastopol	2630	San Mateo	2880
Covelo	2710	Hollister	2890
Petaluma	2740	Kelseyville	2930
Dyerville	2750	Santa Rosa	2950
San Jose	2760	Placerville	2980
Crocket	2840		

TOWN OR CITY	HEAT SUMMATION	TOWN OR CITY	HEAT SUMMATION
Region III (3001–3500)			
Oakville	3100	Pinnacles	3330
Ukiah	3100	Cuyama	3340
Paso Robles	3100	Santa Ana	3360
Calistoga	3150	Camino	3400
King City	3150	Mokelumne Hill	3400
Hopland	3150	Livermore	3400
St. Helena	3170	Potter Valley	3420
Santa Margarita	3180	Cloverdale	3430
Healdsburg	3190	Ramona	3470
Poway	3220	Mandeville Island	3480
Clear Lake Park	3260		
Region IV (3501–4000)			
Martinez	3500	Nacimento	3740
Escondido	3510	David	3780
Upland	3520	Vacaville	3780
Suisun	3530	Sacramento	3830
Colfax	3530	Delta	3850
Turlock	3600	Clarksburg	3860
Linden	3620	Sonora	3880
Vista	3660	San Miguel	3890
Pomona	3680	Fontana	3900
Lodi	3720	Auburn	3990
Region V (4001 or more)			
Ojai	4010	Woodland	4210
Modesto	4010	Reedley	4410
Oakdale	4030	Merced	4430
Brentwood	4100	Chico	4450
Stockton	4160	Fresno	4680
Antioch	4200	Red Bluff	4930
		Bakersfield	5080

SOURCE: Winkler, *General Viticulture.*

Table 4   VINIFERA IN CALIFORNIA—HABITS AND REGIONAL SUITABILITY

VARIETY	WINE COLOR	MOST SUITABLE VITICULTURAL REGION(S)	TIME OF MATURITY*
Barbera	Red	III, IV	Midseason
Burger	White	IV, V	Late
Cabernet Sauvignon	Red	I, II	Midseason
Carignane	Red	III, IV	Late midseason
Chardonnay	White	I, II	Early
Chenin Blanc	White	II—V	Midseason
Colombard	White	III—V	Midseason
Emerald Riesling	White	II, III	Late
Flora	White	I—III	Early
Gamay	Red	II, III	Late midseason
Gamay Beaujolais	Red	I, II, cooler parts of III	Early
Gewürztraminer	White	I	Early
Grenache	Rose	IV, V	Late midseason
Grignolino	Red	II—IV	Early
Malbec	Red	II, III	Midseason
Malvasia Bianca	White	IV, V	Midseason
Merlot	Red	II	Midseason
Mission	Red	III—V	Late midseason
Muscat of Alexandria	White	IV, V	Late midseason
Nebbiolo	Red	III, IV	Late
Palomino	White	IV, V	Late midseason
Petite Sirah	Red	II, cooler parts of III	Early midseason
Pinot Blanc	White	II, III	Early midseason
Pinot Noir	Red	Cooler parts of I	Early

Red Veltliner	Red	III	Late
Royalty	Red	IV, V	Midseason
Rubired	Red	IV, V	Midseason
Ruby Cabernet	Red	IV, V	Late midseason
Saint Emilion	White	II, III	Late
Salvador	Red	IV, V	Late midseason
Sauvignon Blanc	White	II	Midseason
Semillon	White	III	Early midseason
Sylvaner	White	II, III	Early
Riesling	White	I, cooler parts of II	Early midseason
Tinta Madeira	Red	III–V	Early
Zinfandel	Red	I–IV†	Early midseason

SOURCES: Winkler, *General Viticulture*; Weaver, *Grape Growing*; Jackson and Schuster, *Grape Growing and Wine Making*.
*Early grapes require heat summations of at least 1600 to ripen. Late grapes require at least 3500.
†Gives a different style in each region.

Table 5 SUPERIOR WINE GRAPES FOR CALIFORNIA'S HOT REGIONS*

WHITE TABLE WINES	WHITE DESSERT WINES	RED TABLE WINES	RED DESSERT WINES
Chenin Blanc	Mission	Barbera	Carignane (for port)
Colombard	Muscat of Alexandria	Carignane	Rubired
	Muscat Blanc	Grenache	Tinta Madeira
	Palomino (for sherry)	Rubired	
		Ruby Cabernet	

*University of California at Davis, Regions IV and V.

PART 2

GROWING
THE GRAPES

The sun, with all those planets
revolving around it and
dependent on it, can still ripen
a bunch of grapes as if it had
nothing else in the universe to do.

—Galileo

CHOOSING A VINEYARD SIZE AND SITE

After the selection of a variety, the next most important factor in achieving fine wine at home is the selection of a site. It's entirely possible to plant the right variety in the wrong place, and end up with poor wine at best, while a site 100 feet away that would ripen the grapes to perfection lies fallow. It happens all the time. Thousands of years of trial and error with French sites have brought us to an era when we can identify by name the few precious acres that produce the world's finest wines. To show how proper site selection can affect the value of property, ask the price of an acre of Château Lafite Rothschild, or talk to a real estate agent in Napa County about per-acre prices in 1970 compared to the current rates for vine-growing land. You couldn't buy an acre of Lafite, and there are similarly priceless acres developing up and down the coastal spine of California.

Imagine a property for sale on a hill above a river. Four acres and a nice house. On the south slope of the hill is a two-acre vineyard, and the seller pulls the cork on a red wine he made from that vineyard's grapes. It's delicious. How much do you add to the value of the place? Give the buyer another glass and think big.

How Much Wine to Make

Selecting a site begins with deciding how many gallons of wine you want to make each year. That decision affects all the others.

A gallon fills 5 bottles of wine. You'll have to wash 500 bottles to antiseptic purity if you make 100 gallons. Ponder for a moment the triple washing and rinsing of 500 bottles. Now think again about how much wine you want to make. (You can, of course, avoid this task by buying new wine bottles.) Personally, I make about 40 gallons most years.

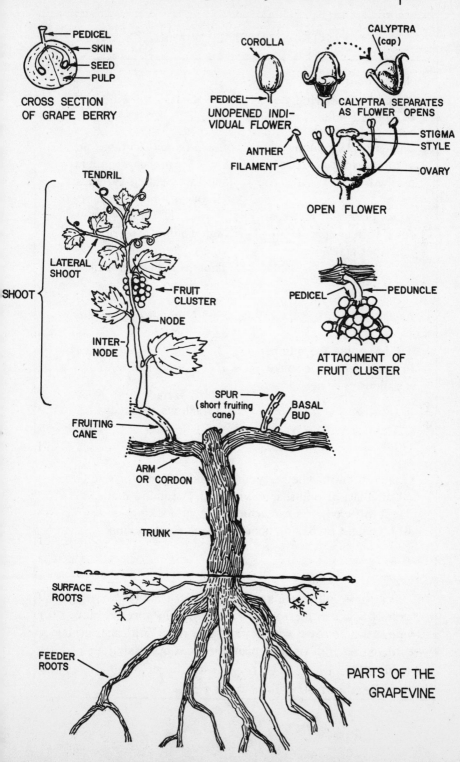

PEDICEL
SKIN
SEED
PULP

CROSS SECTION
OF GRAPE BERRY

COROLLA

CALYPTRA
(cap)

PEDICEL
UNOPENED INDI-
VIDUAL FLOWER

CALYPTRA SEPARATES
AS FLOWER OPENS

STIGMA
STYLE

ANTHER
FILAMENT

OVARY

OPEN FLOWER

TENDRIL

LATERAL
SHOOT

SHOOT

FRUIT
CLUSTER

NODE

INTER-
NODE

PEDICEL

PEDUNCLE

ATTACHMENT OF
FRUIT CLUSTER

FRUITING
CANE

SPUR
(short fruiting
cane)

BASAL
BUD

ARM
OR CORDON

TRUNK

SURFACE
ROOTS

FEEDER
ROOTS

PARTS OF THE
GRAPEVINE

COMPUTING THE SIZE OF A VINEYARD

Assumptions

A mature grapevine yields from 8–12 pounds of grapes

x = Gallons of wine desired

Eleven or 12 pounds of grapes yield a gallon of finished wine

y = Pounds of grapes per vine: *8* for classic vinifera and low-yielding varieties; 10 for most French-American hybrids; 12 for Cayuga and high-yielding American vines; 16 for Mission, Thompson Seedless, and muscadines.

Vines planted 6 feet apart in rows 10 feet apart (650 vines per acre).

Computation

z = Number of vines in each row

To determine the number of vines needed to make x gallons of wine:

a = Number of rows

$$\frac{x \times 11}{y}$$

Example: For 25 gallons of Cayuga,

$$\frac{25 \times 11}{12} = 22.9 \text{ or } 23 \text{ vines}$$

Only you know whether your property allows for a square, rectangular, or odd-shaped vineyard. Assuming that space is not constricted, you can achieve a good-looking rectangular arrangement by having about as many rows as vines in a row.

Example

100 vines would make a vineyard of 10 rows (a = 10), with 10 vines in the row (z = 10). 60 vines would make a vineyard of 7 rows, with 8 vines in a row. You can add the extras to several rows, or plant 64 vines by making an eighth row.

When computing the dimensions of the vineyard, 6 feet must be added all around the outside for end posts and space for mowers and other equipment. This formula does that for you:

$$[(z - 1) \times 6] + 12 = \text{Length of each row}$$
$$[(a - 1) \times 10] + 12 = \text{Width of all rows}$$

Multiply the length of each row by the width of all the rows to get the number of square feet the vineyard will take up.

Here's an example of the whole process, based on the needs of someone who wants to make 40 gallons of Chardonnay per year:

$$\frac{40 \times 11}{8} = 55 \text{ vines.}$$

Since $7 \times 8 = 56$, we will plant 56 vines in 7 rows, with 8 vines per row.

$$[(8 - 1) \times 6] + 12 = 54.$$
$$[(7 - 1) \times 10] + 12 = 72.$$

$54 \times 72 = 3,888$ square feet. Less than one-tenth acre.

Spacing the Vines

The guidelines on page 32 and above allow you to turn this decision into the number of square feet you'll need to produce that quantity of wine. I've made some assumptions—such as a 6 × 10 spacing (vines 6 feet apart in rows 10 feet apart)—that you may want to modify. Six by ten is a common spacing in the East, where water usually isn't a problem. In California, however, UC-Davis recommends 100 square feet per vine for vigorous vines in the hot regions, and about 60 square feet for vines of sparse to moderate vigor in the cooler coastal and Sierra regions.

Many growers in the Napa Valley plant their vines 8 feet apart in rows 8 feet apart. One longtime Napa grower remarked that "I'm planting eight by twelve nowadays. I noticed that the vines on the ends of the rows were always the healthiest, and I figured that's because they have the most room to grow." Where water must be competed for, the extra space is needed for the roots to forage and drink.

Spacing doesn't seem to have any effect on quality according to American scientists, but it can reduce quantity per acre if the spacings are too far apart. As a home grower, achieving top yields per acre isn't very important, so you can leave more or less room as your situation requires. Since a fully mature, vigorous vine will fully use 60 square feet and more, spacings closer than 6 × 10 for wine grapes aren't usually recommended in America, except for the far north. There are always exceptions, though: Muscat of Alexandria produced 32 percent more total crop over eight years when spaced at 4.5 feet than at 7 feet.

The typical acre of California vinifera carries from 440 to 600 vines, a very low number by European standards, where 3,000 (and sometimes many more) vines are crammed onto an acre of—for instance—Champagne's soil. In France, close spacings and low training squeeze every last drop of wine from the acreage. In America, scientists recommend no more than 650 vines per acre trained to a high trellis. They maintain that yields are as high or higher than in Europe, even with the fewer vines. The Europeans, on the other hand, maintain that close spacings reduce yield per vine, but improve the quality and maximize yield per acre. Americans counter that reducing spacings has no effect on quality, and so back and forth the argument goes. As with almost every other facet of grape growing and wine making, there are many and varied ideas about spacing.

FINDING A FAVORABLE SITE

Now that you know the size and shape of the vineyard, where should you put it? To evaluate your property—or a piece

A GUIDE TO VINE SPACING

	FEET BETWEEN VINES		FEET BETWEEN ROWS
West of the Rockies			
Vigorous vines in hot, dry regions	8	×	12
Medium-vigor vines	6	×	10
	or 8	×	8
Low-vigor vines in cooler regions	6	×	8 or 10
East of the Rockies			
Vigorous varieties in dry regions	8	×	10
Low to medium-vigor varieties	6	×	10
Muscadines	20	×	12

of land you may consider buying for planting—it's important to know the site characteristics favorable to grape growth and wine quality.

We'll consider these factors: slope; solar radiation; frost and heat pockets; soil type, drainage and depth; water; wind; and proximity to other growth.

You may have no choice about where to locate your vines, because of space limitations on your property. In that case, the descriptions that follow should help get the most out of what you have. If your property, on the other hand, has many acres of varying flats and slopes, or you want to identify a parcel of land to buy for a vineyard, this information is a guide to site selection.

Sloping Land Is Best

What you're looking for is a slope, oriented anywhere from the southeast to southwest in cooler areas, or northeast to northwest where the sunlight and heat are intense. The best place for the vines is the upper third quarter of the hill.

On clear, cool nights, when the earth's heat is radiated

away from the ground quickly, the layer of air near the soil is cooler than the air mass above. Because this air is cooler, it's denser, and on slopes steeper than 2 percent, it starts to slide downhill. The coolest air collects in pools in the lowest places

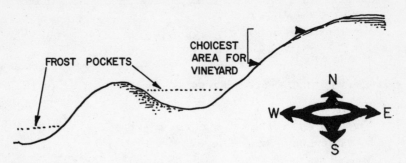

or behind barriers, and when temperatures on the slopes are hovering just above freezing, vegetation in the pockets can be blackened by frost. Valley floor temperatures run from two to four degrees colder than on slopes at night, but about two degrees warmer during the day, since air movement is less and heat buildup occurs in the low spots.

On any slope, rows must follow the contour to prevent gullies and erosion. This automatically produces east-west rows on slopes facing either south or north, and north-south rows on east and west slopes. What *does* have an effect on solar radiation is row *spacing*.

Vineyard temperatures recorded at close spacings are higher on south slopes than at wider spacings. Above 42° north latitude rows on slopes should be reduced from our recommended 10 feet to about 7 feet.

Spacing Vines on Level Land

On level land, you see growers with north-south row orientation, and others with east-west. When choosing yours, keep in mind that sunlight on the exposed soil of level land between the rows causes higher vineyard temperatures and less acid in the grapes, while sunlight on the leaves produces higher sugar in the grape berries. So, in areas where sugar is adequate but acid too high, you'd want to achieve higher vineyard temperatures with a wider spacing oriented so that as much sunlight as possible falls on soil; in northern areas where sugar is too low, closer spacings are indicated to get as much vineyard sunlight on leaves as possible.

Recent computer-aided studies show that closely spaced north-south rows intercept the most sunlight. In the most northerly areas, 7-foot north-south rows on southeastern slopes are probably optimal.

Tables 6 and 7 give a good idea of the magnitude of the effects we're discussing.

Table 6 INDEX* OF SUNLIGHT
RECEIVED BY VARIOUS SLOPES
(45° NORTH LATITUDE)

SLOPE	JUNE 21	SEPTEMBER 21
South 15°	107	122
South 10°	105	115
South 5°	103	108
North 5°	96	91
North 10°	91	81
North 15°	86	70

*Sunlight on a flat surface = 100.

Table 7 INDEX* OF SUNLIGHT RECEIVED
AT VARIOUS LATITUDES (15° SLOPE)

LATITUDE	JUNE 21		SEPTEMBER 21	
	NORTH SLOPE	SOUTH SLOPE	NORTH SLOPE	SOUTH SLOPE
50°	83	109	65	127
45°	86	107	70	122
40°	89	104	75	118
35°	91	101	78	114
30°	93	99	81	111

*Sunlight on a flat surface = 100.

VINEYARD SOIL AND GRAPE QUALITY

All grapes have an affection for gravel, flint, slate, or stony soils, and the best acres are so infertile and stony that a corn farmer wouldn't take them as a gift. In Bordeaux, Château Beau-caillou is so named because of its "beautiful pebbles." Graves, the great region to the south of Bordeaux, means gravel in French. Good California grape soils are flecked with flint, obsidian, volcanic debris. In the East, the hills of the Hudson River valley and shores of the Finger Lakes are stony and poor, without much of the rich humus that most other crops love. One reason why steep hillsides are so good for grapes is that erosion has scoured the land to its poorest, stoniest constituents. Bottomland soils are nearly always richer—often too rich. In addition, low areas have cold air pockets, poorer water drainage, higher humidity, less air movement, and, consequently, more disease.

Types of Soil

Soil is classified as clay, sand, or silt, usually in combinations of these. Vines grow well in all three types, as long as water drainage is good. Look at the soil types in well-known wine regions of France (Table 8, page 39).

It's universally believed in Europe that calcareous—limestone or chalk—soils produce the best wines. This may be true, but not, American scientists say, because they contain large amounts of calcium. Calcareous soils are almost always well drained. Well-drained soils are warmer, hence promote better vine growth and ripening. In any event, in the Cognac region of France, the growers in the most calcareous zones get a higher price for their grapes and wines because of it.

Direct Soil Effects on Grapes

There *are* significant direct effects of the soil makeup on the quality of wines. High-iron soils can produce wines with a ferric *casse*—a slight cloudiness that's impossible to get rid of without sophisticated equipment. Red soils are usually high-iron soils, and are not necessarily good soils for red wines, as legend has it. Too much boron in the soil may hasten maturity and increase sugar content, but it's also known to raise the grapes' pH. An abundance of potassium also raises pH levels—a problem in areas that produce less acidic grapes. Soils high in phosphorus produce wines with a higher iron content.

German studies show that grapes grown on alkaline chalk were higher in potassium and magnesium than grapes from neutral or slightly acid soils. They also underwent a more complete malolactic fermentation.

Table 8 SOIL TYPES IN WINE REGIONS OF FRANCE

WINE REGION	SOIL TYPE
Bordeaux	Predominantly sandy, gravelly loam; some clay soils; calcareous subsoil
Burgundy	Calcareous in Côte d'Or; granitic in southern Burgundy
Chablis	Clay
Champagne	Modified chalk
Moselle	Slate loams

Testing Soil pH

Generally, vinifera likes a slightly alkaline soil: American types like a slightly acid soil; French-American hybrids like a slightly acid to neutral soil. You can test the pH of your soil by contacting your county agent and asking for the soil sampling materials for a pH test. Large land-grant or state agricultural universities perform soil tests for a small fee, and local county agents have the details. A pH under 6.0 shows an overly acid soil, correctable with ground limestone. A pH approaching 8.0 shows an overly alkaline soil, correctable with gypsum.

Determining Your Soil Type

Your soil type will probably be a loam—a mixture of clay, silt, sand, plus stones and organic matter. Grapes most prefer something like a gravelly, sandy, clay, or silt loam, if they could have their druthers; that is, the best soils are a mixture of all the elements. Soil with too much sand, silt, or clay generates problems. An easy way to find out what kind of soil mixture you have is to fill a jar one-third full of soil from the area you intend to plant. Take the soil sample as a slice from the surface to 6 or 8 inches deep. Fill the jar to the top with water, then give it a good shake. Put the jar on a windowsill, or anywhere you'll be able to observe it without disturbing it. The heavy sand will settle out first, followed by silt, and then clay. Organic matter will float. Within two or three days, most of the clay particles will have settled out, and you'll have a good picture of your soil's composition. Good loam contains 45 percent sand, 35 percent silt, and 20 percent clay. If more than 70 percent of your soil sample settles as the bottom layer, you've got a sandy soil. If more than a third settles as the clay layer, or as silt, then you have clay or silt loam. Over 75 percent sand, clay, or silt means you've got a problem soil. We'll talk about correcting these problems later.

Most grape varieties are deeply rooted plants, sending their roots 6 feet or more into the soil. Good drainage sends moisture down to the deepest roots, washes the soil free of injurious salt accumulations, drains away rainfall so that it doesn't pond and deprive the surface roots of oxygen, and carries oxygen deep to the roots.

Problem Soils

For the preceding reasons and others, heavy clay or silt soil is undesirable, as it gives poor drainage and ventilation because of its relatively small pore spaces. Soils rich in humus are often too high in nitrogen for grapes, creating rank, weak growth that's susceptible to pests and diseases. Very sandy soils lose moisture quickly and are also frost prone, due to their low heat capacity and thermal conductivity. They warm up too quickly on sunny days in late winter—encouraging buds to push —but then cool off fast at night, promoting freezing of tender new tissue.

Effects of Soil and Stone Color

If you can find an area with dark stones, it could be an advantage in cooler areas. A study at Geisenheim in Germany showed that temperatures a few inches above dark stones were 10° C (23° F) higher than over light stones. Dark *soils,* on the other hand, usually mean an abundance of humus or organic matter—something to be avoided. A soil that's dark because of its dark rocks, however, would take advantage of extra heat-holding capacity to good effect.

Soil Depth Should Be at Least 30 Inches

Because of the deep-rooting habit of grapes, soils have to be deeper than about 30 inches. That is, there's no bedrock, hardpan, or impenetrable layer within 30 inches of the surface. Up to a depth of 70 inches, the deeper the soil, the better it is for vines. It doesn't seem to improve the grapes if the soil is deeper than 70 inches—meaning that's about the limit of their root length.

To check a site for soil depth, you may want to dig a hole 36 inches deep and inspect the soil profile for a hardpan or rock layer. Hardpans are compacted, impervious layers that act like cement—roots can't grow through them, water can't penetrate. Less compacted layers can still cut water penetration by 80 percent. Both hardpans and compacted layers have to be broken up by a backhoe if they exist where you intend to plant grapes. A

standard soil percolation test will also reveal a hardpan or compacted layer. You can also dig a smaller hole to inspect the first
foot or so, then drive a rod into the ground to see if it penetrates
easily to 30 inches or more. And you can consult the soil maps
at the county agent's office. He or she will have an amazingly
detailed series of maps that show your property, the various soil
types on it, and whether it's over shallow bedrock or is deeply
drained. Also, check the plants that are growing on the site. If
moss and wild strawberries cover the ground, you've got a
poorly drained, acid soil.

Vineyard Drainage

This matter of drainage is supremely important to your
eventual success. Grapes do not like wet feet. Every grower and
scientist I spoke with said the same thing: Warn people not to
plant in badly drained, wet areas. New York State grape scientists go so far as to say that "the site characteristics of rainfall, soil
nutrients, organic matter, high lime, soil texture, and pH are
minor compared with *soil depth, temperature,* and *replant status."*
Soil depth means soil's ability to drain water. Temperature
means winter minimums and length of the growing season. Obviously, planting a tender variety in an area with a −25° F winter
minimum, or planting a 180-day grape in a 150-day region, spell
disaster. Replant status becomes important if you want to plant
where grapes have grown within the past three years. For the
first three years after a vineyard is pulled out, it just won't
support new vines. This is probably an allelopathic effect; that is,
a chemical exuded by grape roots to reduce competition keeps
working for three years after the roots are pulled.

Rootstocks for Problem Soils

Some soil problems can be overcome by using rootstocks.
In the highly alkaline soils of the Southwest, for instance, Dog-
ridge rootstock will grow well and support good grafts of vinif-

era and hybrids. In rich, humusy eastern soils, a Riparia rootstock will hold down vigor. In all but the sandiest areas, vinifera will need rootstock that resists the soil-borne root louse, phylloxera. No rootstock, however, will grow in wet, badly drained soil.

Preparing the Soil for Grapes

If a fine topsoil is underlain by a poor subsoil, vine roots will tend not to grow across the interface. Whenever the soil is in distinct strata, water percolation and root growth problems show up. Here's how I learned the solution to this problem:

On my first visit to Dr. Konstantin Frank, the renegade Russian émigré who showed the world that vinifera could grow well in the Finger Lakes region of upstate New York, I saw him preparing Pinot Noir vines for planting. I asked if I could purchase some for planting at home.

"Do you have your soil prepared?" he snapped.

I stammered something to indicate that I hadn't.

"Go home and get a backhoe. Dig a trench three feet wide and three feet deep and refill it with the soil. Let it sit over winter. Then ask me for vines," he said. "Then, maybe."

He wasn't about to let me take his precious vines home and dig up a few holes in the backyard for them. He was telling me, in his irascible way, that preparing the soil for grapes means loosening, breaking up, and mixing soil layers well below ordinary cultivation depth. The procedure breaks apart man-made compaction layers in the first two feet—these can be caused by foot traffic as well as wheeled vehicles—plus claypans, hardpans, and dense layers below that. In addition, deep mixing disrupts strata of varying soil textures that interrupt root growth.

This can be done by hand, if you like heavy work. More feasible for most of us will be a backhoe that can do the job quickly and well. Just make sure that the backhoe never drives across a turned-up bed. And make sure you never walk on these beds. Feet can and do cause dense layers that turn aside roots and water. A tractor with deep chisel plows can also do the job, but the soil mixing won't be as complete as with a backhoe.

On a slope too steep for equipment, preparing the soil will mean handwork. The process is no less necessary, but you are assured of better water drainage on a slope, so subsoiling doesn't have to be quite as deep. A couple of feet will do.

The planting trench, or holes, as it may be, should be a good 3 feet wide, if you can do it. This large zone of loosened soil allows the vine roots to grow well the first year. In scientific studies of fruit growth in orchards, both grapes and fruit trees responded well to large planting holes. Soil improvement—such as adding manure and compost or other fertilizers—had no beneficial effect, much to the surprise of the researchers. When the holes were filled with improved soil that differed greatly from the poorer base soil, one of those interfaces that deters root growth was formed at the boundary. Not only that, but fine wine grapes in particular don't favor rich soil. Like the herbs that grow most fragrant in poor soil, quality wine grapes are suited to earning their living the hard way. So soil improvement isn't usually necessary unless you want to loosen a thick, heavy clay soil by adding sand. Sand will open up larger pore spaces in such a soil, and can be added when the backhoe is replacing the soil in the trenches. A ton of sand will help loosen about 100 feet of 3-foot-wide trench in heavy clay soil. Also, if your soil pH needs correction, add ground limestone or gypsum at rates recommended by your county agent.

Prepare Soil in the Autumn

The trenching or handwork should be done in the autumn before the spring in which you'll plant. Rains, snows, frosts, and a little time alone are all good for the soil. Trenching in the autumn after weed growth gives you a weed-free planting bed in the spring. On steep slopes, bare soil is extremely prone to erosion, so you may want to terrace now, or at least cover the soil with a mulch that you can remove before planting.

If the planting site must be in a poorly drained area, or the water table is within 2 or 3 feet of the surface, ditches can drain away excess water. A tile drain field under the vineyard may work. Tile for drainage is pretty much like that for a septic system and just as expensive. Your county agent will have literature on putting one in.

OTHER SITE CONSIDERATIONS

Timber too near your site can negatively influence the quality of the grapes. A forest clearing is not a good area for a vineyard. Such sites are subjected to cool, moist air flowing into the vineyard from under the trees during the day and to cool airflows from the tree crowns at night. This effect is more pronounced if the forest is at a height above the planting. Cool, humid air promotes fungus and disease attacks, and the forest is a reservoir of such spores. Edges of forests and woods also harbor multifarious insects. Near large forests, deer can be a nearly impossible problem.

Consider the Prevailing Winds

When picking a site, consider the wind. Very windy sites can mean broken canes during the growing season and dehydrating cold winds in the winter. In northerly areas, especially, choose sites that are sheltered from the prevailing winds. In much of the East, the winds are from the northwest in the winter. Thus a southeastern slope is the most protected. You can also plant windbreaks here and there as needed. A line of arborvitae might do it on the northwest side of a home vineyard. Just don't plant Russian olive or other shrubs that might attract birds. Stone walls and terraces are ideal for wind protection and heat retention.

GRAPE TRELLISES

Now's the time to erect permanent trellises for the grapes. It'll be two years before the vines really need the kind of trellis you'll put in, but if you wait to do it, you'll be digging and working around the young grapes, compacting soil, cutting roots, and generally disturbing the plants. Young plants of almost any type don't like to be disturbed as they take off smoothly into adulthood. Little setbacks frustrate them, and they give up easily. So, after the planting trenches are dug, with no grapes to worry about and the soil loose and easy to work, at least set posts. Stringing wire can wait for the grapes, although stringing it now gives you a year to tighten out any slack that may develop as posts settle in.

If you don't erect trellises now, you'll at least need to insert tomato stakes or something similar when planting your stock. First-year grapes need to be tied up off the soil. Never allow young vines to run on the ground.

Types of Trellis Systems

There are dozens of trellising systems used around the world, each providing a grower with a support suited to his climate and variety. Behind them all is a desire to get the vine up off the ground. In cold winter areas, high trellises keep the fruiting parts away from colder air that tends to lie along the ground. In warm areas, vines are often trained lower. Some trellising systems require four or five wires, crossarms, posts, and end posts. Others require no supports at all after the vine is established.

Probably the best way to help you select the proper trellis for your grapes is to describe the most common types of supports in the United States, and which varieties and climates they're best suited for. We won't be considering arbors and espaliering, as these are for appearance, or shade, or purposes other than the production of fine wine grapes.

• *Single Stakes.* Both head-trained vines and vertical-cordon vines need no wires at all. Head-trained vines are found mostly in northern California, where they are sometimes called *goblets.* They require a stake for the first few years, and after that are supported by the trunk itself. The system is being abandoned in most California vineyards, although it's a sentimental favo-

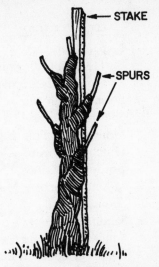

HEAD TRAINING   VERTICAL CORDON TRAINING

rite with me. The vertical cordon also requires only a stake. Head training is used mostly for Petite Sirah, Zinfandel, Carignane, and older California varieties. Vertical cordon is used for Chardonnay and less for Cabernet Sauvignon. UC-Davis viticulturalists are currently frowning on both systems. That's because they're out to maximize production for commercial growers, and in vertical-cordon systems, grapes and foliage can bunch together and promote molds, rots, and fungus. There are some real advantages to no-wire systems, however. Arnold Tudal in St. Helena uses vertical cordon for both Chardonnay and Cabernet Sauvignon and likes it because he can rototill his acres both ways—that is, up and down the rows and up and down the files —without interference from wires. "Keeping the ground turned up all around the grapes keeps the soil warmer. My grapes ripen sooner and I usually harvest two or even three weeks before other growers around here," he says. These systems can be used only in an area where trunks won't freeze—that is, in areas with close to a 300-day growing season. See Table 9 for the growing seasons of some selected cities.

Table 9 GROWING SEASONS
*(Number of days of average daily
temperature over 50° F)*

CITY OR REGION	GROWING SEASON
Napa, California	300
St. Helena, California	290
Livermore, California	285
Fresno, California	285
Sherman, Texas	270
Montpellier, France	235
Hutchinson, Kansas	225
Bordeaux, France	220
Mountain Grove, Missouri	220
Lyons, France	195
Sandusky, Ohio	194
Omaha, Nebraska	189
Reading, Pennsylvania	180
Westfield, New York	173
Minneapolis, Minnesota	170
Madison, Wisconsin	170
Geneva, New York	162
Ithaca, New York	160
Morris, Minnesota	160
Penn Yan, New York	149
Bismarck, North Dakota	145
Duluth, Minnesota	130

• *One-Wire Trellis.* While you occasionally see one-wire trellises, they're best for raisin or table grape production, not fine wine grapes. With only one wire, the new canes droop from the wire, exposing the grapes to the sun. This can produce sun scald, lessen color, lower acids, and otherwise impair the quality of the wine grapes. Also, without a second wire for tying up canes, the grapes' arms can twist under a load of fruit and break. I wouldn't recommend the system.

• *Two-Wire Trellis.* This is the most common type of trellising in the United States today, both in California and in the East. It's the simplest, most effective system for most grape varie-

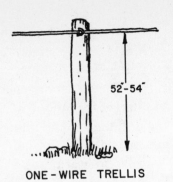

ONE-WIRE TRELLIS

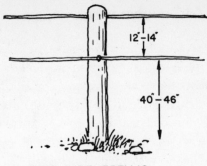

TWO-WIRE TRELLIS

ties in most areas. The height of the two wires above the ground differs from warm areas to cold, with the wires higher in the colder areas. An average height is shown here.

• *Three-Wire Trellis.* This system takes a little more work and a little more wire, but it gives the grower extra places to tie loose canes, and is especially suited to American grape varieties that tend to sprawl and grow downward. It's also a good system for vigorous French-American hybrids anywhere east of the Rockies, and is the most common trellis for new vinifera plantings in California.

• *Geneva Double Curtain Trellis.* Excellent for northern areas when very vigorous vines are grown. GDC has the advantage of allowing more sunlight in the renewal area, the upper-

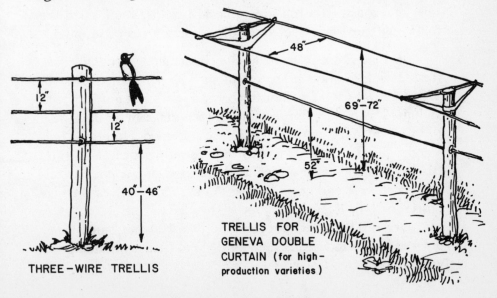

THREE-WIRE TRELLIS

TRELLIS FOR GENEVA DOUBLE CURTAIN (for high-production varieties)

most shoots that will make next year's fruiting canes. Scientists have found that when the renewal area is shaded too much, subsequent canes are weaker and less fruitful. The Geneva double curtain trellis also provides maximum sunlight for the greatest number of leaves and gets the vine high off the ground into the warmest air zone in the vineyard microclimate. This same trellising system can be used for the T-trellis in warm areas where vigorous grapes like Chenin Blanc are grown.

Choosing the Trellis System

We'll see how grapes are set up on these trellises when we look more closely at pruning systems for the vines. You may want to read over that material (page 65) before you finally decide on a trellising system for your grapes. Table 10 gives a good idea of the trellising styles available and the vines and training systems they're good for.

HARDWARE FOR CONSTRUCTING A TRELLIS

To construct a full-scale vineyard trellis, you'll need the following hardware. See Appendix 3 for sources of supply.

• *End Posts.* Use 6- to 8-inch-diameter wooden posts, treated with a wood preservative such as penta or diesel oil. Wood allows a solid anchor for cordon wires when it is drilled and fitted with Wirevise tensioners. (See diagram on page 52.) Pressure-treated commercial posts are also good. Untreated redwood will last for ten years in the coastal parts of California. Black locust and cedar are naturally rot resistant, and are excellent choices for end posts or stakes in the East. Each of the end posts should be 8 feet long; they are needed for the ends of each row over 100 feet long. For rows less than 100 feet, sturdy steel pipes at least 3 inches in diameter or 5- to 6-inch wooden posts will suffice for end posts.

• *Stakes.* Sturdy steel fence stakes in 7-foot lengths are excellent and never rot out. As for wood stakes, I've seen vineyards with two-by-twos, two-by-fours, even four-by-fours. Four-to 5-inch-diameter round posts look nice. Check what's available

Table 10 TRELLISING SYSTEMS

TRELLIS TYPE	TRAINING SYSTEMS	APPROPRIATE VARIETIES
Single stakes	Head training; vertical cordon	Low-vigor vines in California and other 300-day-plus growing season areas
One-wire trellis	Double-arm cordon	Low-yield, low-vigor vinifera. Not recommended
Two-wire trellis	Double-arm cordon; four-arm cordon; umbrella Kniffen; Hudson River umbrella	All types of grapes in all regions. The standard trellis, and the least support possible for vigorous American and French-American hybrids
Three-wire trellis	Same as two-wire, plus Keuka High Renewal and six-arm Kniffen	Same as two-wire, except gives more support points for a better display of the leaf canopy to sunlight
Geneva double curtain trellis (T-trellis)	Geneva double curtain; cordon cane-pruning	American and French-American hybrids of high vigor. Excellent for cold winter areas. Also good trellis for very vigorous warm area varieties

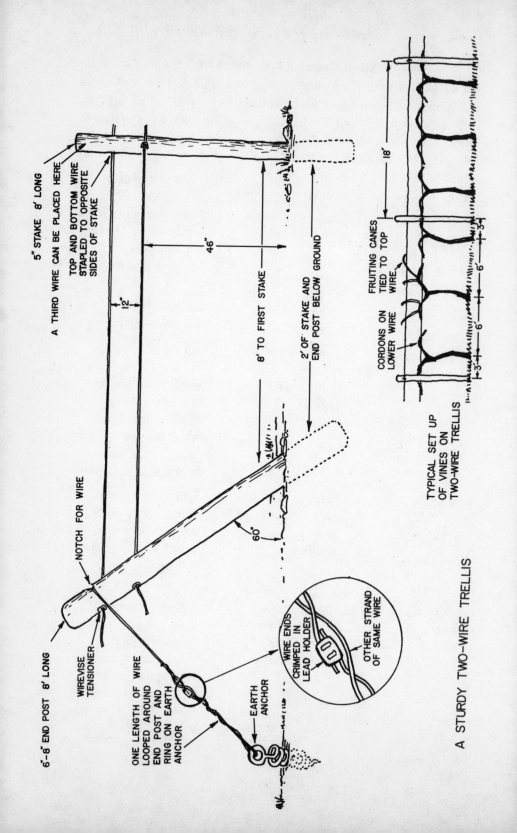

5" STAKE 8' LONG

A THIRD WIRE CAN BE PLACED HERE

TOP AND BOTTOM WIRE STAPLED TO OPPOSITE SIDES OF STAKE

12"

46"

8' TO FIRST STAKE

2' OF STAKE AND END POST BELOW GROUND

NOTCH FOR WIRE

60°

6"-8" END POST 8' LONG

WIREVISE TENSIONER

ONE LENGTH OF WIRE LOOPED AROUND END POST AND RING ON EARTH ANCHOR

EARTH ANCHOR

WIRE ENDS CRIMPED IN LEAD HOLDER

OTHER STRAND OF SAME WIRE

18'

FRUITING CANES TIED TO TOP WIRE

CORDONS ON LOWER WIRE

3'

6'

6'

3'

TYPICAL SET UP OF VINES ON TWO-WIRE TRELLIS

A STURDY TWO-WIRE TRELLIS

at your lumberyard or building supply store. The part that touches the soil must be preserved or pressure treated. If you preserve the stakes yourself, do the job in the fall, so that fresh preservative doesn't contaminate the soil near spring-planted vines. Each stake should be 8 feet, allowing 24 inches in the ground and 6 feet of aerial part—high enough to support any wires you intend to string.

• *Wire.* High-carbon or other high-tensile-strength wire of at least 13 gauge is necessary. Eleven and 12 gauge are thicker, hold more weight, but aren't likely to be needed unless you plan to grow long rows of very high-yielding vines like Concord, muscadine, or viniferas such as Mission.

• *Earth Anchors.* End posts are wired to earth anchors at the ends of each row. Earth anchors are large screws with rings on top. You twist them into the ground with a bar. If you have long rows of heavy crops, an even sturdier anchor is a steel reinforcing rod with a ring on top set into four square feet of concrete poured into a hole at the end of the row. If all this seems like overkill, consider that the trellis under the full weight of summer canes, fruit, trunks, and leaves, standing up to a stiff breeze, will exert tons of pressure along the row. Nothing looks worse or damages trunks and canes more than a jerrybuilt trellis sagging and swaying with each breeze.

• *Staples.* Large galvanized staples or brads are used to attach the wire loosely to the stakes. If the staples are driven down tight on the wire, they can nick and break it. Also, the wire can't be tightened from the end posts. The staples should be driven down to just hold the wire lightly. Plastic wire anchors that are nailed to stakes are available. They are made to hold the wire with the proper tension.

• *Wirevise Tensioners.* These little devices go in the end posts and firmly hold the wire from slipping under full weight. The wire can be drawn through them for tightening, but it can't slip back. They're well worth their cost. The Wirevise people also make Wirelinks, which are handy for splicing broken wires.

• *Tools.* You'll need the following tools: a drill to make holes in the end posts to thread the wires through; a good, large pair of pliers; a breaker or crowbar for twisting the earth anchors into the ground; a hammer for stapling the wires to the stakes; a sledgehammer or hand sledge for driving in stakes; a shovel or post-hole digger to dig holes for posts and stakes, or a farmer with a tractor equipped with an earth augur. Metal stakes can be driven into unbroken ground (just drive them in straight), but wooden posts need to be dug and set.

CONSTRUCTION DIRECTIONS

Set the end posts and earth anchor assembly first. Set the first stake 8 to 10 feet from the end post. Attach the wire to wooden stakes with staples or plastic wire anchors, leaving enough to be put through the end post and the Wirevise. Steel fence stakes have hooks that can be crimped lightly onto the wires. Set stakes 18 feet apart in the row, and continue stringing wire as you set stakes—it helps to keep rows straight. The 18-foot spacing accommodates a 6-foot vine spacing, allowing three vines between stakes, as shown in the diagram. For vines 8 feet apart, stakes can be set at 16-foot intervals, with two vines between stakes, or 24-foot intervals, with three vines between stakes. Twenty-four feet is a long run of wire, though, and could need support in the middle.

Set end posts at a 60° angle, leaning away from the row, at least 24 inches into the ground. Set stakes 24 inches deep. Set posts and stakes in their holes, then block them in place with soil and rocks until the hole is a third full. Tamp. Fill another third, blocking the stakes with rocks and soil. Tamp. Fill to the top and tamp again. Mound up some soil around the stake so there's no water-holding depression left.

Stringing the wire for each stake right after you set it helps to keep the rows straight, but you may also want to stretch a cord the length of the rows to make sure you're setting the stakes in a straight line. Crooked rows will put extra strain on the wires at the staples and cause breakage. When you reach the other end of the row, string the last stake, then the end post. Now go back to the first end post and string that. Pull the wires tight with a breaker or crowbar. Now attach the end posts to the anchors as shown in the diagram.

This work is best done in the fall preceding the spring in which you'll plant.

With only a few dozen vines or a very small vineyard with short rows, you won't need as sturdy an end post or stake as shown in the diagram. However, overbuilding won't hurt, and it will save you the trouble of having sagging wires with no easy way to tighten them.

ORDERING AND PLANTING GRAPESTOCK

Let's suppose that the trellis is up and wired by the end of October. By the end of December your vines should be ordered from a reliable supplier. By reliable, I mean a nurseryman whose stock is guaranteed virus free, has a reputation for supplying strong grafts and vigorous vines, and guarantees to replace any vines that die within a month—free. Studies show that one-year-old vines have a higher success rate in surviving transplanting than two- or three-year-olds, so look for a supplier of young vines. You'll find a list of mail-order suppliers in Appendix 4. Nurserymen send the stock at the proper time for planting—from May in the most northern regions to February in California and the deep south.

When your stock arrives, you'll be ready for it. Now the real adventure begins. Suddenly these babies are in your care. As you watch them flower, fruit, senesce, and shiver their way through the seasons, you'll come to know them very well. The vine will tell you what it needs. You just have to learn how to listen to it.

Handling Bare-Rooted Stock

Chances are you'll be getting bare-rooted stock, wrapped in damp excelsior of some type, then wrapped in the mailing package. If you can get right to the planting job, all to the better. Unwrap the plants and soak the roots in a bucket of water for at least 6 but not more than 12 hours, then plant.

Never let the roots dry out.

The plants will be okay in the mailing package for a day or two, but if it's going to be longer than that before you plant them, dig a shallow trench and lay them down in it out of direct sun. Cover the roots with soil or wet sand, and keep them moist until planting time. This is called *heeling in,* and your plants can last for weeks in fine condition this way.

Whether heeling in or not, soak the roots for six hours before planting, then carry the water bucket with plants to the vineyard. Take the plants from the water and with a pair of sharp cross-cut pruners (anvil-type pruners tend to crush plant tissue when even a little dull), cut back the top, if any, above the graft to two or three buds. Cut straight across, at least a half-inch above the bud you want to be topmost. (Cuts too close to buds will dry and kill them.) Nick out all but the bud or buds you want to keep with a sharp thumbnail or penknife. Make sure to get the whole bud out.

Trimming the Roots

Many years of scientific testing have shown that although trimming roots encourages new root growth, the more of the roots you remove, the more stored carbohydrate food you're taking from the plant, and the poorer growth it makes in the first year. So trim all roots back to 6 or 8 inches, no more, and remove all roots within 8 inches of the top of the pruned plant.

Planting the Grapevines

These cuts will leave plenty of root for the plant and

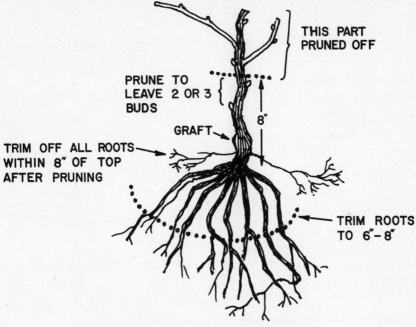

THIS PART
PRUNED OFF

PRUNE TO
LEAVE 2 OR 3
BUDS

8″

GRAFT

TRIM OFF ALL ROOTS
WITHIN 8″ OF TOP
AFTER PRUNING

TRIM ROOTS
TO 6″–8″

TRIMMING BARE-ROOTED STOCK
BEFORE PLANTING

stimulate root production at the cut ends when they contact the soil. Now place the plant in the hole with the roots spread out evenly all around. You can place a mound of soil in the bottom to set the depth and to array roots evenly all around. Try not to let any roots overlap. Press the roots firmly onto this mound, cover with more soil, and press again. It's essential that the roots are fully in contact with the soil, including the space under the center of the roots. The plant should be placed in the hole so that the buds are about 2 inches above the soil surface. If you're planting grafted vines, then the graft should be about 2 or 3 inches above the soil surface. (Roots should never grow from above the graft, or some of the chief purposes of grafting will be circumvented.)

Fill in the rest of the hole and gently but firmly step it down. You may want to leave a slight depression to catch extra rain or hose water.

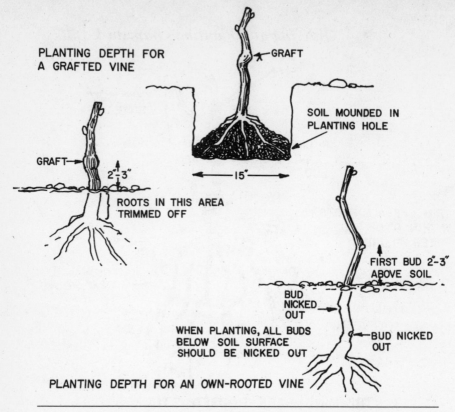

PLANTING DEPTH FOR
A GRAFTED VINE

←GRAFT

SOIL MOUNDED IN
PLANTING HOLE

GRAFT→

2″–3″

←15″→

ROOTS IN THIS AREA
TRIMMED OFF

FIRST BUD 2″–3″
ABOVE SOIL

BUD
NICKED
OUT

BUD NICKED
OUT

WHEN PLANTING, ALL BUDS
BELOW SOIL SURFACE
SHOULD BE NICKED OUT

PLANTING DEPTH FOR AN OWN-ROOTED VINE

Cutting Back Tops of Newly Planted Vines

Some growers cut the newly planted vines back to only one bud, but I think that's dangerous. If that bud turns out to be damaged or dead, the plant can die or be severely set back. I leave two or three buds, which gives me a choice when selecting a shoot to train into a trunk.

If you want to try to train a future trunk up to the trellis in the first year, you can remove all but one shoot from the plant after frost danger is over, leaving the shoot to carry the first year's growth. With vigorous varieties, it should reach at least the bottom wire, if not the top, in the first year.

On the other hand, you may want to let all three buds grow the first year to produce as much leaf area as possible, getting a trunk to the wire in the second year. This will promote photosynthesis and the growth of strong roots during the first year. In the second spring, the plant is pruned back to one bud again. This one bud, supported by a large root system, will explode into an extremely vigorous shoot that will speed toward the top wire and make it with ease. This method can delay fruit production, but that isn't crucial in the home vineyard. I choose the two-year method in my vineyard, but you can use either in establishing yours. I think the two-year method is safer and surer.

Watering and Protecting Young Vines

After planting, soak each vine until the soil in and around the hole is thoroughly wet well past the bottom roots. Keep the soil moist for the first month, if possible. Droughty soil is the prime reason why newly set-out grapes die. In a month, new roots will be striking out for available soil moisture and constant watering after that will only delay new root growth.

For grafted vines, growers in drought-prone areas often cover the entire new plant for several weeks with soil or dip the aerial parts in paraffin heated just to the melting point to prevent the graft from drying out. This gives the plant a chance to get settled in before it has to transpire water. These techniques are recommended in cool, dry regions, and are *necessary* in hot, dry regions. The buds have no trouble pushing through the soil or the paraffin. Once growth starts in earnest, the mounded soil should be pulled away from the plant until the graft and buds (now turning into shoots) are again properly above ground level. Another way to protect grafted vines in their first few weeks is to cover them with pots or boxes of whatever types are available. Own-rooted vines will do well if the soil is kept moist, and will need no hilling or waxing.

While tying a vine to a support isn't absolutely necessary the first year, you should do it—especially in the East where warm, wet weather promotes fungus on vines on the ground. If you haven't constructed a trellis, a slender bamboo cane about 5 feet long, sunk into the soil next to the plant, will do. Tie the strongest shoot to it with a plastic twist-tie, twine, or a strip of cloth. Don't tie it so tight you could damage the tender young shoot—just snug it enough to hold the shoot to the stake.

Nick Off First Flower Clusters

Some very fruitful varieties—Chancellor is one—will send out a few tentative flower clusters the first year. Nick them off with your thumbnail before they flower. You want all the strength of the vine for the first two years to go into root and leaf production. A strong start repays you in the long run.

MANAGING VINEYARD ROWS AND AISLES

The vineyard resembles a new construction site at this point, with the young vines and trellises in place. Vine rows will be planted in the middle of the 3-foot-wide beds dug by the backhoe, leaving 7-foot aisles. The beds should be kept in bare soil through the spring and most of the summer.

Cover Crops for the Beds

Toward the end of July, weeds or a cover crop like grass should be allowed to grow in the beds. This helps the grapes slow down and helps the fruit and wood to mature. Annual grasses, which will be killed by frosts, are a good cover crop. Make sure they're *annual,* not perennial, grasses, or you'll never get rid of the grass. Allowing weeds to grow is simpler. Just make sure to cut them before they can set seed, or you're creating future weed problems for yourself.

To Mulch or Not to Mulch

Mulching the area under the vines is not recommended for any except the very hot and dry areas. The mulch keeps the soil moist, which can stimulate late vine growth—growth that will be weak, tender, and immature heading into cold weather, with a much greater chance of winterkill. Such late growth takes

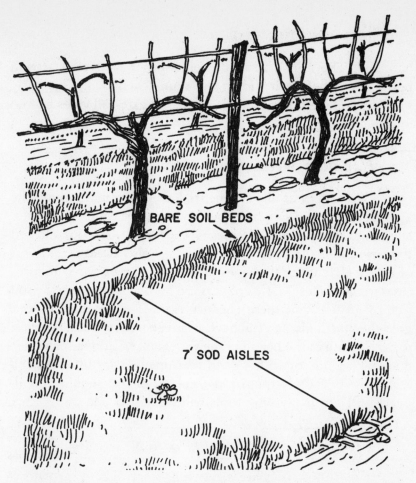

3
BARE SOIL BEDS

7' SOD AISLES

carbohydrates that would better be pumped into the ripening grapes. Also, mulches decay over the summer, washing soluble nutrients down to vine roots, stimulating even more undesirable late growth. Mulch also prevents you from letting weeds grow in the beds after July.

After killing frosts have arrived in late fall and the vine loses its leaves and goes dormant, the weeds in the beds should be turned under and killed. In no case should weeds be allowed to set seeds. The vine bed goes through the winter with bare soil. This allows frost to penetrate deeply into the ground, preventing early bud burst—and the consequent danger of frost damage—in the spring. Dr. John McGrew of the USDA told me that he had two rows of vines along his driveway in Maryland. One was mulched overwinter and through the spring, and the other had bare soil. The mulch kept the soil warmer, and vine growth began there before it did in the unmulched bed. This early growth was killed by late frosts, while the bare-soil vines had no injury at all.

Handling Weeds in the Beds

Bare soil beds allow beneficial air movement around the vines in spring and summer when warm, wet weather can stimulate fungus growth and diseases. Weeds or cover crops allowed to grow under the vines before July can also act as a reservoir of insects that attack the vines directly or carry viruses and diseases to the leaves. Many growers use herbicides to keep the soil free of growth, but these chemicals prevent late season weed growth in the beds, and can have an adverse effect on the grapes, to say nothing of the health of the winemaker. Cultivation is best done with a hoe or with a good rear-tined rotary tiller set to a shallow depth. Only the top two inches of soil should be cultivated, or too many vine roots will be destroyed.

Techniques for Managing Aisles

The 7-foot aisles are a different story. There, growth is often desirable. In the Napa Valley area, spring brings a pale yellow bloom to the wildflowers that grow in the aisles, creating a special beauty with the black trunks and fresh green of new grape leaves. Wildflower mixes specific for various areas of the country are marketed by several firms. One for California, sold by the Clyde Robin Seed Company of Castro Valley, California, includes strawberry and white Dutch clover, California poppies, cosmos, bachelor buttons, Shasta daisies, lupines, coreopsis, gaillardia, rudbeckia, and fescue grass. Ordinary sod grass will do, and can be mowed easily to look good. A pure stand of white Dutch clover is excellent because it mows well and adds nitrogen to the soil. On a visit to Bordeaux, I stopped by Château du Puy near St. Emilion and found turnips growing in the aisles. I asked Monsieur Amoreau, the owner, about it, and he explained that turnips strike deep roots and bring subsoil nutrients to the surface. When the turnips are fully grown in the fall, he tills them, chopping them to bits, and tosses some around the vines to decay overwinter and add subsoil micronutrients to the root zone of his grapes.

Grasses tend to creep into bare soil beds, so some sort of barrier to their underground rhizomes, such as yearly edging, is ideal though time-consuming. The permanent cover for the aisles is important for stopping erosion as well as for looks. I use grass, keeping it mowed and edged carefully.

Stone Mulches

One final note about bare soil beds: a stone mulch is perfect. That is, stones are laid in the 3-foot beds to completely cover the soil. This keeps the weeds down, and the stones retain the heat of late summer and early fall days. There's no way to allow the weeds to grow after July, but the advantages of the stones far outweigh this disadvantage. The trouble is that laying that much stone is a task beyond the ambition of most of us— including me.

STONE MULCH

Irrigation

Irrigation is used mostly by commercial growers, who want to control every aspect of their crop's growth so they can be sure of getting a marketable harvest in order to repay the bank for the money it lent them to put in the irrigation system. Small vineyard owners going for fine wines are out of this vicious cycle. Besides, the home vineyardist isn't interested in turning out a standardized product year after year. If 1986 is wet and dreary and the leaf hoppers eat up the vines, then you'll probably have underripe grapes. That's what vintage wine is all about: the good years are the hills and the poor years are the valleys. There's no way to capitalize on the rare climatic conditions that make truly great vintage years if you're going to standardize everything by irrigating routinely. Irrigation may be okay for wines that elicit an *aaah* from their drinkers, but only vines that have held on during a dry growing season to ripen a crop of undersized, intense berries to perfection will make wine that elicits *ooohs* as well. Arnold Tudal, who turns out treasures from his hacienda on Big Tree Road in St. Helena, refuses to irrigate. "It harms the quality of the grapes," he says.

That said, irrigation may be necessary in desert areas where heat and dryness could kill vines. If that's the case where you live (under 12 inches of rain a year), you can choose between drip and sprinkler irrigation. Drip irrigation is simply a system of water lines laid along the rows, with emitters near the base of the vines. It conserves water, using only half as much— or less—as a sprinkler system. The main advantage to an overhead sprinkler is that you can use it on cold spring nights to prevent frost.

Only enough water to keep the vine from dying or being permanently damaged should be applied. Since vine roots strike so deep, it has to be plenty dry to call for irrigation. You'll see shoot growth slowing in a spring drought, when it should be raging along, with the spaces between the nodes shortening toward the ends of the shoots. Tendrils will become flaccid and wilty, and grape flower clusters will dry out. If you see any of these symptoms, it's time to irrigate. Give the roots a good soaking, rather than watering them just a little. The good soaking will penetrate to the bulk of the plant's root system. Shallow watering promotes the growth of surface roots. Then the next time the soil dries out down through the first few inches, the whole vine suddenly has no water. It could quickly be damaged.

A warning: If the year starts out with low to adequate water, but turns very dry during grape maturation, don't be tempted to irrigate on the theory that a good soaking will plump up the berries for harvest. If the year has been dry, the berries will be smaller than usual, and a good soaking after *véraison* (the time at which the fruit starts to color) will pump the berries full of water, lessening quality and very possibly splitting them. Water only to save vines, not fruit.

The time when you're building trellises and preparing the vineyard for the grapes is the time to install permanent irrigation.

HOW TO PRUNE GRAPES

Now we come to training and pruning the young vines to establish a good fruiting framework on the trellis. This is the heart of grape growing, and the process on which everything else depends.

It took me a while to understand how to prune grapes, because I picked up my information piecemeal. Now I've achieved a reputation among my friends as someone who is privy to the mysteries of grape pruning, and I'm asked several times each spring to rescue vines that have grown into thickets from neglect.

How a Vine Grows

To prune properly—whether to train a young vine or maintain a mature one—it's necessary to understand how a

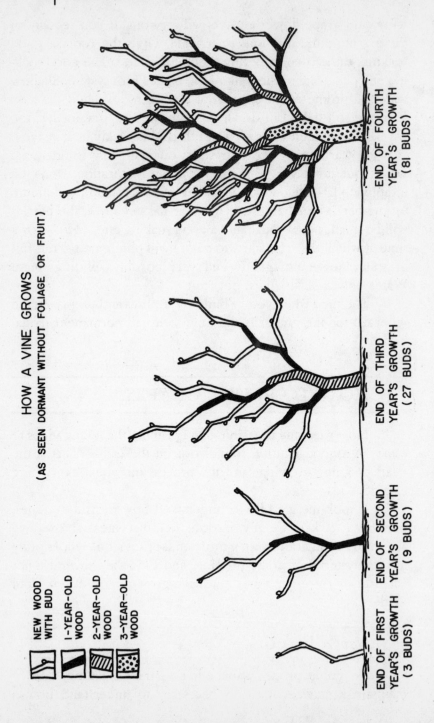

HOW A VINE GROWS
(AS SEEN DORMANT WITHOUT FOLIAGE OR FRUIT)

NEW WOOD WITH BUD

1–YEAR–OLD WOOD

2–YEAR–OLD WOOD

3–YEAR–OLD WOOD

END OF FIRST YEAR'S GROWTH (3 BUDS)

END OF SECOND YEAR'S GROWTH (9 BUDS)

END OF THIRD YEAR'S GROWTH (27 BUDS)

END OF FOURTH YEAR'S GROWTH (81 BUDS)

grapevine grows. Otherwise, a vine is an unintelligible jumble of trunks, arms, canes, shoots, leaves, tendrils, and fruit clusters. The illustration on page 66 shows how a vine grows: from last year's growth, for the most part. Sometimes buds will arise from older wood—these are suckers and should always be removed unless you want to use one to start a new arm or trunk.

Sometimes new shoots will give rise to branch or lateral shoots.

These laterals will seldom, if ever, be fruitful in the following year, and are routinely removed. Removing them helps keep the canopy open and directs growth into the main cane, which will then grow a little longer. If you have the time and inclination, especially in the first year, looking for these branches as they arise and pinching them off will keep growth in the main cane.

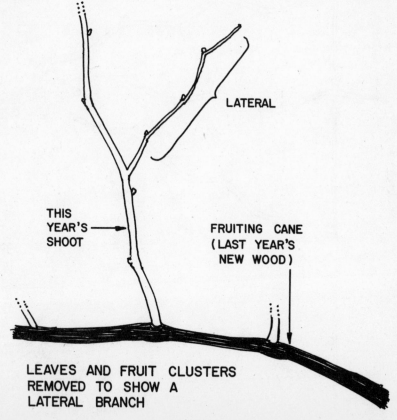

THIS YEAR'S SHOOT

LATERAL

FRUITING CANE (LAST YEAR'S NEW WOOD)

LEAVES AND FRUIT CLUSTERS REMOVED TO SHOW A LATERAL BRANCH

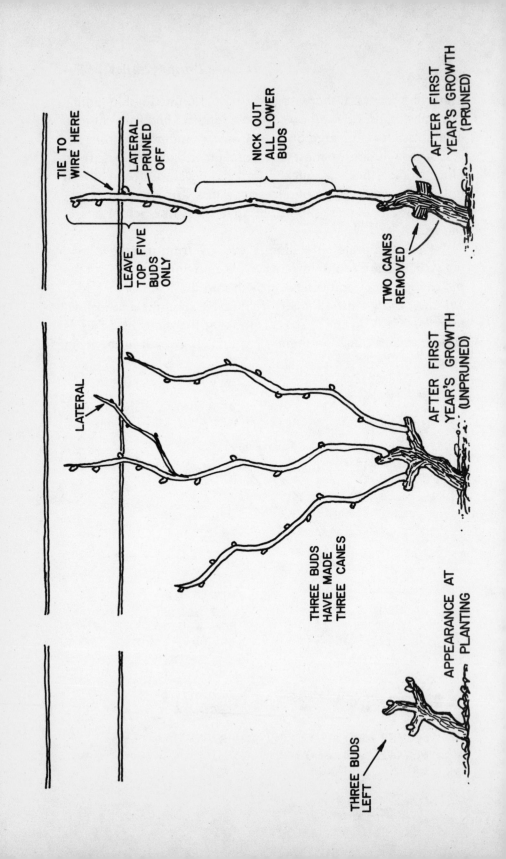

TIE TO WIRE HERE

LATERAL PRUNED OFF

NICK OUT ALL LOWER BUDS

AFTER FIRST YEAR'S GROWTH (PRUNED)

LEAVE TOP FIVE BUDS ONLY

TWO CANES REMOVED

LATERAL

AFTER FIRST YEAR'S GROWTH (UNPRUNED)

THREE BUDS HAVE MADE THREE CANES

APPEARANCE AT PLANTING

THREE BUDS LEFT

Relationship of Training System to Pruning

How you prune will depend, of course, on the training system you're using on the trellis. What's cut off and what's retained is different with different training systems, such as cordon-spur, cordon-cane, umbrella Kniffen, Geneva double curtain, and so on. Pruning and training proceed together, but we'll look at the essentials of pruning first, since you must know them in order to train the vine properly. If you know the variety you'll be planting, consult Table 10, so you have an idea which training system you're going for. Or use this rule of thumb:

Vinifera In California: head, vertical cordon, cordon-spur, cordon-cane. In the East: cordon-cane, Kniffen systems, Keuka High Renewal, Geneva double curtain—often with multiple trunks.

French-American hybrids Cordon-cane in warmer areas, such as California and the Northwest. Kniffen, Keuka High Renewal, and Geneva double curtain in the East.

American varieties Geneva double curtain, four to six-arm Kniffen, umbrella systems.

Pruning in the First Two Years

In the first two years after setting out new vines, all varieties for all training systems are handled the same way. If the vine has made vigorous growth in the first season and reached the bottom wire, prune as shown on page 68.

If growth has not been vigorous, or you want to produce a strong cane that will surely reach the top wire in the second season, prune back to one bud at start of second year, as shown on page 70.

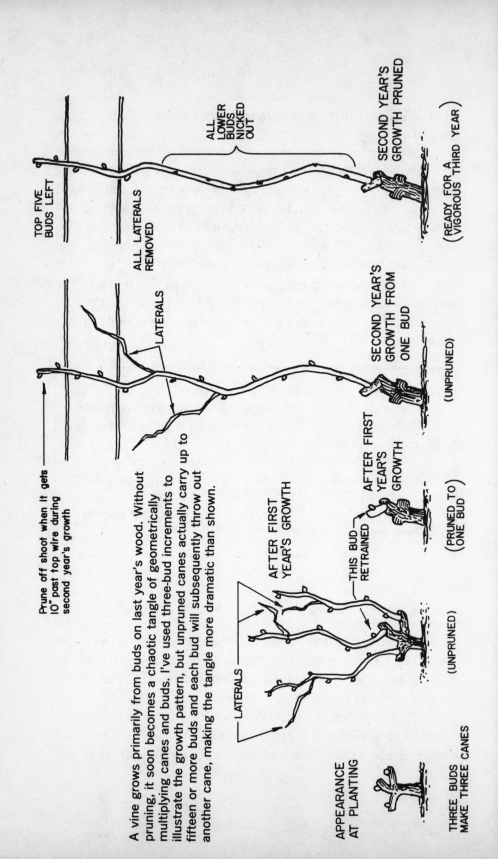

A vine grows primarily from buds on last year's wood. Without pruning, it soon becomes a chaotic tangle of geometrically multiplying canes and buds. I've used three-bud increments to illustrate the growth pattern, but unpruned canes actually carry up to fifteen or more buds and each bud will subsequently throw out another cane, making the tangle more dramatic than shown.

Prune off shoot when it gets 10" past top wire during second year's growth

TOP FIVE BUDS LEFT

ALL LATERALS REMOVED

ALL LOWER BUDS NICKED OUT

SECOND YEAR'S GROWTH PRUNED

(READY FOR A VIGOROUS THIRD YEAR)

LATERALS

SECOND YEAR'S GROWTH FROM ONE BUD

(UNPRUNED)

AFTER FIRST YEAR'S GROWTH

AFTER FIRST YEAR'S GROWTH

THIS BUD RETRAINED

(PRUNED TO ONE BUD)

LATERALS

(UNPRUNED)

APPEARANCE AT PLANTING

THREE BUDS MAKE THREE CANES

When tying vines to the wire—whether trunk, arms, or canes, always tie on the side facing the prevailing winds. This helps reduce breakage of canes.

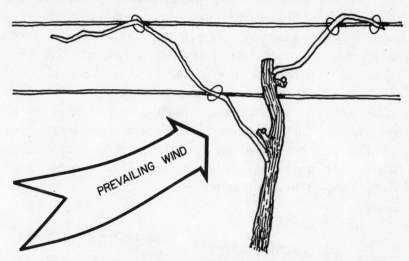

Here's a method of tying canes to wires using plastic-coated twist ties. (Paper-covered ties disintegrate.) Tie loosely rather than tightly.

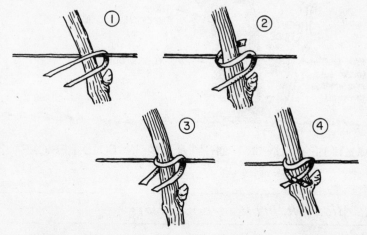

Whenever a vine's first cane reaches the top wire, cut it off about 5 to 10 inches above the top wire and tie it to the wire. This cut allows more of the plant's energy to be channeled into the portion that will eventually be the main trunk.

Multiple Trunks

In the East, especially when working with cold-hardy varieties, some Geneva scientists recommend having no trunk more than five years old, with up-and-coming trunks at four, three, two, and one years old. In other words, each year a cane is brought up from a spur at the base of the vine, which becomes a trunk that bears fruiting wood after five years. New trunks are constantly coming, reducing the problems that old vinifera has with virus, crown gall, and other grape diseases in the East. An additional advantage is that if a hard freeze kills one or more trunks, there'll most likely be one that survives. Double trunking is not seen in the West, as far as I know.

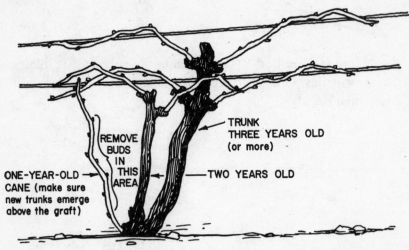

REMOVE BUDS IN THIS AREA

TRUNK THREE YEARS OLD (or more)

ONE-YEAR-OLD CANE (make sure new trunks emerge above the graft)

TWO YEARS OLD

MULTIPLE TRUNKING OF VINIFERA IN COLD REGIONS

Allow No Fruit in First Years

Any flower clusters that show during these first two years should be taken off with clippers or a thumbnail. These are the years when proper training is much more important than whatever small fruit yield the vine will bear. Since fruit yield and vegetative growth compete for the vine's resources, allowing fruit to develop will slow down the training and you'll get less fruit in the long run.

When you've established a strong cane to the top wire, leave about five buds for a vine of average vigor, with a couple of buds just below the bottom wire and the other three between the bottom and top wires. This allows you to proceed into almost every training system with ease.

Later on, we'll describe how to train this single trunk into the many systems, but, first, let's describe the principles of pruning so you'll be prepared to make your cuts with confidence. The single trunk will be the easiest to handle and adequate for all but the coldest regions.

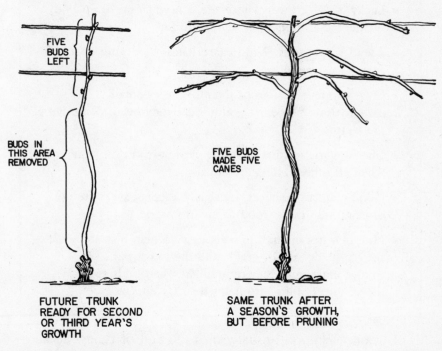

FIVE
BUDS
LEFT

BUDS IN
THIS AREA
REMOVED

FUTURE TRUNK
READY FOR SECOND
OR THIRD YEAR'S
GROWTH

FIVE BUDS
MADE FIVE
CANES

SAME TRUNK AFTER
A SEASON'S GROWTH,
BUT BEFORE PRUNING

Recognizing Winterkill

If you live in the northern part of the East and Midwest, you'll have to come to know the appearance of living wood from

MINIMIZING WINTER INJURY TO VINE TRUNKS

- Wet growing sites reduce root development and consequently vine vigor, making the grapes more susceptible to winter injury. Excess ground water can also raise the moisture level of the trunks prematurely, reducing hardiness.

- Cold sites, such as in hollows and flatlands at the base of hills, prevent canes and wood—as well as grapes—from maturing properly, and properly matured wood is a requisite for warding off winterkill. These places are prone to early and late frosts—both detrimental to vine vigor, hence to hardiness.

- Lucky is the grower whose site is near an unfrozen body of water that moderates temperatures.

- Avoid windy sites. Wind exacerbates the drying effect of subzero temperatures.

- Overcropping vines robs them of the essential carbohydrate phloem sap antifreeze they need to survive the winter.

- Choose varieties that have the earliest-maturing wood when all other factors are equal.

- Good cultural practices, especially keeping vines free of disease, help their wood to mature properly.

- Hill up vines enough in cold areas to help insulate surface feeder roots, grafts, and the lower parts of trunks; make sure they're unhilled when buds swell in the spring. Hilling also helps them avoid "wet feet."

dead wood. Winterkill usually nips the end of canes, because that portion of the shoot often doesn't enter winter with fully matured wood. The cut end of live wood is green and white inside, and the cane is resilient. Dead wood is dark and brittle. Winterkilled buds are brown in the center when nicked off, and live buds are green.

When to Prune

The best time to prune is when the buds start looking plump, but before they swell rapidly toward bud break. In any case, make sure your pruning is done before bud break. Not pruning until the last minute delays bud break and is a good practice to help vines avoid damaging late frosts in the spring. I usually prune in late March here in Pennsylvania. In the Napa Valley, pruning starts in mid-December and continues through February, although late pruning is often done in March. Vines will start to grow when the average daily temperature gets above 50° F (10° C), so watch your vines carefully in the spring.

Recognizing Fruitful Buds

You'll be able to tell last year's wood from older wood easily. Last year's canes are smooth with obvious buds, below which are the scars of last year's leaves. The bark on older wood is shaggy and stringy. The best canes for fruit production are those that received good sun exposure in the previous season and are between the size of a pencil and a little finger, depending on the inherent vigor of the vine. This brings us to the fact that buds on canes that grew in the previous season are fruitful and others are usually not.

John McGrew gives us six rules that help explain the facts of grape growth and the central ideas behind pruning.

1. There are two kinds of buds on a grapevine, those that give rise to shoots that bear fruit, and those that do not.
2. Buds formed on wood of the previous season's growth are fruitful buds.
3. Training puts the crop in an economical and convenient position.
4. A renewal spur gives rise to a vigorous shoot this year that will be retained for the fruiting cane the next year.
5. Pruning controls the size of the crop.
6. Fruit production competes with vegetative growth.

Rules 1 and 2 go together. Buds that arise from wood older than one year generally are not fruitful, with some notable exceptions such as de Chaunac, whose buds on older wood can indeed be fruitful. Buds on one-year-old canes—the smooth ones arising from last year's renewal spurs—are generally fruitful. Scientists have found that vinifera in warm areas generally are fruitful from the first bud—the one closest to the trunk—because of the intense sunlight they receive. In the East and North, fruitfulness increases as you go out the cane, away from the trunk, especially in French-American hybrids and American grapes.

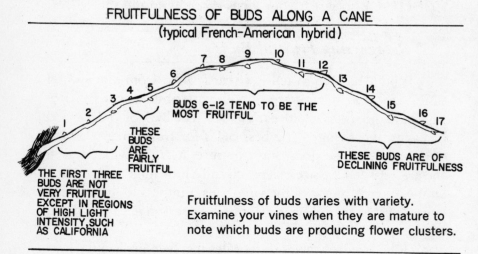

FRUITFULNESS OF BUDS ALONG A CANE
(typical French-American hybrid)

BUDS 6-12 TEND TO BE THE MOST FRUITFUL

THESE BUDS ARE FAIRLY FRUITFUL

THE FIRST THREE BUDS ARE NOT VERY FRUITFUL EXCEPT IN REGIONS OF HIGH LIGHT INTENSITY, SUCH AS CALIFORNIA

THESE BUDS ARE OF DECLINING FRUITFULNESS

Fruitfulness of buds varies with variety. Examine your vines when they are mature to note which buds are producing flower clusters.

As can be seen from the illustration above, buds 6 through 12 are usually the most fruitful. Fruitfulness of buds toward the trunk is enhanced by higher temperatures and intense sunlight when the buds were formed in the previous years—the kind of conditions found in California. That's why cordons with spurs of four or five buds are often found there, while in the East, cordons or Kniffen systems with long canes of up to twelve buds are found. In any event, an open canopy and careful positioning of shoots that will form next year's fruiting canes are important. A common mistake made by new grape growers is pruning and tying their vines in the spring, and then letting them grow as they will during the year. It's important to visit the vines every few weeks during rapid growth to place next year's fruiting canes—the ones that come from renewal spurs—in the open sun. The trigger mechanism for flower bud formation is sunlight, with heat also a factor. Thus next year's fruit is being formed in the primordial stage during this year's growth, starting right from the time when shoots are elongating past their tenth bud.

Pruning Prevents Overcropping

Overcropping in a given year reduces the fruitfulness of buds in the subsequent year. So the best way to guarantee that your vines produce adequately year after year is to prune them properly year after year. You may have noticed that old unkempt apple trees have the habit of bearing large crops of small fruit one year, and few if any apples the next. I at first figured that this was the tree's way of interrupting the yearly cycle of the bugs. And it may well be. But the primary reason is that the tree has run riot, and been left unpruned and neglected. The off year is the tree's attempt to regroup and build up its resources. The same holds true for a vine. An unpruned vine will have from 10 to 100 times the buds necessary for a good crop of quality grapes. The vine struggles for quantity, thus maximizing its chances to reproduce. The vintner struggles for quality, maximizing his or her chances for *vin parfait*. Pruning is the way to avoid overcropping.

Leaving Spurs or Canes

Cordons can be pruned to spurs of anywhere from two to five buds, or to canes of ten to twelve buds. Head-trained vines can also be trained to spurs or canes. Kniffen systems and other eastern training schemes use canes, because spur buds near the trunk under the lower light and heat conditions of the East may not be fruitful (and also because cordon arms may winterkill and are avoided). In addition to the fruiting spurs or canes, many growers leave renewal spurs of two buds—one renewal spur for each fruiting cane on the vine. This year's fruiting cane will be cut off at next spring's pruning, and the shoots that form from the renewal spurs will become next year's fruiting canes.

GRAPEVINE PRUNING ILLUSTRATED

You can look at pruning as a series of rules, but they all come down to this:

> Fruiting canes for next year are grown from this year's renewal spurs. The fruiting canes' length at pruning is determined by the number of buds left on each, which in turn is determined by the fruiting capacity of the vine variety.
>
> (See illustrations on pages 82–88.)

It can be even simpler. Instead of using renewal spurs, it's possible to prune fruiting canes back to several buds each spring. I've seen this method done with cordon-spur pruning in California, where the vintners can get away with it. I might try it experimentally in the East, leaving ten-bud canes rather than four-bud spurs. It's certainly an elegant, simple way to prune. (See illustrations on page 89.)

I like the way Mike Grgich of Grgich Hills Cellar in the Napa Valley sums up pruning: "Pruning every vine in the same style is a mistake," he said. "You can't put the same suit on you and me. I prune all of my vines according to the vine itself." I looked at some of his nearby Chardonnay, recently pruned. He used renewal spurs with canes of about eight buds. "That's because the most fruit comes from the fourth, fifth, and sixth buds," he said. Zinfandel, on the other hand, requires a different suit and gets spur pruned.

BALANCED PRUNING

The most important relationship in pruning is between crop and vegetative growth. One is grown at the expense of the other. If you overcrop by leaving too many fruitful buds, the next year's vegetative growth, including fruiting canes, will be weak and depressed and the fruit inferior. If you overprune, the crop will be reduced, but the vegetative growth will respond with increased vigor. The idea is to find the right balance that allows the vine plenty of wood—where its food resources are stored—and a moderate crop. Grapes of moderate crops are of a much higher quality than those from overcropped vines.

Balanced pruning is a way for eastern grape growers to make sure that they're getting a good balance between vigor and crop, until they develop a feel for a vine's reaction to pruning. This involves weighing the cane prunings from a vine and leaving a certain number of buds, depending on the weight of wood pruned off. To do it, you'll need a small hanging scale that you can hold in your hand, and that measures up to 5 pounds of weight. Tie the canes pruned from a vine with a piece of twine and hang them from the scale. The formula for balanced pruning is given in Table 11 (page 81).

Generally, fewer buds are left than shown in the "Maximum Buds" column in Table 11, especially in California and other areas with mild winters. Forty buds is about average for most vinifera varieties. Cordon spurs are usually four buds on five spurs on each arm, making twenty buds an arm and forty for both arms. Cordon canes are ordinarily ten buds long, and four canes is a typical number retained at pruning. A recent study at UC-Davis recommended ten buds be retained for each pound of cane prunings on small-clustered, cane-pruned varieties like Pinot Noir and Chardonnay.

Pruning Muscadines

In the southeastern states, where *Muscadinia rotundifolia* is being grown, a unique pruning method is used. Muscadines

CANE-LENGTH PRUNING RECOMMENDATIONS
FOR NORTHEASTERN GROWING REGIONS

LC = Long cane (12-plus buds)
MC = Medium cane (7–11 buds)
SC = Short cane (up to 6 buds)

NORTHERN REGION	CENTRAL REGION	SOUTHERN REGION
Beta LC	Aurora LC	Cabernet Sauvignon SC
Swenson Red MC	Buffalo LC	Catawba MC
Edelweiss MC	Cascade MC	Chambourcin SC
	Concord LC	Chancellor SC
	de Chaunac MC	Chelois SC
	Fredonia LC	Delaware SC
	Maréchal Foch MC	Golden Muscat MC
	Ontario LC	Joannes-Seyve 23–416
	Schuyler SC	MC
	Seneca MC	Landot 244 MC
	Seyval Blanc SC	Niagara LC
	Van Buren LC	Seibel 10868
	Ravat 51 MC	Steuben MC
	Worden LC	Verdelet SC
		Vidal 256 SC
		Villard Blanc SC
		Villard Noir SC
		Chardonnay SC
		Pinot Noir SC
		Riesling SC

SOURCE: *Horticulture,* August 1980.

Table 11 BALANCED PRUNING FOR MATURE VINES IN EASTERN AND NORTHERN REGIONS

GRAPE VARIETY	NO. BUDS TO RETAIN FOR FIRST POUND OF CANE PRUNINGS		NO. BUDS TO RETAIN FOR EACH ADDITIONAL POUND OF CANE PRUNING	MAXIMUM BUDS PER VINE AT 6 × 10 OR 8 × 8 SPACING
American Grapes				
Concord	30	plus	10	60
Fredonia	40	plus	10	70
Niagara	25	plus	10	60
Delaware, Catawba, Ives, Elvira, Dutchess	20	plus	10	50
French-American Hybrids				
Small-clustered types such as Foch and Leon Millot	20	plus	10	50
Medium-clustered types such as Aurora, Cascade, Chelois	10	plus	10	40
Large-clustered types* such as Seyval Blanc, Chancellor, Verdelet, Villard Blanc	20	plus	10	45
Vinifera (all types)†	20	plus	20	60

*Needs pre-bloom cluster thinning to one cluster per shoot.
†In years of excellent fruit set or on weak vines, cluster thinning is indicated.

SOURCE: *Misc. Bull. III*, New York State College of Agriculture and Life Sciences, Cornell University.

GRAPEVINE PRUNING ILLUSTRATED

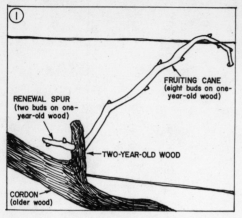

Let's start with this situation and call it year 1. It's early spring, just before the season's growth begins.

After the season of growth, the leaves drop and winter reveals the this situation. We want to prune so that we're left with a fruiting cane and a renewal spur, just as in year 1. Dotted lines show where I'll cut to do this. Cane **X** will become the eight-to-twelve-bud fruiting cane and cane **Y** will become the two-bud renewal spur.

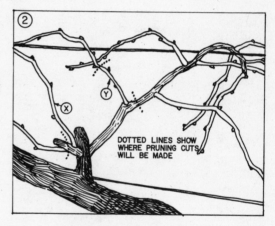

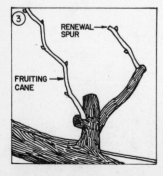

Here's how it looks after the actual pruning. The vine is ready for growth in year 2.

Let's see what happens in year 2. Each bud has grown a shoot that matures into a cane when the foliage drops. The dotted lines show where I'll prune to get back to a renewal spur and a fruiting cane for year 3.

And here's the same area after the cuts are made, ready for growth in year 3. Notice that the arrangement is getting longer and more cluttered with old wood. Eventually we want to get back to the situation in step 1, where we're working with relatively new wood.

This is the same situation as in step 5, except that sucker buds have formed on the cordon at **A** and on three-year-old wood at **B**, and a basal bud has formed on two-year-old wood at **C**. To get back to a less elongated and cluttered situation, we could use either bud **A** or **B** for renewing the area. Using **C** wouldn't allow us to clean up the situation very much. You'll notice such sucker and basal buds forming almost every year in various places on old wood—none, as a rule, will be fruitful. They would be removed when growth starts, unless you use them for renewal. Now let's see how things would look if we used bud **A** to clean things up.

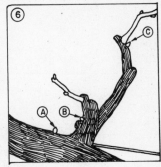

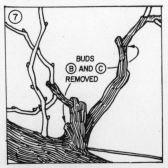

Here's step 6 after a season's growth. Bud **A** becomes a cane that will be fruitful if it gets enough sun; such renewal canes should be positioned for full sun as they grow. Buds **B** and **C** were removed before the season's growth started.

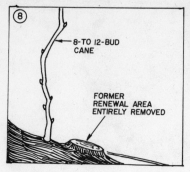

To prune for year 4 growth, the old renewal area is removed and the renewal cane is cut to eight to twelve buds. Let's see what happens when we grow this out during year 4.

After year 4 growth, it looks like this. By pruning at dotted lines, we're back at the situation in step 1 for year 5.

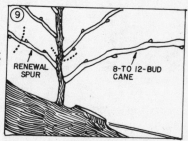

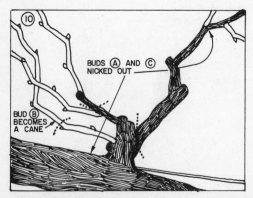

Look back at step 6. What would the situation be if we selected bud **B** for renewal and nicked off buds **A** and **C**? The drawing above shows what we'd have at the end of the growing season (year 4) if we kept **B**.

Here's step 10 after pruning. The vine is ready for growth in year 5.

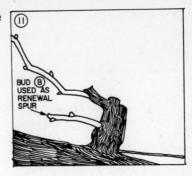

Growth in year 5 produces this situation. Now we can simplify the growing area by pruning as shown by the dotted lines.

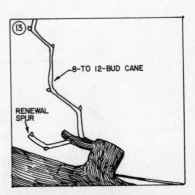

Here's what it looks like after pruning. The growth area is simplified but will become awkward again as years pass. Watch for a sucker bud somewhere on the cordon near the growth area and use it to replace the entire knob of wood (as in steps 7, 8, and 9).

Now we can better see how to train a vine into a cordon-cane system:

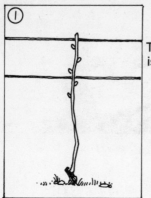

The young trunk
is established.

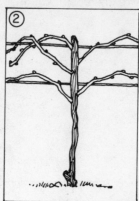

Its five buds grow
into five canes.

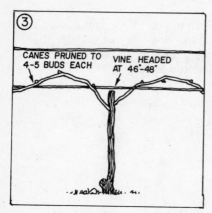

CANES PRUNED TO
4-5 BUDS EACH   VINE HEADED
AT 46"-48"

The vine is headed to 48
inches and two canes are
placed on the lower wire to
begin the next spring's growth.

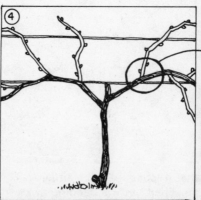

This is an enlargement
of one cane arising
from the cordon.

The lower-wire canes become cordons, or arms,
for the new canes that grew from its buds.

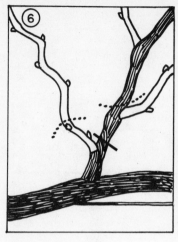

Here's the same situation after a season's growth. The dotted lines show where to prune to achieve a cane-and-spur renewal system. Often California growers will prune at the solid line, leaving a cane and no renewal spurs.

produce scattered berries rather than bunches, and carry an enormous profusion of wood. Thus they tend not to overcrop themselves if left to run unpruned. Pruning a muscadine is more akin to trimming a hedge than to ordinary grape pruning. Because of the profusion of fruiting spurs along the vines' arms, moderate pruning means clipping all wood back to about 12–15 inches from the trellis wires in all directions. Light pruning would be clipping back only the tips. Heavy pruning would be forcing the muscadine to a four-arm Kniffen or similar system. Such Procrustean training methods aren't for the muscadine. Since the vine doesn't harm itself if left to fruit at will, the job of pruning is more that of keeping it generally in place on the wires so you can get through the vineyard. A Geneva double curtain trellis is excellent for muscadines.

Bleeding

Tales tell about the bad effects of "bleeding," or the running of sap from the cut ends of canes when they're pruned late in the season. The bleeding stops naturally within a day or two, and does not harm the vine.

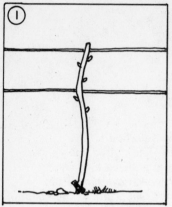

Cordons are dispensed with when starting a Kniffen system, preferred in the East. Here's a typical five-bud young trunk.

THIS CANE REMOVED

The four best-positioned canes are retained after a season's growth. Canes are pruned to ten buds.

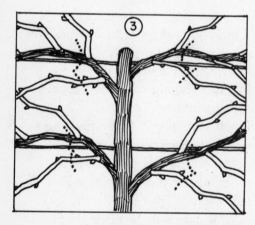

When these buds grow out the next year, they will leave canes as shown above. Dotted lines show where pruning cuts will be made to establish four fruiting-cane and renewal-spur growing areas.

Delayed and Double Pruning

In areas where late freezes occur, pruning is normally delayed until the buds just start to swell. Such late pruning delays vine growth, often until freeze danger is passed. Some variations of this tactic make sense in the very coldest areas. It appears that delayed bud burst is an in-cane, rather than an in-vine phenomenon. Therefore, double pruning is often practiced in the cold areas on tender varieties and those susceptible to late freezes. At

Five four-bud spurs on each of two cordons.

Close-up of one spur.

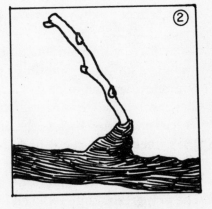

TRIM TO
4 BUDS

Same spur after a growing season. Dotted lines show how the pruner renews the area to a four-bud spur.

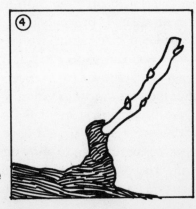

Here's how it looks after the pruning cuts are made.

pruning, twice the number of ten-bud canes are left as are wanted. If no winter damage is evident after buds start to swell, the extra canes would then be removed. If winter damage has occurred, as shown by dead buds, the extra canes are cut back, but not completely, to make up for killed areas. An even simpler method, and one that works just as well, is to prune to the desired number of canes at pruning time, but don't cut the canes back to ten buds, or however many buds you want to develop. Let these canes hang full length until buds swell, then assess damage and prune to the required number of buds. Since delayed growth results from this late pruning of the canes, the effect works to get your vines past freeze danger before major green growth starts.

A New Zealand viticulturalist, Ross Turkington, delayed pruning a group of vines until well after bud burst. As is typical of grapevines, the buds farther out the shoots burst first, while the lower buds, toward the trunk, were still tight. The canes were then pruned back to the unburst buds, usually the first five. Two weeks later, these buds burst. Turkington found that although the crop started to ripen later, final berry maturity was reached about the same time as conventionally pruned vines. The grapes, although reduced in quantity about 50 percent from the conventional vines, were of higher quality. Wine made from the late-pruned grapes scored consistently higher in blind tastings, he reported.

I'd recommend at least delaying pruning until the buds start to swell, or double pruning or late cane pruning in cold winter areas. It prevents freeze damage, improves quality, and helps keep vines from overcropping.

You can expect to get about 2 pounds of cane prunings from vines of low to moderate vigor; 2–3 pounds from moderate to somewhat vigorous vines; 3–4 pounds from a vigorous vine. Vines producing more than 4 pounds of cane cuttings a year are very vigorous and should have their canopy divided into a Geneva double curtain to allow more light to get to the shoots that will be next year's fruiting canes.

After you've cut and weighed the canes, burn them. Insects and insect eggs, parasites, and diseases such as Eutypa die-back can overwinter in the canes.

Managing Vine Vigor

Sometimes growers who've seen the severe European pruning systems will cut back the tips of shoots, or even remove whole shoots, during the summer growing season to manage overvigorous vines with extra light crops. This forces sugars to the grapes where otherwise the very vigorous vine would use the sugars to keep growing shoots. But summer pruning cuts away leaf area and food reserves the plant needs to create fruitful buds for next year's crop. There are other, better ways to manage vigor. First, start the vines with any training system you think is appropriate. If they overrun that trellising system, next year move to a top-wire cordon system with fruiting canes hanging down. If they're still running wild, go to a four-arm Kniffen or cordon system on both wires. If still too vigorous, go to the Geneva double curtain.

Management of nitrogen and water in the vineyard also manages vigor. Too much nitrogen creates weak, lush growth in excessive amounts. Too much water can have the same effect. Both problems can be corrected by using cover crops rather than doing summer pruning. The more vigorous the vines, the earlier you should start the cover crops of clover and annual grasses, or the earlier you should allow the weeds to grow. These cover crops and weeds will compete with the vine for nitrogen and water and help reduce vigor.

The very best way to manage vigor is to allow more buds to push shoots—but how is this done without allowing the vine to overcrop? Cluster thinning is the answer.

CLUSTER THINNING

Cluster thinning is the removal of flower clusters before they bloom, and, combined with lighter pruning, is a perfect way to manage vigor, keep crops to the proper, moderate levels, and get the highest-quality wine grapes. I highly recommend it. I've seen some Alden grapes that never matured properly for me ripen perfectly with plenty of time to spare after being cluster-thinned. For very fruitful wine grape varieties like Chancellor, cluster thinning is a must.

A vine doesn't like to be shorn of its food reserves. "Traditional pruning is too severe. If vineyardists will prune ten to fifteen percent lighter, and thin the clusters early in the spring, they'll have healthier, larger vines and a larger, finer crop," says grape scientist C. J. Alley, who works at UC-Davis. It was at Davis about fifty years ago that scientists proved that a combination of lighter pruning and cluster thinning produces crops up to 50 percent larger than with traditional pruning, with an *increase* in grape quality and no loss of vine health.

If you would ordinarily leave forty buds on four canes, next year leave forty-eight and cluster thin. If you'd leave sixty buds, leave seventy-five. You may even leave an extra cane. Leave more buds on vigorous vines than on weak ones. (By removing *all* the clusters and allowing a very weak vine to grow foliage freely, you can rejuvenate it, although you may pass up a crop.)

Timing of Cluster Thinning

The right time to cluster thin is in early spring, before the clusters' flowers open. As buds break and shoots start to elongate, you'll see little rosy whorls of leaves unfold, and tiny clusters appearing. Most shoots will have two to three clusters. Pinch off one or two clusters on shoots that bear three, or one on shoots that bear two. Large-clustered varieties should always be thinned to one cluster per shoot.

Waiting until after flowering to remove clusters—even *three days* after flowering—will lessen the improved growth you'd otherwise expect, and will not improve the final quality of the grapes.

The lightly pruned and cluster-thinned vine leafs out several weeks earlier than the traditionally pruned vine, due to the lighter pruning. In areas where late frosts can be a problem, delaying the light pruning until buds swell will delay this tendency toward faster leafing. Vines handled this way start the year with more buds and a greater reserve of wood, and thus food, and throughout the season make more growth. The greater growth and longer season in the sun make more nourishment for the grapes, which in turn grow larger and sweeter, and ripen earlier. I realize that larger grapes mean less color and skin extractives in the musts, due to less skin per pound of grapes, but a little longer time in the vat will help to overcome that drawback. The sweeter fruit and better acid-sugar balance are blessings that more than make up for larger berry size.

Positioning Cluster-Thinned Shoots

Lightly pruned, cluster-thinned vines will be stronger growers and may overrun a two-wire trellis and shade themselves. Careful positioning of shoots so that next year's fruiting canes get the maximum sunlight is a very important corollary technique that goes with this method.

Other Benefits of Cluster Thinning

Cluster thinning and lighter pruning also reduce bunch rot in tight-clustered varieties like Chenin Blanc, California scientists have found. In fact, many tightly bunched vinifera would have looser clusters and less rot if pruned to sixty rather than the standard forty buds, then cluster-thinned to control the size of the crop.

Another beneficial effect of cluster thinning is improved berry set, so that remaining clusters will contain more berries and larger berries, in a looser cluster.

Some French-American hybrids are prone to produce clusters from basal buds that arise on older wood—de Chaunac is typical of these. Cluster thinning here is essential to remove any fruit on these suckers, if not the suckers themselves, so that the

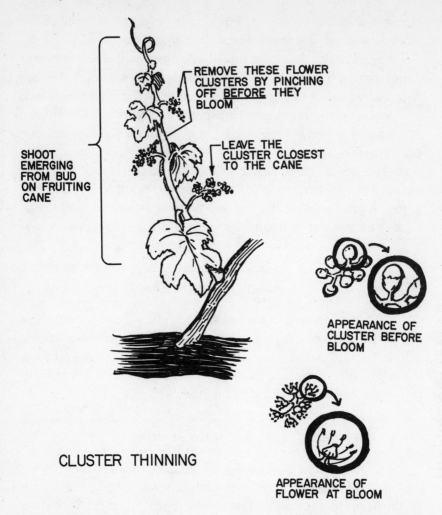

REMOVE THESE FLOWER CLUSTERS BY PINCHING OFF BEFORE THEY BLOOM

LEAVE THE CLUSTER CLOSEST TO THE CANE

SHOOT EMERGING FROM BUD ON FRUITING CANE

APPEARANCE OF CLUSTER BEFORE BLOOM

CLUSTER THINNING

APPEARANCE OF FLOWER AT BLOOM

crop is kept to the buds you've counted. Otherwise, the extra fruit set could mean overcropping, with delayed maturity, higher acid and lower sugar levels.

Cluster thinning can advance the maturity of the grapes by as much as a month, although two weeks is more common. This means late-maturing varieties can possibly be grown where growing seasons are shorter. It can also mean that mid-season or early-maturing varieties may ripen in the hot summer days, which will reduce fruit and wine quality. Thus cluster thinning isn't recommended on early-maturing eastern varieties, such as

TRELLIS SYSTEMS ILLUSTRATED

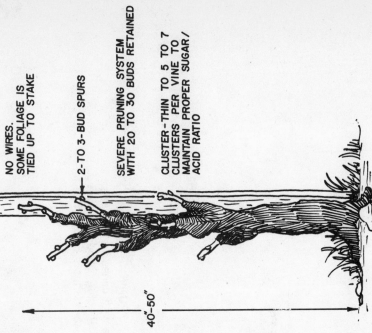

NO WIRES. SOME FOLIAGE IS TIED UP TO STAKE

2-TO 3-BUD SPURS

SEVERE PRUNING SYSTEM WITH 20 TO 30 BUDS RETAINED

CLUSTER-THIN TO 5 TO 7 CLUSTERS PER VINE TO MAINTAIN PROPER SUGAR/ACID RATIO

40″–50″

VERTICAL CORDON

Used in California to save space and avoid wires. Going out of favor.

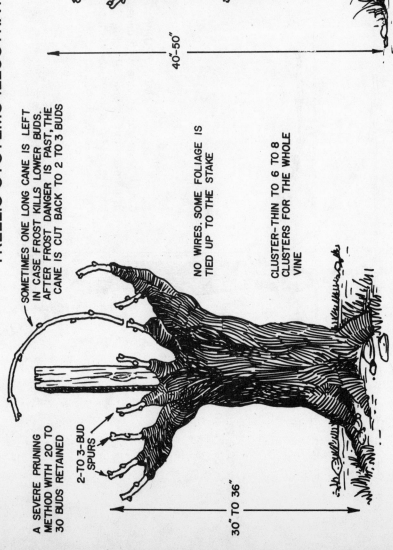

SOMETIMES ONE LONG CANE IS LEFT IN CASE FROST KILLS LOWER BUDS. AFTER FROST DANGER IS PAST, THE CANE IS CUT BACK TO 2 TO 3 BUDS

A SEVERE PRUNING METHOD WITH 20 TO 30 BUDS RETAINED

2-TO 3-BUD SPURS

NO WIRES. SOME FOLIAGE IS TIED UP TO THE STAKE

CLUSTER-THIN TO 6 TO 8 CLUSTERS FOR THE WHOLE VINE

30″ TO 36″

HEAD TRAINING

An old-fashioned method still found in California's northern counties, where it's used for varieties like Carignane and Zinfandel.

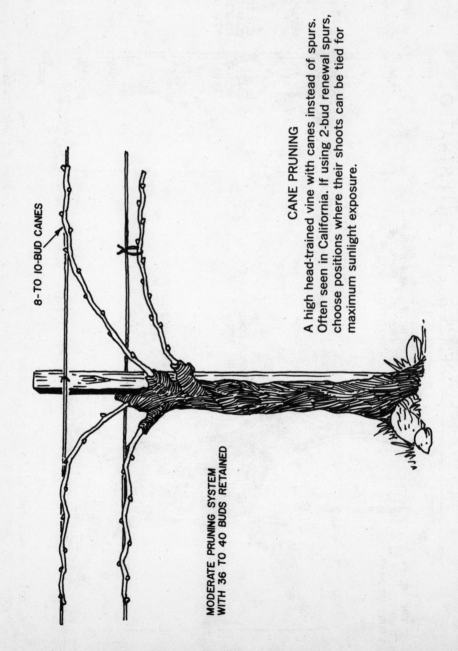

8-TO 10-BUD CANES

MODERATE PRUNING SYSTEM
WITH 36 TO 40 BUDS RETAINED

CANE PRUNING

A high head-trained vine with canes instead of spurs.
Often seen in California. If using 2-bud renewal spurs,
choose positions where their shoots can be tied for
maximum sunlight exposure.

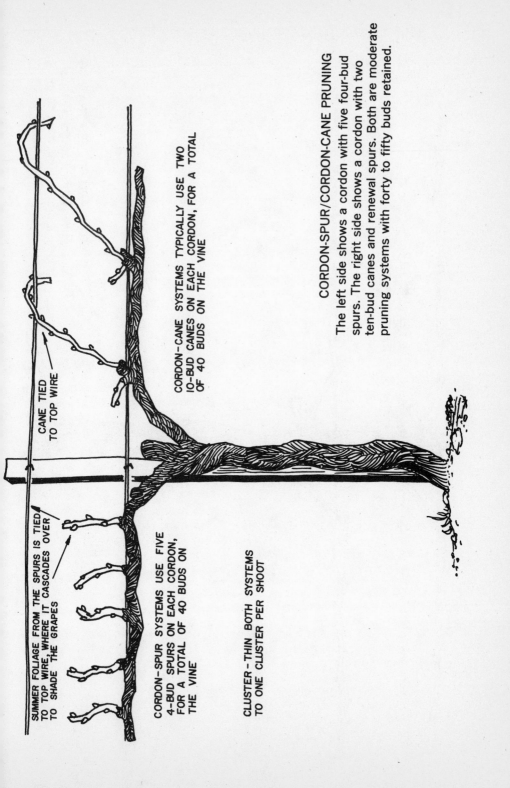

CORDON-SPUR/CORDON-CANE PRUNING

The left side shows a cordon with five four-bud spurs. The right side shows a cordon with two ten-bud canes and renewal spurs. Both are moderate pruning systems with forty to fifty buds retained.

CANE TIED TO TOP WIRE

CORDON-CANE SYSTEMS TYPICALLY USE TWO 10-BUD CANES ON EACH CORDON, FOR A TOTAL OF 40 BUDS ON THE VINE

SUMMER FOLIAGE FROM THE SPURS IS TIED TO TOP WIRE, WHERE IT CASCADES OVER TO SHADE THE GRAPES

CORDON-SPUR SYSTEMS USE FIVE 4-BUD SPURS ON EACH CORDON, FOR A TOTAL OF 40 BUDS ON THE VINE

CLUSTER-THIN BOTH SYSTEMS TO ONE CLUSTER PER SHOOT

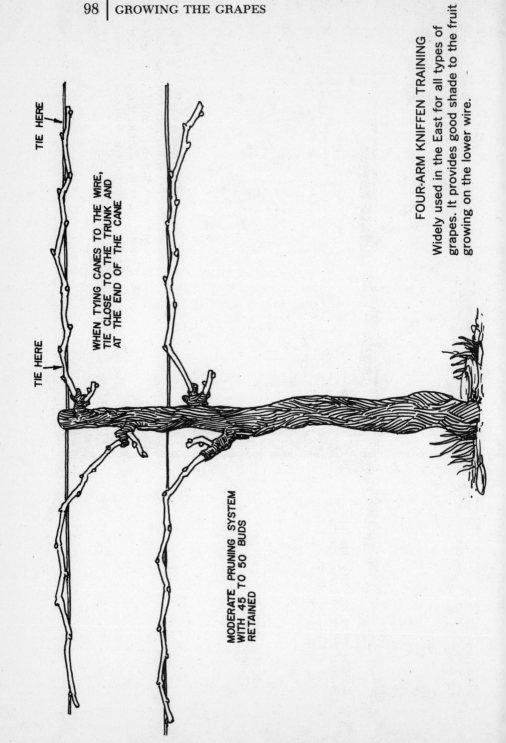

TIE HERE

TIE HERE

WHEN TYING CANES TO THE WIRE,
TIE CLOSE TO THE TRUNK AND
AT THE END OF THE CANE

MODERATE PRUNING SYSTEM
WITH 45 TO 50 BUDS
RETAINED

FOUR-ARM KNIFFEN TRAINING

Widely used in the East for all types of grapes. It provides good shade to the fruit growing on the lower wire.

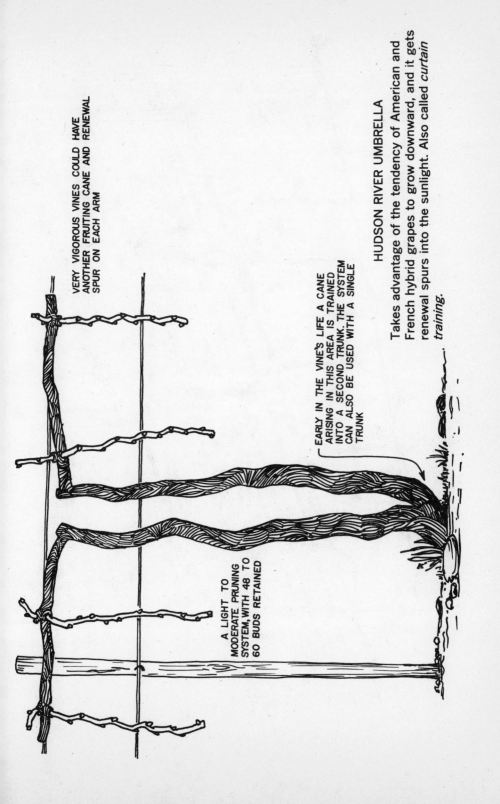

VERY VIGOROUS VINES COULD HAVE ANOTHER FRUITING CANE AND RENEWAL SPUR ON EACH ARM

EARLY IN THE VINE'S LIFE A CANE ARISING IN THIS AREA IS TRAINED INTO A SECOND TRUNK. THE SYSTEM CAN ALSO BE USED WITH A SINGLE TRUNK

A LIGHT TO MODERATE PRUNING SYSTEM, WITH 48 TO 60 BUDS RETAINED

HUDSON RIVER UMBRELLA

Takes advantage of the tendency of American and French hybrid grapes to grow downward, and it gets renewal spurs into the sunlight. Also called *curtain training.*

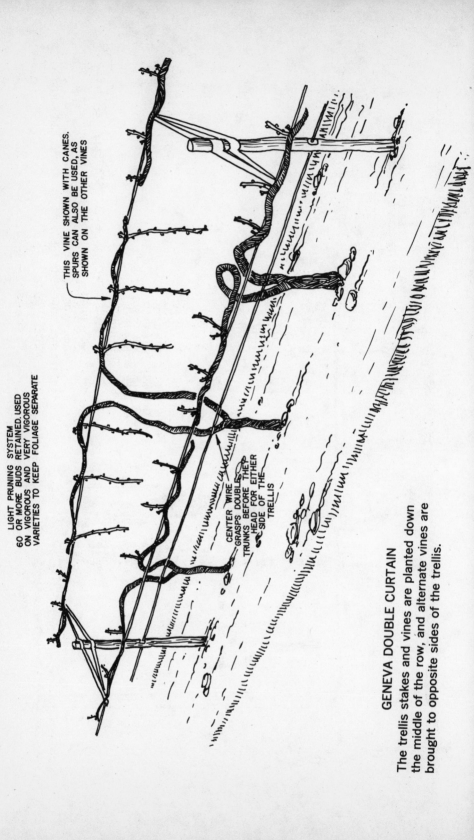

LIGHT PRUNING SYSTEM.
60 OR MORE BUDS RETAINED. USED
ON VIGOROUS AND VERY VIGOROUS
VARIETIES TO KEEP FOLIAGE SEPARATE

THIS VINE SHOWN WITH CANES.
SPURS CAN ALSO BE USED, AS
SHOWN ON THE OTHER VINES

CENTER WIRE
GRASPS DOUBLE
TRUNKS BEFORE THEY
HEAD FOR EITHER
SIDE OF THE
TRELLIS

GENEVA DOUBLE CURTAIN

The trellis stakes and vines are planted down
the middle of the row, and alternate vines are
brought to opposite sides of the trellis.

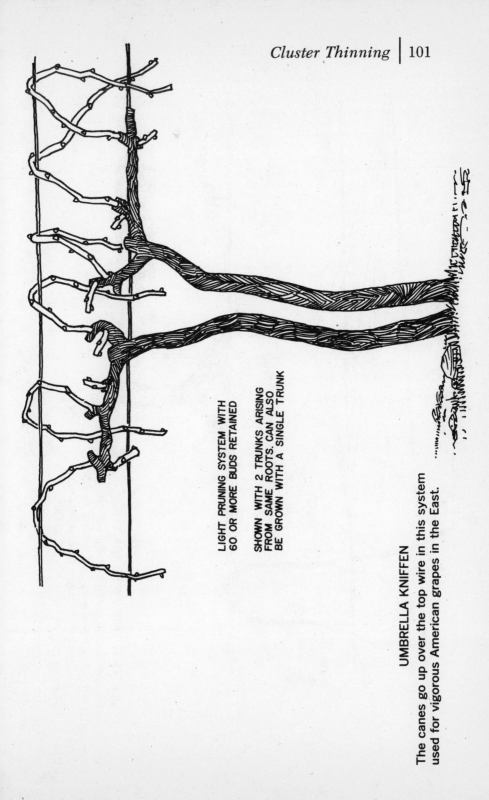

LIGHT PRUNING SYSTEM WITH
60 OR MORE BUDS RETAINED

SHOWN WITH 2 TRUNKS ARISING
FROM SAME ROOTS. CAN ALSO
BE GROWN WITH A SINGLE TRUNK

UMBRELLA KNIFFEN

The canes go up over the top wire in this system
used for vigorous American grapes in the East.

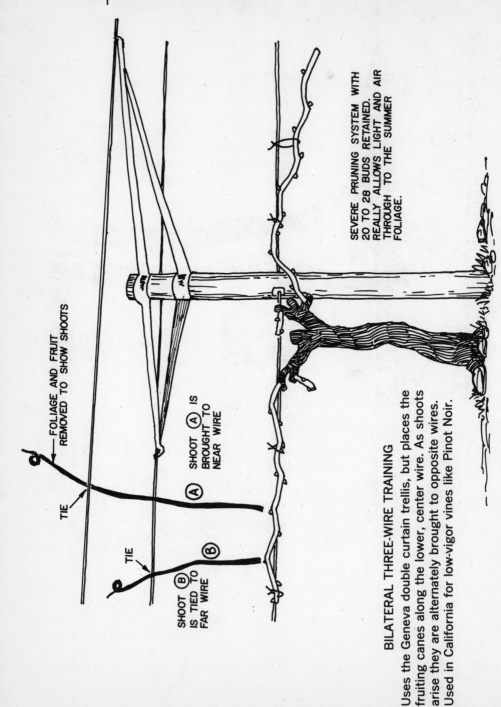

FOLIAGE AND FRUIT
REMOVED TO SHOW SHOOTS

TIE

Ⓐ SHOOT Ⓐ IS
BROUGHT TO
NEAR WIRE

TIE

SHOOT Ⓑ
IS TIED TO
FAR WIRE

SEVERE PRUNING SYSTEM WITH
20 TO 28 BUDS RETAINED.
REALLY ALLOWS LIGHT AND AIR
THROUGH TO THE SUMMER
FOLIAGE.

BILATERAL THREE-WIRE TRAINING

Uses the Geneva double curtain trellis, but places the
fruiting canes along the lower, center wire. As shoots
arise they are alternately brought to opposite wires.
Used in California for low-vigor vines like Pinot Noir.

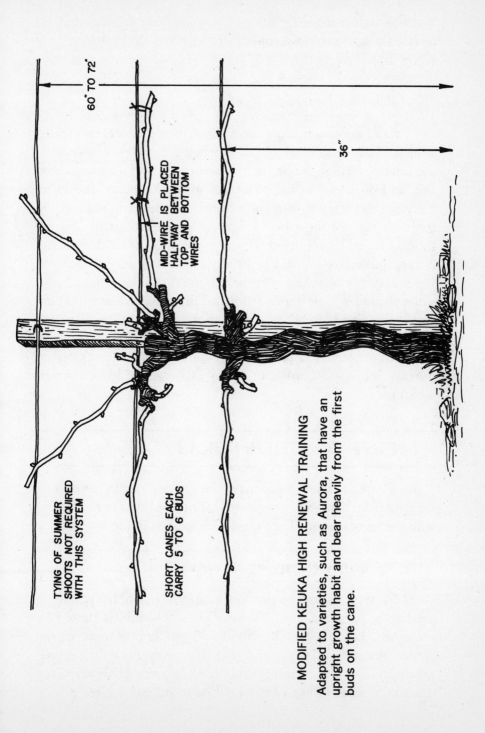

60" TO 72'

36"

MID-WIRE IS PLACED
HALFWAY BETWEEN
TOP AND BOTTOM
WIRES

TYING OF SUMMER
SHOOTS NOT REQUIRED
WITH THIS SYSTEM

SHORT CANES EACH
CARRY 5 TO 6 BUDS

MODIFIED KEUKA HIGH RENEWAL TRAINING

Adapted to varieties, such as Aurora, that have an
upright growth habit and bear heavily from the first
buds on the cane.

Aurora, unless the vine has put out so many clusters that it's obviously going to overcrop, or unless you want to help restore vigor to a weak vine.

Which Clusters to Remove

Let's say that a shoot has two or three clusters emerging. Which of the clusters should be pinched off? The ones closest to the cane or farther out on the shoot? I could find no research on this, so I did some of my own. Last spring I pinched shoots on the east side of my row to leave the cluster nearest the cane. On the west side of the row I left the cluster farthest out on the shoot. I tasted both sides at harvest and I must admit that the call is very subjective—still, I think the clusters closest to the cane were better, everything else being equal. For one thing, they were shaded a little more from the direct sun. Second, those closest received sugar from one more set of leaves than the clusters farther out. Third, the weight of the grapes was a little closer to the stronger parts of the vine. If the cluster closest to the cane looks small, weak, or damaged, however, leave a better-looking one.

PEST CONTROL STRATEGIES

There are many weapons in the vintner's armamentarium, ranging from benign to very deadly. They're listed here, starting with the most benign. They should be applied in the same order.

Naturally Occurring Controls

Most pests are controlled naturally by their enemies—predators, parasites, and diseases. These beneficials should be protected, because they'll provide 80 percent or more of the control that goes on in the vineyard. That means avoiding broad-spectrum insecticides, and giving beneficials good habitat, which essentially means a bit of old field or meadow nearby.

Applied Biological Controls

Parasites and predators of major grape pests can be purchased from insectaries for release in the vineyard. Your county agent may know the addresses of firms in your region that supply beneficial insects or parasites.

Diseases of larval worms and caterpillars are sold throughout the country at garden supply stores, under trade names such as Dipel and Thuricide. The active ingredient is *Bacillus thuringiensis* and the disease affects only caterpillarlike larvae. To be effective, the worms must eat spores of the disease sprayed on the leaves. It kills within three days.

It's possible to make one's own grape pest disease culture by looking for sick or dead caterpillars. If sick, they will lose color and move slowly, if at all. At death, they often hang limp and darkened from a leaf by a spot of "glue." Several of these are all you need to treat an acre of vines. Whiz them in a blender with a quart of water, strain, and dilute to spray your vines. Use right away, as this mixture will start to putrefy after twelve hours. It's a bit grisly, but very cheap and very effective. Just don't forget to clean the blender.

Feeding Repellents

These are safe and sometimes effective—which means that sometimes they're not. Very few are sold—you have to discover ones that work for you. The idea is to spray something on the vines that your target pest can't stand. It drives him away; your problem is solved. Some of the new products made from neem tree seeds are extremely effective repellents. But look around—what plant in your area is seldom, if ever, eaten by insects? Put some of the leaves in a blender with water, strain the slurry well, and spray it undiluted on your vine leaves. Catnip, tansy, pine, garlic, and sassafras are good choices to try. Make sure you know the plant you're spraying isn't something poisonous to you—like elderberry canes or poison ivy. It may take you a while to find something that repels troublesome pests, but when you do, the remedy is safe, cheap, and effective.

Traps

Sex-lure attractants are effective and are widely marketed in the East for Japanese beetles and Gypsy moths. In some, the sex lure is bolstered by food odors. Japanese beetles can quickly turn vine leaves to lace, reducing photosynthesis, and therefore sugar production, berry quality, and plant growth. These traps can be a real help. The pervasive scent of a female interferes with the males' ability to locate females for mating, and the traps actually capture hundreds of males.

Another kind of trap—effective against flea beetles, white fly, and some other insects—is a variation of flypaper. Gallon plastic jugs are painted bright yellow or yellow-orange. When dry, they're coated with a thin coat of Tanglefoot, the sticky stuff put on young tree trunks to catch crawling insects and ants. They can be set among the vines just before buds swell to catch emerging flea beetles, especially. For some reason, the bright yellow attracts them. One every 15 feet of row will do a good job. Set them on the ground (some water inside will keep them from blowing over), or hang empty from trellis wires.

Dormant Sprays

Dormant oil spray is a good preventive and remedy for mites and scale insects. It's applied in northern states when the sun coaxes the late winter or early spring daytime temperature up to the fifties (Fahrenheit), but nighttime temperatures plunge below freezing. Both mites and scale insects begin to stir under the brightening sun, and their respiration quickens. At this stage, they're vulnerable to a thin coat of oil, which covers and suffocates them. The coating is very thin. One-half pint of fresh 10-weight motor oil and one cup of a liquid dishwashing soap or detergent are stirred together in 2 gallons of water. Commercial dormant sprays are available, too, and these usually mix more easily with water. Make sure that the oil is thoroughly dispersed and emulsified. Once I halfheartedly stirred the oil and detergent in my sprayer, then sprayed my apple trees. Everything was okay until I did the last three trees. They looked too shiny. I soon figured out that the oil—not well dispersed—had settled to the bottom of the tank, and I was giving the trees a heavy coat of oil, which could penetrate to the cambium and kill them. I emptied the tank and cleaned it, then refilled it with hot water and detergent, and sprayed the trees again, trying to wash it off. I was lucky—there were no apparent ill effects from the overdose.

When you've made the dormant oil spray (which means an oil spray for dormant wood, not a spray made from something called "dormant oil"), mix it in a clean can or large bucket, then pour the emulsified oil mixture into the tank. My mistake was trying to mix right in the sprayer tank. Spray the entire vine until it's wet. Drenching isn't necessary. Spray *before* bud burst, as the oil will kill new leaf tissue.

Botanical Insecticides

They include rotenone, ryania, and pyrethrum—sometimes found in combination, usually as a dust that's dissolvable in water. These are broad-spectrum insecticides, and should be used as a last resort. Their advantage over chemicals such as carbaryl and malathion is that they are safer for people to be around.

Chemical Insecticides

The pyrethroids—chemical analogs of pyrethrum—are relatively safe but still toxic to humans. Lime-sulfur and flowable sulfur are sometimes used as misting agents and are safe to use. There are thousands of chemical insecticides. Personally, I avoid them. If you want to go that route, your county agent can advise you about which are effective for your particular pest problem. Be aware that they often cause as many problems as they solve in the tight-knit ecosystem of the healthy vineyard. They can be very dangerous to the person applying them. And some will eventually work its way into the finished wine. If you use chemical pesticides, it's wise to wear protective clothing and a mask.

All your pests are food for their parasites and predators. You want to knock an infestation's numbers back down to acceptable levels—where naturally occurring controls can keep them in check—rather than eliminate them completely. If you eliminate them, you'll also eliminate the beneficials that exist by eating or parasitizing them.

Institute no controls unless your vines or crop are in danger. Learn to tolerate a certain amount of insect presence and damage. Use the most benign control first. Only an intractable infestation of insects that threatens to destroy vines and crops would be cause for broad-spectrum insecticides. And maybe not even then: nature may be telling you to find another site for the vineyard.

For specific pest, disease, virus, and other vineyard problems, see Appendix 5.

FERTILIZATION

Observe how your vines grow when young. If the leaves are deep green and they're making good growth, you don't need to fertilize the first year or so. Most ground that's lain fallow for more than three years has enough nutrients to support at least the first year's growth, especially if it's been under sod or meadow grass. If you're planting where nothing was growing, the soil was rocky or poor, or in what was recently a heavily cropped field, fertilize with compost by digging about 4 to 6 inches of it into the top 2 or 3 inches of soil in a 4-foot-diameter circle around each young vine. If all looks well with the young vines, plan to fertilize in the third year and every year or two thereafter. Spread 2 or 3 inches of compost around each vine in a 6-foot-diameter circle and mix it into the top 2 inches with a rake or hoe. This is best done about two or three weeks before bud burst.

When most wine grape varieties are mature and properly fertilized, they'll produce between 3 and 4 pounds of cane prunings each year, or between 2.5 and 3.5 pounds for less vigorous vines such as Pinot Noir. Less than 3 pounds indicates the need for more nitrogen, especially if leaves are showing light green. More than 4 pounds means that the vines may be growing too much wood. Eliminate fertilization until pruning weights drop.

At 6- to 8-foot spacings, properly fertilized mature vines will cover about 90 percent of the trellis with dark green leaves in mid-August. Many growers who see less growth think that nitrogen fertilization will correct the problem, but that's not necessarily so. The problem may be overcropping. If over-cropped, highly fruitful French-American hybrids eventually lose vine size. Reduced vine size leads to even more fruitfulness. This causes yet more vine stress and even smaller vines. As long as overcropping is happening, extra nitrogen will only cause more problems than it solves.

Proper fertilization of grapes with nitrogen—such as is achieved with moderate applications of good compost—supplies the right level of nutrients in the berries for wine yeasts to eventually grow on.

Too much nitrogen produces free amino acids in the grape juice, which is a cause of hydrogen sulfide production in the wines. This is usually a consequence of using highly soluble commercial nitrogen fertilizers like ammonium sulfate, urea, or nitrates, or fresh manure in excess.

Making Compost

You don't have to make a hot compost pile to get good fertilizer for grapes. A large pile of leaves mixed with other plant matter will slowly and coolly decay over a few years by itself until it turns into a rich humus. It's likely to be low in nitrogen, so you may want to supplement it with some horse manure—ten parts old humus to one part horse manure, mixed together and applied around the vines. Applied by themselves, fresh manures give too much nitrogen to the vines, causing excessive vegeta-

Table 12 LEAF DEFICIENCY SYMPTOMS OF FOUR TRACE ELEMENTS IMPORTANT TO QUALITY GRAPE PRODUCTION

ELEMENT	MILD SYMPTOMS	SEVERE SYMPTOMS	LOCATION OF MOST SEVERELY AFFECTED LEAVES	CORRECTIVE MEASURES
Potassium	Yellowing between veins and on margins	Leaf scorch from margins inward	Midportion of shoot	Dust soil under vines with wood ashes or add ashes to compost
Magnesium	Yellowing between veins does not extend to margins on some leaves	Increasing yellowing with rusty blotches and dead spots on leaves	Base of shoot	Add dolomitic limestone to compost or dig in 1 pound under each vine
Manganese	Yellowing between veins in an intermittent pattern	Same as mild, only getting worse	Base of shoot	Add compost made with manure to soil under vines
Iron	Yellowing extends to the veins	Yellowed areas become intensely creamy white, then die	Shoot tips	Add compost made with manure to soil under vines

SOURCE: New York State College of Agriculture and Life Sciences, Cornell University.

tive growth that's slow to mature, and reducing the quality of the fruit crop. Old, well-rotted manure is good, but it may or may not have had most of its nitrogen leached. Go sparingly with rotted manure until you know that you're not overfertilizing. With vines, underfertilization is much preferable to overfertilization.

Some people make a large bin and toss in all the plant matter from their property. They take rotted material from the bottom continually, and add material to the top continually. It should take a couple of years for top material to reach the bottom, at which point it has been transformed from trash to humus, the first step toward the megachange—into wine.

With good compost, you don't have to worry about whether you have phosphorus, potash, manganese, zinc, or any other mineral. It contains everything the vines will need, including all the trace elements. Using compost fertilizers solves a host of problems at once, and in my view it is so far superior to commercial fertilizers (which contain only nitrogen, potassium and phosphorus, and tend to kill off earthworms) that I strongly recommend it for home vineyardists.

If you intend to use commercial fertilizers, despite my recommendation, you'll need a soil test arranged through your county agent and his recommendation for rates of fertilizer to apply.

HANDLING GRAPE CROPS

All flower clusters are picked off vines in their first year. In the second year, very vigorous and fruitful vines may be allowed to ripen a few clusters, just so you can taste the berries. In the third year, a light crop may be had, and you can make your first batch of wine, which will probably be less than half of what you'll get when the vines reach maturity. Four-year-old vines are capable of producing a crop, but if you allow more than one cluster per shoot, you'll have trouble reaching good sugar levels.

About eight weeks after bloom, you'll see the grapes start

to change color. This point is called *véraison,* and is the beginning of the ripening process. From here until harvest, your job will be to keep the clusters hanging airily in their redoubts under the leaves. On trips to the vineyard, pull away any dense foliage that's crowding the grape clusters and place it in better positions. Pull off any dead leaves that might be near a bunch. Repositioning rather than detaching green leaves that are crowding bunches is best. The leaves that arise nearest the bunch produce the most sugar for the bunch if positioned well to intercept light. Direct sunlight on the bunches can scald them and reduce color, so position shoots to allow elbow room under the canopy, but not so that sunlight can strike them.

Grapes in top positions where there's more air and light will ripen first, and the grapes lowest and in the densest shade will ripen last.

DETERMINING RIPENESS

From *véraison* on, sugar and acid levels in the grapes can be measured and plotted so that you can see the moment of perfect ripeness approaching and be ready for the day when it arrives.

The concept of perfect ripeness needs some explaining. Some say perfect red grapes give the following readings: 22 Brix, 0.75 acid, and a pH about 3.4. That's like saying the perfect poker hand is a royal flush. You don't see it very often. Sometimes you're dealt a pair of fours, sometimes a full house.

There are three factors—sugar, acid, and pH—that can be tracked weekly after *véraison* and that will reach optimum levels when the grapes are ready to harvest for winemaking.

For years I made wine without measuring these factors. Some wine was excellent. Some was poured out as undrinkable. For consistently good wine from grapes of optimum quality, I'd suggest getting the equipment necessary to make these tests. Taste the grapes as you test them weekly, so that you can learn to associate certain tastes with certain changes in the measured factors. Eventually, you would like to be able to walk into the vineyard, taste the grapes and decide whether or not to harvest. As far as I know, nobody interested in producing great wine does that. They're too interested in knowing the numbers.

The factors to be measured are Brix, titratable acidity, and pH.

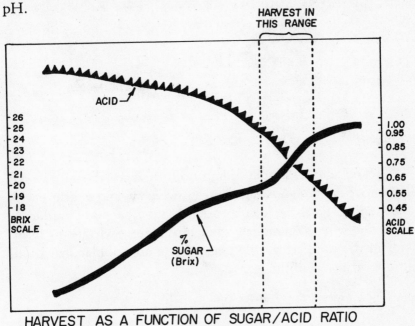

HARVEST AS A FUNCTION OF SUGAR/ACID RATIO

Brix

Also known as degrees Balling, it is really the percentage of sugar in the grape juice. Its presence raises the specific gravity of grape juice above 1.000, which is the specific gravity of distilled water. Therefore, we can use a hydrometer that measures Brix or Balling to get sugar content. These are found at most winemaking supply shops (see Appendix 3). Some hydrometers are Baumé hydrometers. Don't use a Baumé, or you'll have to do cumbersome conversions.

Two separate 100-berry samples, each crushed, sieved, and measured with a hydrometer, with their specific gravities then averaged, will give an accuracy of plus or minus 1° Brix for the grapes in the whole vineyard. Five 100-berry samples will give an accuracy of plus or minus half a degree.

The berries should be selected from the middle of the bunches, taken randomly from vines of the same variety, avoiding end vines and obviously diseased or stunted vines.

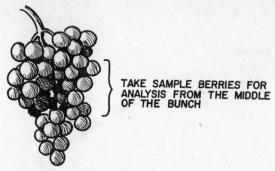

TAKE SAMPLE BERRIES FOR ANALYSIS FROM THE MIDDLE OF THE BUNCH

The samples should be lightly crushed and the juice sieved to remove any free-floating particles, which would interfere with the reading. Pour the juice into a glass tube, such as a graduated flask, that will accommodate the hydrometer. Swirl the hydrometer in the juice to rid the glass of any air bubbles that could throw off the reading.

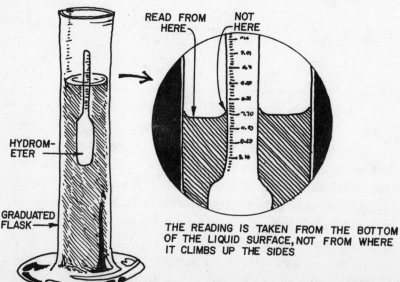

READ FROM HERE

NOT HERE

HYDROM- ETER

GRADUATED FLASK

THE READING IS TAKEN FROM THE BOTTOM OF THE LIQUID SURFACE, NOT FROM WHERE IT CLIMBS UP THE SIDES

Table 13 converts specific gravity to degrees Brix. This table also shows potential alcohol. It gives one an idea of final alcohol if the grapes are fermented to dryness—all sugar converted to alcohol. The actual final alcohol may differ slightly, but not by much. Winemakers' supply stores also have tables for conversion of specific gravity to Brix.

 Hand refractometers take sugar readings right in the vineyard, and they need only a drop of juice. They're reasonably accurate, extremely handy, and expensive. They measure soluble solids (sugar) by the degree to which light is refracted as it passes through the juice. The instrument can be ordered from suppliers listed in Appendix 3.

 Hydrometers usually come calibrated at 59° F, meaning that any deviation from that temperature will expand or contract the liquid, throwing the reading off. Take the temperature of the grape juice and use Table 14 to make conversions.

 Over the years, scientific experiments have shown that there are optimum Brix readings for ripe grapes of various varie-

Table 13
HYDROMETER READINGS/BRIX EQUIVALENTS

SPECIFIC GRAVITY	BRIX	% POTENTIAL ALCOHOL	SPECIFIC GRAVITY	BRIX	POTENTIAL ALCOHOL
1.040	10.4	5.4	1.100	24.2	14.2
1.045	11.6	6.1	1.105	25.3	15.0
1.050	12.8	6.8	1.110	26.4	*
1.055	14.0	7.6	1.115	27.5	
1.060	15.2	8.3	1.120	28.5	
1.065	16.4	9.0	1.125	29.6	
1.070	17.6	9.7	1.130	30.6	
1.075	18.7	10.4			
1.080	19.8	11.1			
1.085	20.9	11.9			
1.090	22.0	12.7			
1.095	23.1	13.1			

*At about this point, the alcohol concentration becomes sufficient to kill remaining yeast, and any residual sugar will stay unfermented.

Table 14 CORRECTING HYDROMETER READINGS BASED ON TEMPERATURE

TEMPERATURE OF THE LIQUID	SPECIFIC GRAVITY WILL BE RAISED OR LOWERED BY	BRIX READING WILL NEED TO BE RAISED OR LOWERED BY
41° F	−0.002	−0.05
50° F	−0.001	−0.25
59° F	—	—
68° F	+0.001	+0.25
77° F	+0.002	+0.50
86° F	+0.003	+0.75
95° F	+0.005	+1.25
106° F	+0.007	+1.75

ties in varying climates that give wine of the highest possible quality. Don't worry if your grapes don't reach these sugar levels when your measurements say harvest time has arrived. It is possible to add sugar in order to bring up the alcohol level—although sugar additions add nothing to the taste of wines. American and French-American hybrids in the East are best at Brix 19–23, with the optimum of Brix 21–22. In cooler areas or when the weather hasn't cooperated, they may often be below the minimum Brix and may need additional sugar for balance in the final wine. For vinifera, the optimum Brix is between 20 and 22.

Titratable Acidity

Acids give crispness, brightness, and thirst-quenching qualities to wines and are essential components of the balance in a fine wine. Most of the acid will be tartaric, and some will be malic, with some tiny amounts of other kinds, such as citric and succinic. Grape acids protect the must from the growth of spoilage organisms.

Just as sugar has an optimum level around 22 Brix, so acid has arguable optimum levels of 0.60 to 0.80 for reds and 0.65 to 0.85 for whites. Harvest is indicated when the acid comes closest to these optimums at the same time that sugar comes closest to its optimums. In many cases, the optimums will not be reached, so later in this section I'll be giving rules of thumb for judging readiness for harvest.

"Titratable acidity" is a measure of total acid in the grape juice expressed as the tartaric acid content. Tartaric is a sharply sour acid with by far the largest effect on taste, while malic acid is softer, with a less pronounced effect. The procedure for determining titratable acidity isn't complicated, but it must be done carefully. TA kits are available from most home winemaking supply stores, and there are several mail-order suppliers listed in Appendix 3. If you live in a town where there's a wine laboratory, such as North East, Pennsylvania, or St. Helena, California, you can have juice tested for a nominal cost.

Determining titratable acidity involves neutralizing a predetermined amount of juice with an accurately measured standard alkaline solution. The point of neutralization is confirmed by use of an indicator, usually phenolphthalein.

Your apparatus will include two 20-ml. syringes, one for juice and one for alkaline solution. These should not be used interchangeably, so mark them if they're not differentiated in your kit. You'll need a beaker that should be kept with the kit and used for no other purpose.

Your reagents will be a high-accuracy 0.1 Normal (decinormal) solution of sodium hydroxide, which is the alkaline neutralizing agent. You'll also need distilled water, although Dr. McGrew says he uses tap water that he measures with his indicator kit to make sure it isn't either acid or alkaline. I'd stick with a bottle of distilled water, obtainable at most drugstores. Your kit will also have a bottle of phenolphthalein solution.

Using one of the syringes, draw up 15 ml. of juice and squirt it into the beaker. Then add from three to five drops of phenolphthalein solution—follow your kit's instructions for the proper number of drops. Using the other syringe, take up 20 ml. of the sodium hydroxide solution and add it drop by drop, swirling the liquid in the beaker to mix it thoroughly. Continue the drops of sodium hydroxide one by one until you first see a pink color in white juice or a blue-gray-black color in red juice, which doesn't disappear when the liquid is swirled. This is the *end point*. When the addition of more sodium hydroxide doesn't change the color further, you've overshot the end point. The color appears only when the acid is neutralized. Some practice will soon make you as expert as you need to be. When the end point is reached, note the number of milliliters used.

The number of milliliters used is divided by 2. This gives you tartaric acid in parts per thousand, or tenths of a percent, equivalent to grams per 100 milliliters. For instance, if you've used 10 ml. of sodium hydroxide solution, that will be $10/2 = 5$ ppt of tartaric acid, or TA of 0.50 percent (five-tenths of one percent usually shown without the percent sign or 0.50 gm/100 ml.). Our optimum acid of 0.70 for white wine would thus have required 14 drops of sodium hydroxide solution; an acid reading of 1.00 would have required 20 drops, and so forth.

Obviously, very dark red juice or wine is going to create end point identification problems, since it's hard to see a color change occur in a dark red liquid. The answer is to add 5 volumes (75 ml.) of distilled water to the 15 ml. of juice placed in the beaker. The water will reduce the color, but not the total amount of acid in the beaker, which will require the same amount of sodium hydroxide to neutralize as the pure juice. This is more of a problem when finding TA for wine, since it's not hard to get a clear juice even from red grapes, as long as you don't squeeze the skins enough to break the color sacs. White juice from red grapes will turn pink when the endpoint is reached.

Most winemakers do the TA test twice, then average the results. If the results of the two tests differ by more than 0.05 percent, something has gone awry, and you should start again with new juice. The same grape berries used for determining sugar content should be used for TA, since these are randomly picked from the whole plot and will give the most accurate results.

At this point, you will know the Brix and the TA of your grapes.

pH

As you probably remember from high school chemistry, pH is a measure of the number of free (H+) hydrogen ions in a solution. This is related to TA, but differs from it in significant ways, and the pH of grape juice may or may not be correlated with the amount of tartaric acid. As with our other measurements, there are optimums: pH 3.1 or 3.2 for white grape juice, and 3.4 for reds.

pH papers are made to test juice, but most are hardly accurate enough for fine winemaking. We need to know pH to 0.1, which means the use of a pH meter. These cost somewhat more than a hand refractometer. If you don't want to buy one, I'd suggest talking to the chemistry teacher at your local high school about going in after school hours to test juice with one of the department's pH meters. Colleges, too, of course, have them. And most towns have commercial laboratories that do chemical analysis, and will probably charge a minimal amount, if anything at all, for plunking their pH meter's measuring rod into some juice. Make sure that the meter gives readings with an accuracy of plus or minus 0.1. If you have access to one that gives an accuracy of only plus or minus 0.15, which many do, run several measurements and see if they differ. If they do, average them. Use clear, strained juice, as solid particles in the juice will distort the reading.

Even when TA is within a good range, pH can run high —above 3.3 for whites and 3.5 for reds. High-pH juice can lead to wine defects from spoilage organisms. If the pH is high, your grapes may be overripe, or your soil may have too much available potassium in it. High soil potassium is directly linked to high pH in the juice. Such juice can be given extra tartaric acid and malic acid during winemaking. The pH of finished wine will be higher than that of the juice, as some acid is reduced and some precipitated, while still more is changed during fermentation to less acid substances.

With an accurate pH reading, you now have the three factors you'll need to determine when to harvest.

Brix:TA Ratio Measures Ripeness

The balance between sweetness and acidity is a basic concept in judging the quality of fruits and other foods, and grapes and wine are no exceptions. When connoisseurs speak of "balanced" wine, that balance is most of what they're talking about, even if they aren't aware of the chemistry of the balance.

The *ratio* of Brix to TA is a better indicator of ripeness and quality than sweetness or tartness alone. Researchers at the University of California at Davis have found that wines are most in balance when the Brix:TA ratio is between 30:1 and 35:1. So let's say your grapes are ripening. You've been taking weekly measurements of Brix and TA since *véraison,* and you see these values changing toward the moment of perfection when harvest is indicated. Let's say your grapes are at 16 Brix and 1.10 acid. The Brix:TA ratio is about 15:1—nowhere near the harvesting point. But now let's say your grapes have developed to 22 Brix and 0.75 TA. The ratio is now about 30:1, and you can start harvesting anytime. Keep plotting this ratio from *véraison,* doing it more frequently as the grapes near the 30:1 ratio. You can let them hang after they reach 30:1, but don't let them go beyond 35:1 unless you're making botrytized or sweet dessert wine.

During ripening, the sugar levels go up and the acid levels come down. At some point they will reach a ratio of 30:1, and that's your cue to harvest. However, especially in cold, eastern regions where high acidity is a problem, they may only get to a 25:1 ratio and stay there. Now check the pH. If it's approaching 3.4 to 3.5, harvest and crush before it goes above those numbers, no matter what the Brix and TA are doing. The pH reading thus gives a check against total reliance on the Brix:TA ratio.

A Better Measure of Ripeness

There is another, probably even more accurate, measure

of harvestability, and it is especially good to use in high-potassium soils where there's a danger of high pH. Since you have readings for Brix, TA, and pH each week, it takes only a moment on the calculator to get this alternative measure, which is Brix times pH^2. That is, you multiply the pH by itself, and then multiply the product by the Brix. Harvest grapes for white wines when this number gets as close as possible to 200, and grapes for red wines when this number approaches 260. Here's an example for each:

WHITE

Brix = 20	3.3	10.89
pH = 3.3	×3.3	×20
	99	217.80
Goal = 200	99	
	10.89	

217.80 is not bad for a white. If the number has been rising steadily, harvest. It will only go higher.

RED

Brix = 19	3.5	12.25
pH = 3.5	×3.5	×19
	175	11025
Goal = 260	105	1225
	12.25	232.75

Again, not bad for a red. If the number has been rising steadily, check again tomorrow. Don't let the pH go any higher than 3.5, however, before harvesting.

HARVESTING BOTRYTIZED GRAPES

Given all these measurements, you should have no trouble knowing just when to harvest. You may, however, want to wait, no matter what the scientific recommendations are, because you want to make a high-sugar, late-picked wine, or are waiting for botrytis rot to do its thing. You should pick botrytized white grapes when the pH reaches 3.2, no matter what the other measurements are. Within three days of reaching 3.2, the pH of such grapes will take off and shoot up to 3.6–3.8, way too high. The grapes will turn to mush and you'll lose the harvest. Also be aware that botrytized grapes are hard to ferment and often "stick," that is, stop fermenting. They are also prone to quick oxidation, as are all late-picked grapes.

Ravat 51 presents a different picture, however. In the Finger Lakes, this variety will reach 25 Brix with acid levels still up around 1.2–1.3. Even at 30 Brix, this variety will have acid levels of 1.0, with a good pH. In the cold portions of the East, this is the variety to grow if you want to utilize the benefits of botrytis.

Keep measuring. Don't let the pH go above 3.3 with whites or 3.5 with reds. Harvest when the Brix:TA ratio is as close as possible to 30:1–35:1, and when Brix $\times$ pH^2 is as close as possible to 200 for whites and 260 for reds.

WEATHER AS A HARVEST FACTOR

Weather is an increasingly important factor as you approach harvest. If your grapes are slightly less than optimum, but the weather forecast calls for three days of drenching rain, get the grapes in. Rain just before harvest can swell berries, cracking them, diluting the flavor factors, and allowing openings for spoilage microorganisms. Weather must be factored into your harvest decision, but it's always a judgment call. Sometimes in rainy years the acid will always be too high, the sugar too low, and the flavor factors poor. In France in such years they used to make nonvintage wine, but this happens less and less these days as even the great châteaux vintage date their poor wines.

Some years will be better than others. That's what sharpens the home winemaker's ability to be philosophical. Measure, check, watch the weather, taste the grapes, and harvest when you've got as many of these ducks in a row as possible.

HARVESTING

When picking, cut the clusters off with shears, and look them over for small green shot berries, rotten or diseased fruit, and trash and dead leaves, and pick these out. Soon, the leaves will start to turn shades of light green, yellow, and red as they approach leaf fall and dormancy. Any late mildew should be checked. Your cover crop will turn brown after frosts. Leaves will drop. Now's the time to check the past season's shoots to see if the canes have properly matured. Most shoots, especially those from the renewal area, should be brown almost all the way —if not all the way—to their tips. Unripened cane will not overwinter. But let it go. You'll take care of winterkill when you prune the vineyard in the late winter or early spring. From now on, your attention is going to the grapes that will soon be wine. The plants have kept their part of the bargain and have delivered to you a harvest of sweet fruit. Taste it and relish it fresh. Of all juices, grape is the sweetest of nature's nectars.

PART 3

MAKING THE WINE

God makes wine. Only the ungrateful or the purblind can fail to see that sugar in the grape and yeast on the skins is a divine idea, not a human one.

Father Robert Capon,
The Supper of the Lamb

MAKING CONSISTENTLY FINE WINE

There are three ways to make wine: dumb luck, by recipe, and from know-how. It's possible to make great wine by dumb luck or recipe, but not consistently. Only by understanding what's going on in the vineyard, measuring several factors, and using careful skills such as cleanliness and timing can you make the best possible wine year after year. As Tom Cottrell, enologist at the Geneva, New York, Experiment Station, said, "Using a recipe may produce 'safe' wine, but cannot optimize or bring to excellence any wine with characteristics that lie beyond the scope of the recipes. Great wine produced by recipe is truly great luck."

On a recent California wine tour, I brought home several bottles of homemade. My most treasured was a bottle of Cabernet Sauvignon from grapes grown in Oakville and vinified by Peter Forni. His label reads:

1980 Oakville Cabernet Sauvignon

TA .65   Alcohol 13.5%

pH 3.65   Total SO_2 82

It is just these measurements that we'll need to know in order to maximize the quality of our homemade wines, and we'll be describing what they mean for winemaking later in this section. Now, however, it's back to the vineyard where our grapes are picked and lie in boxes ready to be taken in for crushing. A word about the boxes: commercial growers use plastic containers that hold about forty pounds of grapes each and stack on top of one another without crushing the grapes beneath. These are ideal, but in a small vineyard sturdy cardboard boxes that are clean and dry are fine, as long as you don't set them on top of one another. The last thing you want to do is crush or split any grapes before you're ready to, as unwanted molds and yeasts could colonize them.

Crush Immediately After Picking

Time, for the moment, becomes of the essence, as the grapes should be taken to your winemaking area and crushed into a fermentable slurry or pressed into juice as soon as possible. Immediately is ideal. If it's a hot day, and you must hold the grapes for any length of time, get them out of the sun into a cool place. Don't try to cool them by hosing them with cold water. That'll cool them, but it will also immediately reduce the quality of the grapes by producing conditions for bad mold spores and off-flavored yeasts to multiply, and by washing away the microscopic spider nests and other goodies that contribute their *je ne sais quoi* to the finished wine. Have everything ready for the crush before you pick, and see how fast you can turn them into crushed grapes. The shorter the time from vine to crusher, the higher the quality of the wine. Many home winemakers in the East get shipments of "fresh" California grapes. The packers stuff forty pounds into boxes and nail on the lids, crushing many of the berries. Then they're refrigerated (a condition that the worst molds favor), shipped east, and days or even a week or more later, are carted home in the back of a hot station wagon. By the time they're crushed, many of the grapes are little vinegar pots, and it's almost impossible to make quality wine from them. Flash-frozen chunks of mashed grapes are now being sold by Wine & The People in Berkeley, California, and shipped around the country. These make a much better wine, but not up to the quality of wine from fresh-picked grapes, since freezing reduces total acidity and elevates pH—not desirable in California grapes.

As soon as the fruit is picked, it's likely to draw fruit flies, especially *Drosophila melanogaster,* the little fly with the giant chromosomes that geneticists are so fond of diddling with. So, it's important to get the fruit to the crusher quickly. From this point until the wine is safely bottled away, make every effort to keep fruit flies off the grapes, and out of the must. These flies, because they're always walking around on split and decaying fruit of all kinds, carry the acetobacter bacteria—the one that turns alcohol into acetic acid (vinegar). This chemical transformation can take place only in the presence of air, which is why winemakers keep their developing wines away from air except in the first stages of the process.

Decisions of the First Few Days

Crushing immediately after picking means being ready to crush before you pick. Let's quickly go over what's going to happen during the first few days after picking, so you'll have an overall idea of the process. Also, consult chart, "Winemaking Process Simplified," on page 129. You're going to bring in the picked grapes and make some important decisions: whether or not to take the berries off the stems; whether to do a light pressing of whole or crushed grapes to capture the finest juice; whether to have the juice ferment in a vat, barrel, or glass carboy. In any case, you're going to end up with a container of grape juice, with or without stems and crushed skins. Now you'll read Brix, TA, and pH. From these you'll know whether to add sugar to increase final alcohol, and whether to adjust the acidity. Also from these readings you'll figure the amount of potassium metabisulfite to add to the must—if you decide to add any at all. Then you'll cover the container and forget the juice until the next day, when you'll add the yeast.

From crushing through the end of the primary fermentation a few days later, the must can be exposed to air without harm, although you'll cover the vat with cloth to keep out fruit flies. In fact, you'll be punching down the cap that forms on your fermenting must in order to get some air into it and keep the must homogenized. White wines are much more prone to oxidation than reds, but, even so, some air contact is important when the primary fermentation is going on. Although Tom Cottrell says "oxidation paranoia is a relatively sane state" for the wine-

WINEMAKING PROCESS SIMPLIFIED

(All steps are fully explained in the text)

RED WINE	WHITE OR PINK WINE

FIRST DAY

Stem and crush grapes into fermentation vat

Stem, crush, and press juice from white or red grapes into vat, or into carboys two-thirds full.

Then: Test TA, adjust if necessary.
Test Brix, adjust if necessary.
Test pH.
Add potassium metabisufite.

(Whites left on skins are pressed after 8–16 hours. The juice is vatted or put into carboys two-thirds full.)

SECOND DAY

Add yeast.

Punch down cap twice a day during this period.

PRIMARY FERMENTATION

(Just after primary begins to slow, add malolactic starter culture.)

Brix reduced by two-thirds. Fermentation slows.

3–12 DAYS LATER

Press and transfer juice to carboys filled to shoulder. Attach air locks.

Transfer vatted whites to carboys filled to shoulder. Attach air locks.

SECONDARY FERMENTATION

(Whites in carboys can be given an optional racking 5 days after primary ends to increase freshness.)

1–2 MONTHS LATER

Secondary fermentation ends. All bubbling ceases.

Rack into clean carboys filled to within an inch of the cork. Add oak chips, if desired. Or, rack into an oak barrel at this time.

Cold stabilize during this period.

2–3 MONTHS LATER

Rack wine again. Top up.

3–4 MONTHS LATER

Rack again. Test pH, TA, residual sugar, percentage alcohol.
Bottle the wine or top up carboys or barrel and bottle at leisure.

maker and the wine, "at the beginning of the life of the wine, some oxygen is actually helpful. By causing early browning of some phenolic compounds that subsequently precipitate when the wine ferments, the final wine is lighter and more resistant to oxidative browning in its later life. Having made clean, light Chardonnays from oxidized musts that looked like lentil soup, I can assure you that even severe early browning of juice is not necessarily bad."

After the primary fermentation, when the furious action of the yeast on sugar starts to settle down and wine has emerged from grape juice, then will be time enough for oxidation paranoia.

Process only one grape variety at a time. Dumping several kinds of grapes in the hopper at once leads to mediocre wine in most cases. The exception would be when you're including some teinturier grapes for added color. Otherwise, I'd strongly recommend vinifying each grape variety separately, and blending much later in the process—just before bottling. It's a matter of control. Blending pure variety types later gives you microfine-tuning capabilities that are impossible once everything's dumped together in the fermentation vat.

The First Day's Procedures

Now let's go back and look at the first day's procedures in more detail.

First, what kind of grapes do you have? And what kind of wine do you have in mind? The answers to these questions determine how you're going to handle the grapes you've just picked.

Most likely you'll have either red or white grapes. Pink grapes like Gewürztraminer or Catawba are usually handled like a white—although you may want to vinify them like reds after you possess enough winemaking skill to try knowledgeable experiments.

• *Red Grapes* Since you've already picked the trash off the bunches in the vineyard, it's possible to toss them in the vat without stemming them. They can then be mashed to a pulp with feet, hands, or a pestle of some nonporous material like stainless steel, porcelain, or plastic. Wood can be used if it's coated with paraffin to fill the pores. With any such pestle, cleanliness is important. Wash in hot ammonia water and rinse *thoroughly* before using. You don't want to add any bacteria or mold spores or add other material that could harbor decay microorganisms. Personally, I think feet do the best job. My wife, Marilyn, scrubs her legs and feet until they're squeaky clean. Then from the shower, making sure all soapy water is rinsed off her feet, into clean socks. These she strips off one by one as she steps into the vat of grapes. Given the size of our vats, the juice and pulp reach above her knee, and she treads in place until the grapes have been crushed and are all off the stems. The sight of her thighs dripping with grape juice never fails to quicken my pulse. This is not a bad time to put your Bo Diddley record on the turntable and pass around some wine that's good for gulping.

Treading about 150 pounds of grapes in a 30-gallon vat of some kind (we'll discuss "kinds" a little further on) shouldn't take more than ten minutes. Make the most of them.

Leaving the stems in the must will give you more bitter principles, such as tannin, and some herbaceousness, too. These may be to your taste, and they will help the wine age the way a big red is supposed to. Many vintners stem the bunches by hand, but that's too much work for me. I think red wine benefits from some stems, so here's what I do. After Marilyn exits the vat, I go through the slurry with my (thoroughly washed and rinsed) arms and hands and remove most of the stems, which are floating free. I'd say that about one of every ten original stems remains in the must after this is finished. Doing this also gives you a chance to detach and squeeze open any berries still clinging to the stems, or, if the berries are underripe or mummified and cling tightly, discard them with the stems.

Many winemakers have a stemmer-crusher, especially those who do any volume of wine, such as 50 or more gallons a year. Small versions of these sit on top of your vat and do the stemming and crushing at the turn of a crank or, in some models, at the flick of a switch. While I like the hand-done (or foot-done) approach just for the tradition and fun of it, I'd probably invest in a stemmer-crusher if I made any more wine than I usually do (about 40 gallons a year).

Allowing pulp, skins, some stems, and juice to ferment leads to a big, deeply colored red wine. This is because so much of the flavor and color is in the skins, and it's extracted into the wine during the primary fermentation. The juice is then pressed out after the primary.

A lighter, fresher red wine can be made by stemming and crushing the grapes right into a wine press and immediately pressing out the juice. Because the skins don't stew in the must during the primary fermentation, very little color and little of the subtle flavors of the grapes suffuse into the juice, which will probably be a shade of pink—or in the case of de Chaunac, light orange. The resulting wine will be light, fruity, fresh, and drinkable next year. It won't age for more than another year before starting to lose quality. Such wine can be delightful, but it is almost always ordinary. Great reds, however, come from lots of skin and some stem contact in the fermenting must.

• *White and Pink Grapes* To get all the flavor and subtlety you can from a good, ripe Chardonnay, Seyval Blanc, or other white that can yield big wines, stem and crush by hand or foot, or use the stemmer-crusher. The juice is allowed to sit on the skins 12 hours before being pressed, to pick up extra flavors. The benefits of soaking whites on the skins for about 12 hours go beyond enriching flavor. Susan Freas, a graduate student in enology at Penn State, described an experiment in which her department crushed three batches each of Seyval Blanc, Vidal 256, Chardonnay, and Riesling. One batch was immediately fermented. A second was left on the skins for 8 hours, and a third batch sat on the skins for 16 hours. These batches were then fermented and the resulting wines evaluated. With 16 hours skin contact, all the varieties gave a greater yield of juice (due to the softening and breakdown of cells in skins and pulp), higher sugar, color, and flavor components, while acid levels were lower, than wines from batches with less skin contact time or none at all.

If possible, the juice and skins should be kept between 55° and 65° F. At higher temperatures, there's a greater chance of oxidative browning and production of bitter phenols.

White wine makers after a light, clean, fresh, and fruity wine de-stem and crush the grapes and immediately press out the juice. All the juice can be pressed out at once or you can make two grades of wine. The finest and lightest grade comes from grapes that are de-stemmed, then put *uncrushed* into the wine press for squeezing. A light-medium pressure is applied. The juice that comes from this light squeezing will be very clear and fine, and will make an exceedingly light and pleasant wine. This "first-run" juice is then fermented separately from the juice that runs from harder pressure. At the second pressing, don't press too hard—just enough to get the bulk of the juice out. Some winemakers who are running both reds and whites toss the white's solids into the red's fermenting vats, but I don't recommend this.

Cleanliness

Everything that contacts the crushed grapes or must should be thoroughly clean, and rinsed with a sterilizing solution. I usually wash everything with hot ammonia water—never soap. Rinsing well is imperative, since you don't want even a molecule of ammonia in the wine.

Most winemakers use a sterilizing solution of sodium or potassium metabisulfite, rather than ammonia. After I use ammonia and several clean water rinses, then I finish with a rinse of the sulfite sterilizing solution. The air is swarming with all manner of bacteria and spores, so you can't be antiseptic. Just make sure that everything is clean. And that includes the room you're in. The image of mold-encrusted walls in a dank wine cellar may seem romantic, but that isn't the way it is in the winemaking room, unless you want all that dankness to add its ugly bouquet to your wine.

A STERILIZING SOLUTION FOR WINEMAKING EQUIPMENT

Use either potassium metabisulfite or sodium bisulfite. *Two ounces of the white sulfite powder dissolved in a gallon of water* makes a strong sterilizing solution for winemaking equipment. This should be used as a final rinse, as further washing would allow the surfaces of the equipment to be recolonized immediately by yeast and mold spores and bacteria. Stainless steel, however, should be rinsed, as sulfite may pit its surface if left standing. Keep the sulfite solution tightly stoppered. The sulfite solution will give off a smell like burning kitchen matches, which is the characteristic smell of sulfur dioxide gas. Ventilate the room where you're using it, since the sulfur dioxide is poisonous in large concentrations.

Primary Fermentation Vats

At this point, you've got a vat of juice, or juice and pulp, or juice, pulp, and stems, depending on how you've crushed the grapes. The best vat for the first few days of primary fermentation is an open-topped barrel or cylinder. Here's a rundown of possibilities, their pros and cons, from the most to the least recommended.

• *Stainless steel drum.* Ideal. These are easy to clean, nonporous, and in all ways superior. You'll find a listing for them in Appendix 3. They come in many sizes, but a 55-gallon drum lets you ferment a little or a lot.

• *A large vitreous crock.* As long as the inside surface is not cracked, revealing the porous crockery underneath, these are excellent. It's sometimes difficult to find them in sizes large enough to hold the amount of juice you're vatting, and they do get heavy when they're large. I use a 15-gallon crock for 10-gallon batches.

• *Fresh whiskey barrels.* These come from the distilleries bunged, clean, and smelling strongly of whiskey. Their insides have been burned to charcoal before the whiskey was put in, and the charcoal can help absorb some impurities—and possibly some flavor or color constituents—from the must. I've used these with excellent results to vat 40 gallons. You must cut out or knock in one end of the barrel, then rinse with clean water before putting in the grapes. This is an expensive route, since you can vat only one primary fermentation in them. After that, they're impossible to clean well enough to store for future vattings. They do make great planters.

• *Five-gallon glass carboys.* While glass is always excellent, due to its nonporous nature, these are less than optimum for reds due to the small neck, which makes it difficult to punch down the cap of bubbles, spent yeast, and grape detritus that rises during the primary. It's also difficult to introduce air into the must, which would help disperse odors and gases during the rapid fermentation of the first few days. They're good for fermenting white juice, however, as they prevent overoxidation. I keep the top stoppered with a loose wad of sterile cotton that allows gases to escape. Two or three times a day I remove the cotton, put my (washed) hand over the opening, tip the carboy, and shake it to mix down the cap. Then I blow a puff of fresh air into the carboy for luck, wipe off the rim with a paper towel moistened with the sulfite sterilizing solution, and replace the stopper with fresh cotton.

• *Plastic garbage cans.* Many winemakers use large plastic garbage cans purchased especially for the purpose of vatting wine during the primary. I don't recommend it at all. Plasticizers and plastic flavors can leach into the fermenting must—even from food-grade plastic.

The primary fermentation will be vigorous and rapid, and the bubbles and cap will rise as much as a third above the level of the must. Therefore, never fill your container—whether drum, barrel, or carboy—more than two-thirds full for the primary.

When the must is made, cover the vat with a clean towel kept stretched tight across the top of the vat by a board wide enough to hold the towel straight. The arrangement lets gases out and air in, and keeps the must secure from fruit flies.

Remove the towel only when adding sulfite, taking juice to measure pH, adding sugar, or adjusting the total acidity in low-acid musts—all operations done this first day.

For some reason, musts and wines don't like being disturbed. "Don't mess with it," is surely engraved over the lintel of heaven's chais. This rule becomes more important after the primary, when the wine is set aside to finish working, and more important still when the wine is resting in carboys before bottling. The less you do to wine, the better. The steps listed in this book are the minimum needed, I think, to produce fine wine. And doing the minimum is not only thrifty, the wine benefits.

Adding Sulfite to the Must

As soon as the grapes are crushed and vatted, they are susceptible to unwanted yeast and microorganism growth, and to oxidation. The grape skins are abloom with wild yeasts, which will immediately start to reproduce in the sweet must. In some wine-growing regions of the world, especially Europe, winemakers will sometimes allow these wild yeasts to go ahead and ferment the must, and some winemakers feel that the wine will be more natural if it ferments using the yeast that nature grew on the skins. This is wrong—for several reasons. We want to stun or kill off all yeasts and microorganisms in the must in order to get it ready for the yeast strain we want to use.

It's wrong first because wild yeasts are unpredictable. Some wild strains found on the grape skins may indeed make acceptable wine, but most will stop working and die off at low (4–6 percent) alcohol concentrations, well before the fermentation has proceeded to dryness. Others may produce huge amounts of volatile acids, which give a vinegary taste to the wine. Others introduce bitter tastes into the wine. And the worst of them form hydrogen sulfide gas that makes the wine smell like rotten eggs. There's absolutely no good reason to use the natural yeasts, even if they do it in Bordeaux (which they seldom do). In wine-growing regions that have been fermenting grapes for thousands of years, selected yeast strains abound. The best yeasts are used, and the spent yeast is poured out, or fed to pigs, where billions of still-live spores enter the air, just waiting to colonize next year's grape crop. The wild yeasts present in America are not these selected strains.

So winemakers have taken to using potassium metabisulfite to kill off all yeasts and microorganisms in the must as soon as it's pressed. The sulfur dioxide that's released in the juice both prevents oxidation and cleans the juice of unwanted organisms. The sulfite is added to the juice as soon as it's crushed, and then allowed to sit for about a day, at which point the desired wine yeast is added.

The yeasts we use today have been selected for complete fermentation, meaning they can still work and exist in alcohol concentrations up to about 15 percent and SO_2 concentrations that kill or stop wild yeasts from working. The best of them are also resistant to the formation of hydrogen sulfide. They form compact lees when they settle (a bad yeast settles lightly and clouds the wine as soon as you try to move it for racking; such wines are usually very difficult to clear later in the winemaking process).

Adding sulfite takes precision. You should understand exactly how much you need to add so that you don't oversulfite the wine. I once ruined 10 gallons of the most beautiful Chardonnay by misplacing a decimal point and adding 10 times more sulfite than I should have. Once it's in, there's no way to get it out. Since sulfite can be harmful to humans, we want to add as little as possible. Some commercial winemakers use the Walthari method, in which no sulfite is used. But the method involves keeping everything under CO_2, including a special air-proof bottling machine. The only way to do away with sulfite in the home situation is to take your chances with the wild yeasts, hoping that your addition of a selected yeast will overpower the wild ones, and the increasing alcohol levels will kill them off. And this may be the answer if you are allergic to or sensitive to sulfite and the sulfur dioxide it produces. There are rare individuals who are violently allergic to sulfite, and others who get headaches, flushed feelings, or other low-grade reactions to just a glass or two of wine. Most people, however, are not allergic to sulfite at all, and if the amounts are kept to a minimum, it won't be noticed or harm the drinker, as generations who have used wine as a healthful beverage can attest. The problem with commercial wines is that winemakers tend to go overboard with the sulfite. The FDA allows up to 350 ppm of sulfite in wine. In California, the Wine Institute proposes an upper limit of 175 ppm in reds and 225 ppm in whites. These amounts will grossly oversulfur a wine.

Even 100 ppm can be detected by a sensitive nose. I remember sitting with one of the most respected winemakers in the Napa Valley. I'd tasted his Sauvignon Blanc the day before and smelled sulfur in the nose—the faint aroma of sulfurous match fumes. During our discussion of sulfur, he pulled out a bottle of the same vintage of Sauvignon Blanc I'd wrinkled my nose at and poured out glasses to show how clean the smell was, even at the 100–150 ppm sulfite he was using. It smelled like sulfur to me and I told him so. He sniffed at it, and said that his very trained nose could detect no sulfur. It was then that I formulated my theory that sulfur can burn out well-used noses to the point that it makes itself undetectable.

Wines made using the recommendations in this book will *not* smell like sulfur dioxide. Besides the problem of sulfur smell, too much SO_2 can destroy tannins and flavor constituents in the must. You'll notice that when you clean up a red wine spill with a sulfite solution-soaked cloth, it immediately bleaches out the color. It does this in the must, too.

"A general recommendation is to add 50 ppm total SO_2 at crush," says Tom Cottrell, "but if you've got a high pH, that may not be enough. Conversely, if you've got a low pH, that may be too much."

I'm going to recommend that you add 50 ppm of potassium metabisulfite—sodium metabisulfite can add a bitter taste —to the must. Fifty ppm is enough to kill spoilage microorganisms, act as an antioxidant, and stun wild yeasts, so that tomorrow when you add your strain of yeast, it can take over without challenge. It's also low enough so that the red will be able to undergo a malolactic fermentation at the end of the primary, when you may decide to add a malolactic culture to the wine. At concentrations higher than 50 ppm, malolactic fermentation is inhibited by the SO_2.

Be aware, however, that this figure of 50 ppm is for a must with a pH in the ideal ranges of 3.2 for whites and 3.5 for reds. At pH 2.8, 15 ppm may be perfectly adequate, as more sulfur dioxide stays in active form at lower pHs. As the pH rises to 3.3, 25 ppm can be adequate. At 3.5, 50 ppm is enough. But at pH 3.6, you will have to use 75 ppm, and at pH 3.8, it will take 100 ppm of sulfite to achieve the desired effect.

At pH 3.5, more than half of the potassium metabisulfite will quickly *combine* with organic molecules in the musts and be rendered unfit for active duty. About 40 percent will be *free* bisulfites and other salts, and a small percentage will be *active* SO_2. At lower pHs, the percentage of active SO_2 is higher. At higher pHs, almost all additions of potassium metabisulfite are turned into unavailable compounds, so more is needed to get enough active SO_2 into the must to gain its benefits.

Whites, because they need more antioxidant, and because they are not usually inoculated with malolactic starter, take about 70 ppm at a pH of 3.4, as do reds immediately pressed into juice.

Scientists have discovered a lot about sulfur dioxide in wine, but most of what they've learned is applicable only to the commercial winemaker who can measure molecular, free, combined, and total SO_2 in a wine. For the home winemaker at the crush stage, it's enough to shoot for the 50 ppm for reds and 70 ppm for whites, adjustable as the pH deviates from the optimums (see Table 15). Most winemakers add more sulfite later in the winemaking process, and we'll address further additions when we get there.

To get the desired amount of sulfite in the wine, you can use Campden tablets, available at any wine store or from the suppliers listed in Appendix 3, or pure loose crystals of potassium metabisulfite, usually sold in bags of 1, 2, and 4 ounces. Campden tablets have the virtue of being premeasured doses—each tablet contains 0.44 grams of sulfite and will bring a gallon of must to about 50 ppm total SO_2, which is what we're after for a must of about pH 3.5. Five tablets treat 5 gallons, and so on. These must be crushed and added to some of the juice, and stirred until totally dissolved. I usually dissolve them in a little warm tap water because the must is so murky that I can't see whether there are any undissolved particles. Once dissolved, in juice or water, the dosed liquid is stirred thoroughly into the vat of must so that the sulfite is dispersed evenly through the whole vat. This is most important, so stir until you know it's thoroughly mixed in.

If using the potassium metabisulfite crystals, figure 2 grams to 5 gallons of must. Dissolve them in a little warm water before adding to the must, and mix thoroughly as with Campden tablets. Unless you have a very accurate scale, I'd strongly recommend sticking with premeasured Campden tablets for additions of sulfite to musts, and reserve the powdered form for making sterilizing solutions. That way you can hardly go wrong.

When dealing with badly overripe grapes or botrytized berries, some winemakers recommend adding up to 150 ppm of total SO_2 to achieve the sterilizing effect. That's just too much. I'm assuming, however, that you've got grapes at the peak of ripeness in wonderfully sound condition, having just picked them from your vineyard. In such a case, 50 ppm for reds and 70 ppm for whites is sufficient. If the whole idea of adding this chemical to your wine bothers you, add at least 25 ppm at crush and 25 ppm before bottling at mid-range pHs. Or add none at all and trust to luck.

Table 15 pH EFFECT ON SULFITE ADDITIONS

pH OF MUST	TOTAL SO₂ NEEDED FOR EQUAL STERILIZING POWER*	CAMPDEN TABLETS TO ADD PER GALLON OF MUST
Red Wines		
2.80	15	⅓ tablet
2.90	20	½ tablet
3.00	25	½ tablet
3.10	30	⅔ tablet
3.20	40	⅔ tablet
3.30	50	1 tablet
3.40	50	1 tablet
3.50	50	1 tablet
3.60	60	1⅓ tablets
3.70	70	1½ tablets
3.80	100	2 tablets
White Wines		
2.80	20	½ tablet
3.00	40	⅔ tablet
3.20	60	1⅓ tablets
3.40	70	1½ tablets
3.60	80	1⅔ tablets
3.80	120	2½ tablets

*In ppm potassium metabisulfite. For those who can't measure pH, figure underripe and tart grapes at pH 3.0, ripe grapes at pH 3.2–3.6, and overripe grapes at pH 3.8.

Adding Sugar to Musts

As a very rough approximation, the amount of alcohol in the finished wine will be a little more than half the Brix. In many lackluster years, growers in the northern half of the country will find that Brix reaches only 17, 18, or 19—or less if the weather has been disastrously cold and cloudy. The grapes just don't ripen. That's one reason why the right variety—one that ripens well in your climate—is so important to choose for the backyard vineyard. Low-sugar grapes produce low-alcohol wines: a must of Brix 17, for instance, will yield a dry wine of just a little more than 9 percent alcohol. Low-alcohol wines are soft, prone to wine disorders and to infections by organisms that would otherwise be discouraged by adequate alcohol content. It makes sense to add sugar to the must in order to produce wines of 12.5 percent alcohol—the optimum for a fine wine.

For the first few years that I made wine, I avoided adding sugar, or *chaptalizing,* as it's called in France, where there are laws against it. I thought that if the French eschewed the practice, they had good reasons. And they do: grape-growing areas of France are planted with vines that almost always reach sufficient sugar for an alcohol content of about 12 percent. Besides, I thought, white sugar is terrible, tooth-rotting, body-buzzing stuff, and I didn't want it in my wine.

I've since learned that although I may add sugar, I don't get it in the finished wine. It's entirely converted to alcohol by the yeasts—the self-same ethyl alcohol that they produce from the natural sugars in the grape. There are no flavor components in pure sugar to affect the taste of the wine either way. All it does is raise alcohol toward desired levels.

Pure, white table sugar is perfect for this task. Wine yeasts are excellently equipped with the know-how to convert almost every molecule to alcohol. This sugar—sucrose—is cheap, and every bit as good as dextrose, fructose, and other kinds of sugar. In fact, it's superior to most and costs less. Exotic sugars may or may not be suited to the taste of your yeast. Grape sugar, or d-glucose, is ideal; so is fructose. Maltose, lactose, and others shouldn't be used. When sucrose—ordinary table sugar—is dissolved in water (which comprises most of the grape must, of course), it dissociates into d-glucose and d-fructose. Wine yeasts go right to work on it. (A lot of beer makers go wrong by adding sucrose to their malt. Beer yeasts have trouble converting sucrose to alcohol, and that's why so much homemade beer has an unpleasant sweet aftertaste.)

Only pure white table sugar should be used. Brown sugar, "raw" sugar, or turbinado sugar contain molasses, which will add nothing to a fine wine but a suspicious taste.

Of course, there's something to be said for a natural wine —one with only 11 percent alcohol made from a must with a Brix of 19. That way you can say, "This is the way it was that year—a little light on the sugar, but a nice year nevertheless." Eleven percent alcohol is a little light, but still enough to preserve and protect the wine. Anything less than 19 Brix, however, needs extra alcohol for balance as well as protection, and sugar should be added. My personal rule is to add sugar to any must under 20 Brix.

> A must with a specific gravity of 1.088 contains 230 grams of soluble solids (sugar) per liter. The finished wine will contain 12.5 percent alcohol. This is what we're shooting for.

Now read the Brix of your must with the hydrometer. (The hand refractometer isn't accurate enough for this purpose.) Let's say that the reading is a specific gravity of 1.070. By consulting Table 13 (page 115), which gives percentages of "potential alcohol," you'll see that this must will produce a wine with about 9.70 percent alcohol. Sugar should be added. Now consult Table 16 (page 144) to convert specific gravity to grams of sugar per liter. A specific gravity of 1.070 means the must contains about 182 grams of sugar per liter. The must needs 48 grams per liter more sugar to bring it from 182 to 230. Now multiply 48 times the number of liters in your must to get the total grams of sugar to add. If you've got 60 liters, you'd add 2,880 grams. A thousand grams is a kilogram, equal to 2.2

pounds. Put another way, a pound equals 455 grams. Dividing 2,880 by 455 gives us 6.33 pounds of sugar.

Table 16 FIGURING SUGAR ADJUSTMENT

SPECIFIC GRAVITY OF MUST	=	SUGAR GRAMS/LITER OF THAT MUST	=	BRIX
1.047		124		12.0
1.051		135		13.0
1.055		145		14.0
1.059		157		15.0
1.063		168		16.0
1.068		178		17.0
1.072		188		18.0
1.076		201		19.0
1.081		213		20.0

Remember to adjust the specific gravity for temperature variations from the norm. See Table 14.

When figuring specific gravities between the above numbers, interpolate other numbers. *Example:* S.G. of 1.065 would contain about 173 grams sugar/liter and represent a Brix of about 16.5.

To figure pounds of sugar to add to a must, use this formula.

$$\text{Pounds sugar} = \frac{(230 - x)y}{455}$$

$x =$ grams sugar/liter figured from specific gravity of the must

$y =$ liters of must

Example: S.G. = 1.071, equivalent to 186 grams of sugar/liter in a 20-liter must.

$$\frac{(230 - 186)20}{455} \qquad \frac{(44)20}{455} \qquad \frac{880}{455} = 1.94 \text{ pounds of sugar}$$

Adding 1.94 pounds of sugar to this 20-liter must will raise the specific gravity to about 1.088, equivalent to about 230 grams/liter, or final alcohol content of 12.5 percent.

Adjusting Acidity

It's extremely important that the acid (titratable acid, or TA) content of a wine be at least 0.55 for reds and 0.65 for whites. Most home winemakers won't experience such acid-deficient musts unless their grapes are overripe. Those who live in hot regions may, however, have acid-deficient grapes. Adjusting the acid up to appropriate levels should always be done in such cases. Low-acid wines don't live very long and are subject to wine disorders. Worse, they are flat and flabby, unbalanced, and short on thirst-quenching power. The reason why a cold glass of unsweetened lemonade seems to work better on a thirst than plain water is that the acid in the lemon juice gives that slightly sour edge that slakes a thirst.

Most of the acid in a must will be tartaric—usually somewhat over 50 percent. About 30–35 percent will be malic, and the rest will be citric with traces of a few other organic acids. Acid blend, found at most wine stores or available from suppliers listed in Appendix 3, is a mixture of tartaric, malic, and citric acids in about those proportions. Tartaric acid is very sour; malic is milder, and citric is for balance. Because citric acid can be converted to vinegary acetic acid during fermentation, it's best not to use it for musts, and so many winemakers adjust acid using only tartaric acid.

We're going to assume that you want to bring the acidity to an optimum 0.60 for reds and 0.70 for whites—figures slightly higher than minimum additions mentioned above. We know that 18 grams of tartaric acid will raise the TA of 5 gallons of must by 0.10 percent. Thus it's easy to figure how much acid to add to your acid-deficient must. On page 146 is an example for 5 gallons of red.

It's much more common for northern home winemakers to run into *high-acid* grapes. Some commercial winemakers reduce the acidity of musts by adding alkaline substances such as calcium carbonate, or by adding low-acid grape juice concen-

ADJUSTING ACIDITY

Desired TA = 0.60

An increase of 0.10
= 18 grams tartaric acid.
$\frac{7}{10}$ of 18 grams
= 18 × 0.7

Actual TA   = 0.53

Difference to be made up
by tartaric acid = 0.07, or
$\frac{7}{10}$ of 0.10 percent

= 12.6 grams of tartaric acid
per 5-gallon must

Let's do another example, this time for a white must that measures 0.58 TA. And let's say we're vinifying 20 gallons.

Desired TA = 0.70

An increase of 0.10
= 18 grams tartaric acid
per 5 gallons

Actual TA   = 0.58

Difference to be
made up per 5
gallons = 0.12

An increase of 0.12
= 18 × 1.2
= 21.6 grams/5 gallons
For 20 gallons of must, multiply
21.6 × 4
21.6 × 4 = 86.4 grams tartaric
acid

This amount of tartaric acid will
raise the TA of 20 gallons of must
from 0.58 to 0.70

trates to dilute the acidity. Both methods are a way to turn a promising wine into something mediocre, and in the case of using calcium carbonate, something undrinkable.

The two safe ways of reducing acid are (1) to inoculate the must with malolactic bacteria toward the end of the primary, so that a percentage of the malic acid is converted into lactic acid —a much milder acid on the tongue, and (2) to cold stabilize the wine, which precipitates tartaric acid out of the wine. We'll describe both these operations later, as we get there.

Other than using these methods, I'd let the natural acidity be. That may mean making wine with somewhat higher acidity than is perfect, but it will be a clean wine, unadulterated with chalk or concentrates.

pH SCALE

14.0—Most alkaline
7.0 Neutral
4.0 ⎱ Range of wine
3.0 ⎰ pHs
1.0 Most acid

Acid Adjustment and pH

TA above 0.90 usually unbalances a wine, making it too acid to the taste. Some whites, such as champagne-base wine or botrytized Ravat 51, can carry slightly higher acidities, but 0.90 is considered an upper limit for high-quality, balanced wine, white or red. One would think that high TA would correlate with the pH of a must or wine, as pH also measures acidity. But pH is the negative logarithm of positively charged hydrogen ions, while TA measures the acid content of must or wine by weight. They do not correlate perfectly. In Washington State, for instance, growers often experience a grape crop with high acid *and* high pH.

Tartaric acid dissociates in a liquid into positive H ions

and negative ions more easily than malic acid, which is why it is stronger to the taste. The free H ions are atomic mousetraps, just waiting for anything they can chemically grab to bump into them. This includes the human tongue, and it's their presence that the tongue interprets as sour: too sour and you spit it out fast.

If you add tartaric acid to a low-acid must, you'll also beneficially decrease the pH by a hard-to-predict amount toward the acid side of the scale. Robert Byloff of Penn State tells of a poor-nosed, off-color wine of high pH (4.0) that was brought to pH 3.4 by the addition of tartaric acid, then was cold stabilized. He claims it won a bronze medal at a national tasting.

TA correction with tartaric acid has a beneficial effect on high pH, bringing it down, but *the correction is always made to adjust the TA, not the pH.* If the TA is just right but the pH is a little high, a smart winemaker would leave it alone. TA has 10 times more effect than pH on a wine's taste, so it's TA that's adjusted, and pH is left to fend for itself. Even though we don't adjust much for pH, that measurement is important to know for its effects on wine quality, and for the addition of the proper amount of sulfite. After adjusting with tartaric acid, the pH should be read again, as it will change.

Wines under pH 3.0 are hard to ferment, and ferment more slowly when they do start. They have dipped into the acid range where wine yeasts start to give up. Wines at pH 4.0 or more taste poor and flabby, lack character and fruitiness. They are also susceptible to the growth of wine spoilage organisms that like conditions tending toward the neutral. A pH of 3.5 stops almost all growth of bad microbes. For this reason, some wine scientists say that 3.5 should be the upper limit of any wine pH.

Here are some other effects of pH: as the pH rises above 3.5, wine color tends toward the violets and purples; below pH 3.5, toward reds and typical claret colors. Wine connoisseurs consider a ruby red color superior to shades of purple. And according to scientific tastings, they have every reason to correlate color with quality, since wines at pH 3.5 or lower consistently score higher in flavor categories than wines of higher pH.

Also, as we've seen, lower pH helps potassium metabisulfite do its job, as more SO_2 is preserved in its free and active forms. At pH 4.0, almost all SO_2 is changed to bisulfite ions. A high-pH wine is also much more prone to oxidation, which reduces flavors and adds brownish colors to both red and white wines. Finally, reds with a pH of less than 3.3 tend to resist malolactic fermentation.

The pH of a must will go up as fermentation progresses. "Musts of pH 3.2 to 3.4 end up as 3.6 to 3.8 as wine," says Byloff, "so I'd say that 3.1 or 3.2 is the ideal must pH for whites, and the ideal for reds is something like 3.4."

We've already factored proper pH into our decision (made earlier in the day) to harvest, so most likely you'll have a must with pH close to ideal, or at least as close to ideal as allowed by the other factors of Brix and TA. And yet, it's good to check the pH of the prepared must, so you can be aware of all the important conditions as you replace the towel for the last time and head off for a well-deserved beer in front of the TV.

Harvest Day Summary

This, then, is harvest day:

1. Read Brix, TA, and pH of a sample of vineyard grapes in order to decide to harvest.
2. Harvest.
3. Make the must.
4. Read Brix, TA, and pH of the must.
5. Add potassium metabisulfite now if TA is above 0.55.
6. Adjust the sugar, if necessary.
7. Adjust the TA with tartaric acid, if necessary.
8. Reread the pH after addition of tartaric acid to get the final pH before fermentation.
9. Add potassium metabisulfite now if TA was below 0.55 and has been adjusted.
10. Clean up all equipment and spills.

If, at this point, you've got a crock of whites soaking on the skins, plan to press out the juice eight to sixteen hours later —usually the next morning before work. What's getting up two hours early compared to the thrill of a home-made Chardonnay with character? Otherwise, you're off duty for twenty-four hours.

The bride is prepared for the bridegroom. Tomorrow, grape juice will be introduced to yeast. The courtship will start slowly for a day or two, then skyrocket into a fountain of sparkles. And after this mad passion of first meeting, the yeast and grape juice will be no more—spent and exhausted from their wild revel. In their place will be grape juice transformed and yeast fulfilled: wine. If the wine is well made, the marriage will improve with age.

Pressing Whites for Fermentation

After eight to sixteen hours, whites that have been left on the skins overnight should be pressed out. You'll want a grape press, because while you can squeeze the must by pouring it through cheese cloth, then press by hand, that's a long and messy procedure. Presses are usually wood, although occasionally one of stainless steel will pop up. No other materials will really do, and aren't likely to be found. A basket press (see illustration) is best for the home winemaker.

I find that extra hands make pressing go much easier. One person dips the must into the press's basket—which should always be lined with a fine-mesh nylon bag sold at all winemaking stores or from the mail-order suppliers listed in Appendix 3. It's a good idea to have two or three bags, and while one is being emptied of the pressed skins—called *pomace*—the other is in the basket being filled. Then it's nice to have someone on the crank and someone else selecting records, tapes, or radio programs, watching out for spills, and helping as needed. You can, however, do all these things yourself. From long practice, let me encourage you to enlist at least one other person.

As you pour the must into the nylon bag, a lot of free juice will run out, down into the press's sluice, and then into a waiting vat. The vat can be a carboy if you want to do the primary in glass to give white wines extra protection against oxidation, or an open-topped vessel of the types already described. Wide funnels, available at wine shops, get the juice into the carboy, and not all over the floor. A wide funnel may be the most useful piece of equipment of all this first week. In any case, the press needs to be placed on a table, or somewhere above the vat or carboy. For up to 50 gallons of wine production, the smallest presses will do.

BASKET PRESS

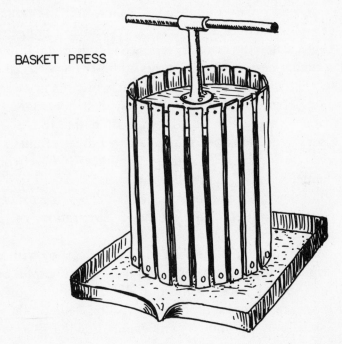

You can choose to save the free-run juice and vinify it separately, looking for an extra measure of quality. Such a white will be lighter and fresher, but not necessarily more flavorful. I think a more well-rounded wine results when the free-run and pressed juices are vinified together. If the pressed must contains lots of solid particles, and you're looking for a light and delicate wine, you can let the must settle for another day and rack the juice off the lees before adding yeast.

When the nylon bag is about three-quarters full of juice and loose skins, fold the top over and start applying pressure. Firm squeezing is enough. Pressing too hard adds the worst of what the skins have to offer, such as bitter principles, and the bitter contents of broken grape seeds. Just get most of the juice out and let it go at that. The pomace cakes are good for the compost pile. They'll also lure bees and yellow jackets and other "sweet-toothed" insects.

Some European vintners use the pomace—there called *marc*—to make a low-quality distilled drink called marc or *grappa*. Usually they dump sugar, water, and the pomace together and ferment it. It is nearly always a bad drink. In aristocratic ages, when the ordinary fellow had little of anything, marc was certainly better than no spirits at all. It's a personal test of macho to down a shot glass full of marc without a grimace. I say forget it. It will make better compost than beverage. In fact, Austrians are using ground grape marc in humus toilets—waterless toilets with a tank of rotting marc that digests human wastes to a clean, odorless state within a month. The heat from a 5-cubic-meter block of marc will warm a small room or stable over a five-month winter, and the Austrians and French are investigating its uses as a fuel. These are better applications for it than making a beverage.

After pressing, clean the rim of vat or carboy with a clean cloth or paper towel moistened with the sterilizing solution, and wash any spilled juice off the outside. Cover with towel and board, or cotton in case of the carboy, then clean up the equipment and floor. Puddles of grape juice left lying around or splashed on surfaces will become nurseries for grape molds and fungi. The press should be given a final rinse of sterilizing solution and the nylon bags should be made as clean as when you bought them, then air-dried and stored away.

Adding the Yeast

About a day—more or less, the hours aren't critical—after you add the sulfite, you add the yeast.

When the grapes come from the vineyard, the skins are colonized by any one of hundreds of possible yeasts. But researchers in Europe found that these were mostly low-alcohol-tolerant strains such as *Kloeckera apiculata.* In fact, one scientist who microscopically identified yeast strains from vineyards from north and south in Europe said that good, alcohol-tolerant wine yeasts "are inhabitants of wineries, not grapes on the vine."

Occasionally, however, *Saccharomyces cerevisiae,* a true wine yeast, does occur on ripening grapes, but it can't be depended on to be there. Many home winemakers routinely use a popular strain of *S. cerevisiae,* known commercially as Montrachet 522, or just Montrachet, to ferment their musts.

Here I must add a word of caution. It appears that Montrachet 522 is implicated in production of hydrogen sulfide. Although this yeast works fast, does a complete job of fermentation to dryness, and makes compact lees, hydrogen sulfide production is intolerable. There's some dispute on this. Dr. John McGrew at USDA shook off the suggestion that Montrachet yeast causes H_2S (hydrogen sulfide). "It's more likely due to the lack of yeast nutrients in the must, or elemental sulfur left on the grape skins at harvest," he said. Similarly, Theo Rosenbrand, winemaster at Sterling Vineyards in the Napa Valley, said, "I use Montrachet for all our wines, white or red."

On the other hand, Mike Grgich told me that "Montrachet does produce H_2S. I use Pasteur Institute yeast." That's a strain of *Saccharomyces bayanus,* known widely as Pasteur Champagne yeast. "I use Pasteur Champagne yeast from the Wine Lab [in St. Helena, California; see Appendix 3] for all my wines," said Arnold Tudal. And many others I've met agree that Montrachet, for all its virtues, is the single greatest reason for H_2S in wines. I've personally used Montrachet and made wines completely free of its awful smell; but then I've also had the problem in other batches using this yeast. I think the condition of the grapes has a lot to do with it; the fresher the grapes, the less likelihood of H_2S. But recently, after hearing a number of horror stories about Montrachet, I've sworn off in favor of Pasteur Champagne.

Types of Wine Yeast

There are many other commercial yeasts available to wine-makers, and the subject of their subtle differences would take up a book in itself. Here's a summary of the most popular types:

Montrachet. (Saccharomyces cerevisiae). Most widely used yeast; numbered UC-Davis 522. A vigorous strain with high SO_2 tolerance. Implicated in hydrogen sulfide production.

Pasteur Champagne. (Saccharomyces bayanus). A yeast developed by the Pasteur Institute and numbered UC-Davis 595. Moderately vigorous with high SO_2 and alcohol tolerance. Used for all wine types, but especially for sparkling wines and stuck fermentations.

California Champagne. (Saccharomyces bayanus). Another strain of bayanus, number UC-Davis 505. Slow to moderately vigorous with extremely rapid, compact precipitation of spent yeast lees. Facilitates riddling of bottle-fermented sparkling wine.

Epernay 2. (Saccharomyces cerevisiae). Slow-fermenting general-purpose strain of *cerevisiae,* as opposed to Montrachet's fast fermentation. Used for reds, whites, and sparkling wine.

Flor Sherry. (Saccharomyces fermentati). UC-Davis 519. The culture needed to produce flor or fino-type sherries in hot, dry regions.

Most of these are found at good winemaking supply shops, but if you can't find the one you want, there are a number of companies that specialize in wine yeasts, including these basic types. There's a list of mail-order suppliers in Appendix 3.

Many growers of Pinot Noir recommend the use of Ass-manshausen wine yeast for that variety. It's a slow-acting yeast and gives a long fermentation under cool conditions. Pinot Noir can be left on the skins as long as two weeks with use of this yeast and fermentation temperatures in the low sixties or upper fifties.

One study done by the Taylor Wine Company evaluated the length of fermentation and quality of Seyval Blanc, de Chaunac, and Vidal 256, each vinified with four yeasts: Pasteur Champagne, California Champagne, Montrachet 522, and Epernay 2. Epernay took sixty-seven days to ferment to dryness, compared with twenty-two days for Pasteur and California champagnes, and even less for Montrachet. Montrachet and Epernay produced better-tasting Vidals than either Pasteur or California champagnes, but flavor differences among the other grapes and yeasts were not discernible.

If you're vinifying any species of *Vitis rotundifolia,* the muscadine grape, be aware that musts of this grape are usually deficient in natural available nitrogen, which yeast needs to work properly. In musts of other varieties, there's ordinarily enough nitrogen from proteins that the yeast breaks down. But muscadine musts should be given added yeast nutrients, available at most winemaking shops or any of the mail-order yeast suppliers in Appendix 3.

The yeast usually comes in a freeze-dried powdered form and is dormant. Some winemakers will start the yeast in lukewarm water charged with a little sugar on harvest day, so that the yeast is awake and beginning to work when it's added to the must the next day. It does get the fermentation off to a faster start —but the value of doing that is debatable, except when the air temperature is very warm and it's desirable to have wine yeast colonize the must as soon as possible to prevent spoilage by other organisms.

Usually, I simply dissolve the yeast in lukewarm water— *not hot water*—and pour it into the must, then stir it in thoroughly. Hot water can kill the yeast, so make sure the water temperature is less than 100° F. Yeast usually comes in packets, with a packet good for 5 gallons. Bulk jars of yeast are available, but are probably much more yeast than a home winemaker needs, and it's not a good idea to keep yeast for a year. Buy just what you need. If you do add from a jar, figure about a tablespoon per 5 gallons, since even one yeast cell will, in time, multiply enough to colonize the must.

A Stuck Fermentation

Sometimes the fermentation will stick before the sugar is entirely converted to alcohol—that is, fermentation will just stop. This is often due to a shortage of yeast nutrients. Most winemakers in this strait will add some more wine yeast, plus some yeast nutrient, and hope that the must starts working again. A light aeration by racking will help the new yeast charge get going.

THE PRIMARY FERMENTATION

Now the must is charged with yeast. There's no turning back. Your grape juice is on its way to becoming wine. Within 12 to 24 hours, the must will start to bubble; by 36–48 hours, it will be fizzing strongly; at 70–80 hours, the process will peak, and then the bubbling will slow down and taper off. Exactly how long all this will take is determined primarily by the temperature. At 50–55° F, it can take several weeks for the primary fermentation to finish; at 85–90° F, the must can rush to a violent completion in three days.

Punching Down the Cap

Once fermentation starts, you should punch down the cap at least twice a day. The cap comprises the skins and other material that floats on the fermenting must. I wash my left hand and arm, then reach into the vat and swirl the cap down into the wine, breaking it up and making sure that liquid covers it all. This adds some air to the must, which helps the yeast to work and carries off any odorous gases. Keeping the cap punched down also prevents bad bacteria or molds from colonizing the skins that float on top. White wine has less of a cap, since there are no skins, but needs stirring of the surface scum twice a day too.

This is a very important step and shouldn't be shirked. I

shirked it on one of my first batches of red simply because I didn't know I was supposed to do it. After five days of primary, the cap looked very unsavory and the wine eventually tasted the same way. Keeping some air in the must during the primary also reduces the chance for hydrogen sulfide production. Finally, keeping the skins mixed into the must elicits the most color and flavor extractives from them.

Fermentation Temperature

The art of winemaking comes into play now, as the wine-maker determines how long the skins will remain in the working must, and how long the primary will take. In commercial winer-ies, the temperature is often controlled—I've seen stainless steel tanks wrapped with hoses, through which flows water of prede-termined temperature, to cool down warm-weather fermenta-tions or warm them on cold days. I've seen whole rooms of vats that are temperature controlled. The furious fermentation of a primary creates *heat,* and at the gallonages vinified commer-cially, enormous heat, which must be controlled. Small batches such as 5 to 40 gallons heat up only a little. We home winemak-ers are pretty much limited to temperatures we can find around the house. Many basements stay at about 60° F, if they're well insulated from the first floor. Check the temperature there if you've got a clean place to put your vat. I ordinarily use my living room. To keep the temperature of red musts up, I place the vat near a hot-air vent—but *not* so that the air can blow directly on the vat. Whites are sheltered in a corner near the bookcases, where the stone walls keep temperatures down. Some people use a porch, garage, or other place subject to outside ambient air temperatures. But these places are exposed to large temperature swings between days that may reach 80° F, and nights that could get down in the fifties. A steady tempera-ture is much preferable to wild swings. The latter can result in a stuck fermentation as the yeast—alternately pushed toward action in the daytime and dormancy at night—gives up.

As a general rule, Tom Cottrell says, "The lower eighties

is a happy place to be for fermenting reds. At higher temperatures, you can get off flavors. If the temperature is much cooler, you get less color extraction." The general rule for whites is a range from 55° to 65° F, although Chardonnay will be excellent at temperatures in the 65–75° F range.

Skin Contact Time

At this point, your intention—what kind of wine you want to make—comes into play. If you're going for a big, intense red, you'll want more skin contact time; light, fruity reds will take less contact time. A lot of winemaking involves creating conditions and letting natural processes work, but the decision of wine style is yours alone, and is one of the points in the process that allows your art to flow in. If it's your first time with reds, shoot for three to five days on the skins, depending on how fast your fermentation is proceeding. If the air temperature in your fermenting area is only in the low seventies, don't fret. That temperature will do fine for reds, too, although the fermentation may take a little longer. As you're about to see, winemakers do their fermentations at all kinds of temperatures and skin contact times, and end up with wines to their taste.

Dr. John McGrew, for instance, talks about how he achieves a fruity red that can be drunk early, while more "important" reds are aging in the bottle. "If you want some reds to drink early and don't mind reducing the ultimate quality a bit, let the must ferment until just a third of the sugar is gone [If you started at 21 Brix, that would mean when the must is reduced by fermentation to 14 Brix measured with the hydrometer]. Then press the must to take the wine off the skins and finish fermenting the wine with no more skin contact. You'll get softer and earlier wines using this technique.

"For excellent fruitiness in whites, I stem and crush, add the sulfite, let it sit on the skins overnight, then press the juice out lightly and let it settle for twenty-four hours. Then I rack off the lighter juice, leaving the thick solids behind. I add the yeast to this lighter juice," he said.

This early racking is unusual, but it adds to the freshness and fruitiness by getting rid of solid particles quickly. As is so often the case in winemaking, opinions differ wildly: I know of one California winemaker who leaves his white wine on the gross lees for *nine months.* And he stirs it up every two weeks! More commonly when making whites, vintners count it a virtue to get the wine off the lees quickly.

To extract full flavor from reds like Cabernet Sauvignon or Petit Sirah, which have so much to give, long skin contact times are called for. I know a winemaker who keeps his Cabernet on the skins for six days at a fermentation temperature of about 80° F. He feels this extracts all the color and flavor he needs, and longer contact would only extract undesirable amounts of bitter principles. Arnold Tudal in the Napa Valley, however, ferments his Cabernet Sauvignon at cooler temperatures, 70–75°, but leaves the wine on the skins for eleven days. Still others have told me of leaving it on the skins for two weeks at 55°. Tom Cottrell says he believes most wine will have too much tannin with that long a skin contact time, especially if there are stems in the must. Tudal's wine, however, is not overly tannic, although it is very big and bursting with flavor and color intensity. The fermentation of big reds at very cool temperatures, such as 55–60°, is undergoing a vogue now in California, but one risks stuck fermentations at those levels. One home winemaker told me that he had made a Zinfandel fermented at 60° and it took two months to work down to 1.2 Brix—then it stopped working. Although it still had this residual sugar, he bottled it, and—of course—it started working again in the bottle. "It started pushing all the corks out," he said. "I thought about wiring them on, but the wine was in regular bottles, not champagne bottles that can stand pressure, and I had visions of bottles exploding in the cellar." He finally stood the bottles up, removed the corks and plugged the tops with cotton for two days to let the residual sugar finish fermenting, then put the corks back in. But the spent yeast from this last fermentation kept that wine cloudy forever. So, it's important to make sure that your wines ferment at high enough temperatures to keep the yeast from quitting on you. I think Tom Cottrell's figures of about 65° for whites and 80° for reds are about right.

A word here about Maréchal Foch. If it's fermented on the skins, it often develops musky, metallic flavors. Some people like Foch that way, but I find the flavors less than subtle. Foch can be handled like Chardonnay—crushed and allowed to sit on the skins overnight, then pressed out and fermented—to make a strawberry-colored "nouveau" that's ready to drink in a few months and is quite delicious.

Malolactic Fermentation

When the primary starts to slow down—perhaps a day before transferring the new wine to glass carboys or a barrel—add a culture of *Leuconostoc* bacteria to red musts. This causes a malolactic fermentation. The culture has one effect—it converts malic acid in the wine to lactic acid. This reduces the acidity of the must, with a concomitant rise in the pH. Adding the culture is always called for when acid levels in red are high (over TA 0.70). If you've adjusted the TA with tartaric acid, you wouldn't need to induce a malolactic fermentation. Cultures are obtainable at wine labs, some wine stores, and from suppliers listed in Appendix 3. Winemakers in the West tend to use a strain developed at UC-Davis, available from The Wine Lab in St. Helena, while eastern winemakers tend to use PSU-1, a strain developed by Penn State, and available from Tri-Bio Labs in State College, Pennsylvania. Putting white wines through a malolactic would reduce the acid considerably, possibly leaving the wine flabby.

Incidentally, once a barrel has held a wine undergoing malolactic fermentation, enough leuconostoc will lurk in the wood to cause a malolactic reaction in future young wines put in it.

There's a notion in France that new wine starts to ferment again, after sitting overwinter, due to rising spring temperatures. Winemakers there are actually noticing a naturally occurring malolactic fermentation, which can start all by itself in young wine when it gets warmer in the spring. Adding malolactic culture at the end of primary will head off this spring spritzing—which can push corks out if you've already bottled the wine, or at least make wine pétillant—prickly with tiny gas bubbles. To prevent this, I never bottle any wine until it's at least six months old. If it's going to undergo a spontaneous malolactic fermentation in the spring, it will happen while the wine is still in the carboys or barrel and the gas can escape through the airlocks with which they're fitted.

After adding the malolactic culture, this special conversion of malic to lactic acid should be entirely completed within ten days.

Pressing the Must

I let my big reds ferment on the skins until the primary starts to slow down—anywhere from three to five days. If the Brix has dropped by about two-thirds, or the specific gravity is between 1.030 and 1.040, it's time to press the wine off the skins and into carboys for further, slower fermentation to complete dryness (the secondary fermentation). Five days on the skins is about my limit, and I find the color and flavors are optimum then. I've done reds with more skin contact time, and some have been so inky that they threw deposits over the inside of the bottles after bottling.

With whites, when two-thirds of the sugar has fermented or the specific gravity is about 1.010, transfer the wine into clean carboys with airlocks.

After your first few batches, you'll get a feel for how length of primary and temperature affect the final wine.

Once the bubbling in the primary vat slows down and you've determined by hydrometer that about two-thirds of the sugar is gone, the primary is over. The new wine—for it's qualified to be called wine now—is more exposed to air than it was when billows of carbon dioxide were coming off. At this point it's necessary to transfer it to glass or barrel to keep it away from air for the rest of the fermentation. Vinegar-producing organisms need air to survive, and they'll start working if the new wine is allowed to contact air for any length of time.

Reds with skins will have to be pressed out now. As you're dipping the must out of the vat into the basket of the grape press, don't stir up the bottom of the vat. The bottom will contain a thick layer of grape seeds and spent yeast. Once your dipper starts to contain an abundance of grape seeds, stop and discard the rest. It should be only about a tenth of the vat or less, depending on how much gunk is down there. Only pressed-out new wine should go into the 5-gallon carboys. For whites, you've already pressed the skins, but try not to transfer the thick gunk on the bottom of the vat to the carboys. Again, you should leave only a tenth or less of the vat's contents of spent yeast and solids that could impart off flavors to the wine. If your primary was done in a carboy, siphon it into clean carboys, leaving the gross lees behind. A large siphon hose of high-quality clear plastic, available in all winemaking stores, can be used to transfer the whites from the vat. A big funnel helps to catch splashes, even during siphoning.

THE SECONDARY FERMENTATION

The secondary fermentation can be done in 5-gallon glass carboys or in an oak barrel. Many winemakers employ a combination of these, finishing the secondary in glass, and then, when the wine is completely fermented and relatively clean, racking it into an oak barrel for three to six months, or more. I recommend allowing the fermentation to finish before putting the wine into barrels. Here's why:

Barrels are used primarily to impart oak flavors to a wine. That can be just as easily achieved—or even more easily achieved—after the fermentation's finished. The secondary fermentation deposits lots of sediment, and this is far more easy to deal with in glass. Consider: After a month in a carboy, you decide to siphon (rack) the wine off the deposits into clean carboys. You can see the deposits (lees) in the bottom, easily defined from the clearer wine above. In a barrel, you can't see demarcation between wine and lees at all. So let the secondary fermentation finish in glass. When the wine is finished working, then put it in a barrel if you desire. You can add oak flavors to wine in glass carboys, too, avoiding barrels altogether. We'll consider this in detail when we discuss oak and barrels, but let's first describe how to set up your new wine in carboys.

New Wine

New wine, indeed. Although it's just past the primary, it is wine. Sample it as you would castor oil—just get a quick impression of the taste. It will be awful. Even Romanée-Conti is awful at this stage—full of yeast, living and dead; all kinds of fresh volatile compounds produced in the fermentation; possibly laced with *Leuconostoc* bacteria. In France, in November, the new wine is sold as *vin nouveau*. When it's *really* vin nouveau (and not the filtered jug Beaujolais the French are happy to ship to people who think it's important to taste the new vintage before someone else does), it can be quite rough. I remember ordering vin nouveau in Angers and getting a raw, chalky-looking mixture of yeast and wine that gave me the sulfur burps for a day.

The new wine is the baby, by yeast out of grape juice. Just like a human baby, who's all squawks and bubbles and elimination at first but develops into a remarkable creature, so too will the new wine develop over time and with experience.

Using Airlocks

Five-gallon glass carboys are familiar to anyone who's seen a water fountain with a large bottle of water upside down on top. So, if you have a friend in the bottled water business, now's the time to draw on that friendship. Most of us, however, will buy our carboys at the winemaker's shop.

Because it's so important to keep air off the wine from now on, the carboys are stoppered with a cork that has a hole in it. An airlock will fit into the hole, and allow CO_2 and other gases from the fermenting wine to pass out, but no outside air to pass back in. There are many types of airlocks. The most common are illustrated below. My favorite, for aesthetic reasons, is the one-piece glass airlock. They are very breakable and costly, though, so mostly I use the plastic one-piece airlock.

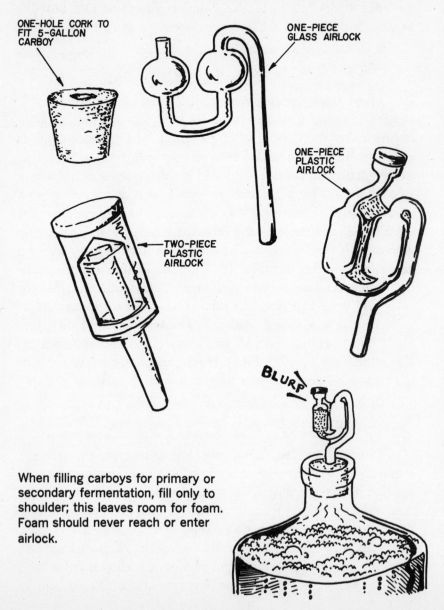

ONE-HOLE CORK TO FIT 5-GALLON CARBOY

ONE-PIECE GLASS AIRLOCK

ONE-PIECE PLASTIC AIRLOCK

TWO-PIECE PLASTIC AIRLOCK

BLURP

When filling carboys for primary or secondary fermentation, fill only to shoulder; this leaves room for foam. Foam should never reach or enter airlock.

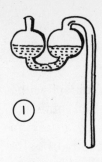
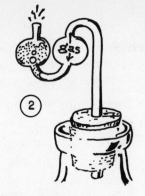
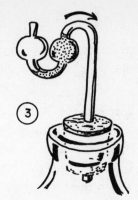

① ② ③

The airlock is filled with sulfite solution to a little less than half full in each chamber.

When fitted to a carboy with fermenting wine, the carbon dioxide from fermentation forces itself through the first chamber and bubbles through the second.

If you see the sulfite solution being drawn back toward the bottle, then fermentation has stopped and a slight vacuum has formed in the bottle. Immediately top up the carboy.

When topping up the carboy after fermentation, bring the wine into the lower neck, about an inch from the bottom of the cork.

Fill the carboys to the shoulder so there's plenty of room for foam in the bottle. Never let the foam reach the bottom of the cork, or it will go up through the airlock, and even out of the airlock all over the floor, where it will draw fruit flies and encourage molds to form. The illustrations above show how to use sterilizing solution. If wine does bubble into the airlock, clean and replace it and lower the level of wine in the carboy.

The secondary should proceed in a room with relatively cool temperatures—from 60° to 70° F. Try to keep the carboys away from cold drafts. I throw a blanket over my bottles, so autumn is characterized at our house by a blanket in a corner of

the living room from which protrudes a group of airlocks bur-
bling a gaseous rondo.

When the secondary fermentation ends completely, the
space in the bottle may form a slight vacuum, which pulls the
sterilizing solution back toward the wine. Don't let this vacuum
make the airlock work in reverse, pulling air (and drops of
solution) into the bottle. The way to prevent this problem is to
watch the secondary very carefully. After anywhere from a few
days to a month or two, the bubbles through the airlock will slow
from many a minute to just a few a day. A few days after that,
all bubbling should have stopped. As soon as you're sure the
bubbling has stopped for good, rack the wine off the lees into
a clean carboy and stopper it with an airlock that's been well
washed and recharged with sulfite solution. This time, fill the
carboy with wine to within an inch of the bottom of the cork.
This will leave only a minute amount of air in the bottle, which
can be removed by giving the carboy a little shake. Some of the
gases dissolved in the wine will come off, the airlock will give
a few bubbles, and then all will be quiet and ready for aging.

Cleaning the Carboys

All carboys should be scrupulously clean. I remove spots
from the inside by pouring a handful or two of clean sand into
the bottle, then adding about 3 inches of hot water and ammonia. Stoppering the end with one hand and grasping the bottom
of the bottle with the other, I swirl the sand-ammonia mixture
throughout the bottle, so that it scours the sides and bottom.
Then I pour out the contents, fill with a few inches of clean
water, swirl again, pour it out, and fill, swirl and pour twice more
until I'm sure that the carboy is *clean* with a capital K.

I also wash the corks and airlocks with ammonia and hot
water, and rinse them in a similarly fanatic manner. After filling
the carboy, I wipe the rim and down inside the neck a little bit
with a paper towel moistened with sterilizing solution. Then I
put in the clean cork. I put the cork in first, add sterilizing
solution to the airlock, then fit it down into the cork. That's

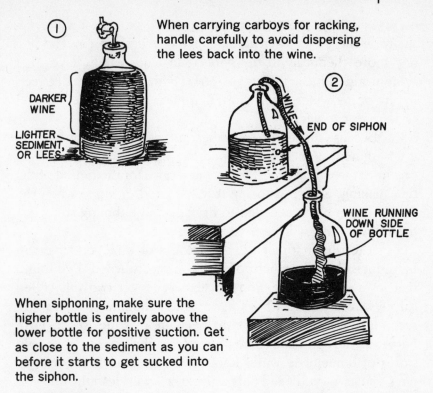

① When carrying carboys for racking, handle carefully to avoid dispersing the lees back into the wine.

DARKER WINE

LIGHTER SEDIMENT, OR LEES

②

END OF SIPHON

WINE RUNNING DOWN SIDE OF BOTTLE

When siphoning, make sure the higher bottle is entirely above the lower bottle for positive suction. Get as close to the sediment as you can before it starts to get sucked into the siphon.

③ Sometimes it's hard to see the end of the siphon in the murky wine, but it will usually curve to the side of the bottle, where it looks like this. Avoid stirring up the lees when jiggling the siphon to find the end.

easier than trying to get the right amount of solution into the airlock after it's in place on the bottle.

The First Racking

Many winemakers add more sulfite to the wine at the first racking. If you've added the minimum that I recommended before, you could add half a Campden tablet per gallon—or two or three tablets per 5 gallons, which would give you another 20–30 ppm sulfur dioxide in the wine. Many claim that this

cleans and helps preserve wines, especially those that will eventually be laid down when aging. Since I have a bug about adding
any more chemicals to my wine than I absolutely have to, I
seldom add sulfite at this stage—so far with no apparent ill effects
to any of my wines, even those that have reached ripe old ages
of four to five years.

Because the length of the secondary fermentation and the
establishment of a clearly defined lees can take anywhere from
one to ten weeks, it's hard to give any rules for the timing of the
first racking. Suffice it to say that it should be done when the
fermentation has proceeded to dryness and bubbling stops. Almost always this will be before Christmas.

After the first racking, the amount of wine you have will
be reduced by the amount of lees you've discarded. I've found
that, as a general rule, you can expect to get two fully filled
carboys from three carboys filled to the shoulder, undergoing
secondary fermentation. If you need more wine to top up a
bottle, use a sound and similar wine from the store or your own
stores of homemade wine. Racking involves having extra carboys on hand—you need only one extra if you clean the one you
just emptied, then use it for the next bottle you have to rack.
Over the years, I've collected about four or five extras. They
come in handy and allow me to clean the used bottles of their
lees at my leisure after I've finished racking, rather than cleaning
as I go.

Cold Stabilization

My basement receives the new, fully filled carboys. They
go down anywhere from late October to December, depending
on how long the secondary takes. My basement is in the low
fifties at that time of year, but by January will get down to the
lower forties or thirties, where it will stay until late February.
This cold period has a beneficial effect on the wine. Not only do
suspended solids settle, leaving a relatively clear wine after this
two-to-three-month period, but the wine is cold stabilized, too.

Cold stabilization precipitates bitartrate—cream of tartar or tartaric acid—out of the wine, and crystals of the compound settle to the bottom, putting a hard crust over the lees. This greatly simplifies the next racking, which should be done in March, or about two to three months after the first racking.

The lees at the first racking are loose and prone to billow up into the wine, and are easily sucked up into the siphon hose. At the second racking, after cold stabilization, the lees are fairly well sealed and don't billow. I still use care, though.

If you don't have a basement like mine that naturally gets down into the low to mid-thirties for two months, I'd suggest investing in an old refrigerator that will hold a carboy when the shelving is removed. About two or three weeks in a refrigerator set for around 32° F should be enough to precipitate out the potassium bitartrate. If you're doing larger batches that make this method impracticable, and there's no nook or corner of your house that gets down to the right temperature, you might consider asking the owner of a walk-in refrigerator to let you store your bottles in there. If you don't know anyone with a walk-in, or don't want to bother, forget about cold stabilization. The potassium bitartrate in solution doesn't harm the wine—it doesn't *need* to be precipitated. If wine that hasn't been cold stabilized is later bottled, and then cooled to near freezing, the crystals will precipitate out in the bottle. It's not a defect and it doesn't affect the taste. Many an experienced wine drinker has occasionally noticed crystals in the bottom of a glass when finishing up certain wines, especially big reds from small wineries. Cold stabilization has these benefits, however: it gets rid of the crystals, which is nice in a cosmetic sense. It reduces the acidity slightly and softens the wine. This latter benefit is the chief one.

Before going on to more aging and, finally, bottling the wine, we must go back to the end of the secondary and talk about oak and the use of barrels.

Using Barrels

I must admit that the idea of an ancient barrel filled with

gorgeous homemade wine tucked away in a corner of the cellar is romantic. Romantic, yes; practical, no.

The chief purpose of barrel aging is to add subtle oak flavors to a wine. Long-term aging in a new barrel—particularly a new American white oak barrel—will leave a wine absolutely stinking of wood. Unless you want to have your wine taste and smell like a sawmill, oak aging will take anywhere from a few weeks to a few months, depending on the age of the barrel.

French oak barrels from Nevers or Limousin oak are the finest money can buy, and I've seen them used by many home winemakers in the Napa Valley. But these lucky guys are able to purchase them from wineries that are ordering them by the thousands, and they get the economy of scale. These barrels are very expensive, but worth it if money isn't the object. There's really not that much difference between American white oak and the oaks used in France. The difference is that French coopers expose the wood to the elements for many months. The sun, rains, frosts, and snows leach the heavy oaky volatiles from the wood. Then they are made into barrels that are capable of imparting delicate nuances of oak to a wine.

American white oak barrels are not so leached. The wood is sawed out and used as is to make the barrels. Such a barrel, without proper preparation, can over-oak a wine in a day.

Barrel aging fine-tunes the taste of wine, imposing light oak flavors that make up what the wine doesn't deliver. It will take experience to determine exactly how much oak to give red wines and Chardonnays, but the general rules given below will get you started.

I routinely oak my red wines. Chardonnays, among whites, benefit from oaking, unless you're going to make champagne. Reds handled like whites and whites themselves, other than Chardonnays, don't usually benefit from oaking. And Chardonnays need less oak flavor than red wines to round them out.

Beaulieu Vineyard in the Napa Valley is one of the few premium wineries in California to use American white oak barrels. Gary Wu, a genial young man who works there, told me that the company ages its Beau Tour wines in new oak barrels

—that is, their most ordinary wine goes in first when the oak is new and harshest. After the Beau Tour is aged, they refill the barrels with their Rutherford wines, which are of better quality. When the Rutherfords are done, their Reserve wines go in. By this time, the barrel has held several wines and imparts only nuances of wood flavor to the wine. Their Reserves can stay in the barrel for a year without getting over-oaky. Surprisingly, Gary said that they don't top up their barrels during this time. *Topping up* means taking out the bung and filling any air space that's present with a sound and similar wine. While Beaulieu may not top up their barrels, I'm going to recommend that you do. That air space is too easily colonized by acetobacter, and their vinegary presence can spoil a wine.

Barrels come in many sizes. The smaller the barrel, the greater the wood-to-wine ratio. That is, more wood will be in contact with any given gallon of wine. Wine will therefore extract more wood flavors and need less aging time in smaller barrels. Barrels are heavy and difficult to move when filled with wine, so consider where you're going to store the barrel and fill it in place. Also think now about getting the wine out of the barrel later on. The best way is to siphon it out, but if your barrel is on the floor, it's going to be very difficult to siphon it. What I've done is build a frame, from scrap wood, that holds the barrel a few feet above the ground, high enough to siphon the wine into 5-gallon carboys when the aging is through. To siphon wine from carboys *into* the barrel, you'll have to set the carboys on a high table, or even on a box on a high table, but that's not hard to rig up.

Obviously, the size of the frame will depend on the size of the barrel. I've used 15-gallon, 20-gallon, 30-gallon, 40-gallon, and 55-gallon barrels, and I'd say that a 30-gallon barrel is the minimum. Smaller ones tend to leak, and they can put too much wood on the wine. Barrels of 40 to 55 gallons are ideal.

The barrel size you choose will depend on the amount of wine you're making. Since only wine that's finished working will go in the barrel, make sure that you take the reductions from wasted lees into account when estimating barrel size, or you may

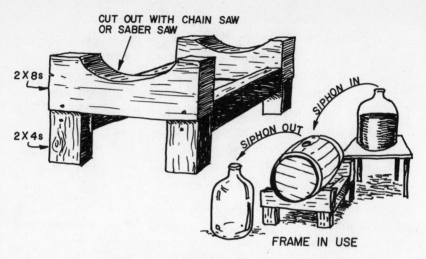

A FRAME FOR HOLDING A WINE BARREL

have to add a lot of store-bought wine to top it up. Buy the barrel just before using it. It will take a few days to prepare the barrel, but then, once it's ready, fill it. Don't let it sit around wet and unused, or the moist wood could become colonized with mold.

Let me add here that I would not use any old barrel that's been used before, unless it's yours and it's been handled properly. Using old barrels is dangerous. Any off smell in a barrel will be transferred to the wine, and a barrel that's been emptied and not refilled immediately can become colonized with all kinds of bad microorganisms in a few days. Old barrels make great planters, especially when cut one-third of the way from an end. That way you get two planters—one shallow and one deep.

Preparing New Barrels

New barrels must be prepared before filling, or they will sprout leaks. First, fill the barrel with water. The moisture swells the wood, closing the gaps between the staves. The leaking should stop within three days. If it doesn't, you may have a leaker. Leaking is a big problem in barrels, and, personally, I've just about sworn off using them for that reason. Make sure that if your barrel turns out to be a leaker you can return it for a sound one. Local winemaking supply shops usually carry barrels. Sources are also listed in Appendix 3.

Since the wine has finished working, you won't need an airlock in the bung. A wooden bung will do, but wooden ones have some problems. They can split; they can wick wine up their sides and expose this residue to air, promoting mold growth. High-grade silicone bungs are much better. They won't wick. They're flexible and so are much easier to insert and remove than wooden bungs. They don't mash the edges of the hole when driven in. And their infinite life span ends the periodic replacement necessary with wooden bungs. The silicone bung is

TURN BARREL SO BUNG IS IN
CONTACT WITH WINE WHEN
STORING

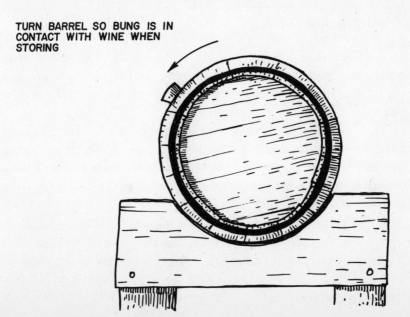

made by the Boswell Company, 305 San Anselmo Avenue, Suite 313, San Anselmo, Calif. 94960. Order well before you want to use your barrels so that you have them when you need them.

Pages 176–77 show the steps necessary to prepare a new barrel—French or American—for wine.

Siphon wine from the carboys into the barrel, with the hole at the very top. Don't fill to the point that makes wine squish out when the bung is inserted, but just before that point is reached. You want as little air as possible in the barrel. If some wine does squish out and run down the barrel, remove a little wine and clean up the spills with sulfite sterilizing solution. Insert the bung snugly, then turn the barrel slightly so the bung and hole are covered by wine inside. If it's a wooden bung, knock it in with a sharp blow from a wooden stick. The silicone bung can be seated by hand pressure, and removed by hand, too. To remove a wooden bung, use a wooden stick and knock the bung from side to side, firmly but gently so you don't shatter any wood. The bung will slowly work its way out with this technique. I always clean up the bung with sterilizing solution, then rinse it, before reinserting it.

Reusing Barrels

The second time you use your barrel, and every year thereafter, you can let the wine spend longer amounts of time on the wood. Older barrels give the most delicate oaking to a wine.

If your barrel develops mold on the outside when storing wine, or when stored filled with water and sulfite, wash it off immediately with sterilizing sulfite solution. Smell your barrel before filling it with wine. It should smell sweet and fresh. If it doesn't, discard it.

"The major failure of home winemakers in my opinion," says Earle Presten of St. Helena, "is they get all enthusiastic about the excitement of the crush, but forget about the racking and topping up during the aging period." I agree with him. Rackings are necessary, and so is topping up.

A big temptation is to open up the barrel or carboy, siphon a little wine out for sampling, and then replace the airlock or bung without topping up. Air is the enemy of wine, and I've personally spoiled at least 50 gallons over the years by not topping up. There'll be two or three inches of air space in the carboy and everything will look okay. But one day the wine will have a whitish skin on it, and then I know I've blown it. The whitish skin is acetobacter happily turning my wine into vinegar. It means the wine is spoiled. It won't even make very good vinegar. All you can do is pour it out as lost.

If you want to have a little wine for tasting, fill a couple of gallon jugs with new wine and put on airlocks. Taste from these. If one of these develops acetobacter, you've lost only a gallon. Keep everything else topped up at all times.

Oak Chips in Glass Containers

I promised to discuss adding oak without using a barrel. I learned the technique from Dr. John McGrew, who also gave up using barrels ("they leak"). The idea is to use oak chips or pieces of oak in the carboys. Oak chips are available from most winemaking supply stores, and they're perfectly good to use. I prefer going to the forest and finding a white oak limb or sapling, looking for a billet about a foot long and an inch or so around. White oak *(Quercus alba) only.* Don't take chances. Red oak smells like cat pee, and you know what that's like. Other oaks are not suitable and won't give you the flavor you're after. If no white oak grows in your area, use the commercial chips, a few grams per gallon, for a few weeks.

Use straight-grain white oak with all the bark removed. Split the billet. If it smells good, take about five slivers from it, about 5 inches long, about a half-inch wide, and maybe a quarter-inch thick. Put the five pieces in a paper bag, then put the bag and a couple of cups of water in a pressure cooker, and pressure cook them for about ten minutes. This will remove the harshest tannins and tastes, and will sterilize the pieces. Then discard the paper bag and put the pieces in a sterilized muslin or cheesecloth

PREPARING AND MAINTAINING OAK BARRELS

To prepare a new barrel for wine

Step 1.

Fill the barrel with water (hot or cold) and put in the bung. Turn the barrel so the bung and hole are in contact with the water. All leaking should stop within three days. If the barrel is still leaking, give it a day or two more to stop. Then, if still leaking, return the barrel to the store and get a new one. Repeat this step with the new one, until you get a barrel that's filled with water and doesn't leak.

Step 2.

Pour out this water and fill halfway with hot water.

Step 3.

Add washing soda (soda ash) according to this table:

BARREL SIZE	WASHING SODA
50 gallons	1 cup
40 gallons	¾ cup
25 gallons	½ cup
20 gallons	⅓ cup
15 gallons	5 tablespoons
10 gallons	3 tablespoons

Dissolve the washing soda in the least amount of water possible, then add to the half-full barrel. Bung the barrel securely.

Step 4.

Roll the barrel back and forth vigorously, sloshing the solution inside over all parts. Do this for at least a half-hour. The washing soda will be leaching harsh, intense oak components from the wood.

Step 5.

Fill the barrel the rest of the way with hot water, then rebung. Allow the barrel to stand for twenty-four hours.

Step 6.

Empty the barrel and fill halfway with cold water. Bung it, then roll it back and forth vigorously for five to ten minutes. Roll it from side to side and end to end. Empty and repeat this rinsing three times. Empty for the final time.

Step 7.

Immediately fill the barrel with wine. If you don't have quite enough to fill, top up with a sound and similar wine.

To store the barrel when not in use

Immediately after emptying the barrel of wine:

Step 1.

Rinse by filling one-fourth full with cold water, bunging, rolling, and emptying. Repeat at least three times.

Step 2.

Fill halfway with cold water.

Step 3.

Add sodium bisulfite or potassium metabisulfite and citric acid in the following proportions:

BARREL SIZE	SULFITE	CITRIC ACID
50 gallons	1½ cups	1 cup
40 gallons	1 cup	¾ cup
25 gallons	¾ cup	½ cup
20 gallons	⅔ cup	⅓ cup
15 gallons	½ cup	5 tablespoons
10 gallons	⅓ cup	3 tablespoons

Dissolve the sulfite and citric acid in water before adding it to the water in the barrel.

Step 4.

Mix thoroughly by bunging the barrel and rolling it for five to ten minutes. Then fill the barrel completely with cold water, bung it securely, and place it in storage.

Step 5.

Top the barrel every month with cold water.

Step 6.

If the barrel will continue in storage after a year, repeat the above steps. If you're going to use it for wine, rinse it several times with cold water, rolling it vigorously each time, before filling.

bag (just a piece of material to hold the wood, tied so it doesn't come apart) with a couple of sterilized marbles to make it sink. Drop this in the carboy and let it stay for three or four months.

Taste the wine at the end of that time. It should have just a nice hint of oak. If you think the oak flavor is too strong, cut down on the time for the next batch. If not strong enough, allow an extra month. But try three to four months to start.

As for barrel aging, I'd allow a wine no more than six weeks in a new barrel prepared the way I indicated on page 176. A barrel that's been used before can hold wine for four to six months, or up to a year or more if it's held several batches of wine.

The Importance of Oak

Oaking is important. It's your chance to add an extra, intriguing, quality taste to the wine, but it should not be overly obvious. Neither should it be undetectable. Try some good California Chardonnays or a Beaulieu Rutherford if you want to taste commercial oaking to give you a benchmark to shoot for. Good red Bordeaux has also been oaked, usually with great finesse, and you can sample them for benchmark oak flavors, too. I think it's easier to adjust the oak flavors by using chips or slivers rather than a barrel. Some say barrel aging provides other benefits, that water works its way out of the wine and through the wood, concentrating the wine that's left. That may be, but that kind of long aging is possible only if you're using old barrels with little flavor to impart to the wine.

FURTHER RACKING AND AGING

After oaking, siphon the wine into clean glass carboys for further aging. You'll be automatically racking the wine at this point. When siphoning finished wine, place the end of the siphon hose under the surface of the bottle that's filling, so the stream doesn't bubble into the wine already in the bottle. The bubbling incorporates air into the wine, and while some air was good for the wine during the primary fermentation, it will only reduce quality and oxidize the wine now. Try to get as little air as possible into the wine when racking. This is especially critical with whites. Rather than stoppering the carboys with a solid cork, I reattach airlocks. If the wine undergoes a natural malolactic fermentation, or otherwise decides to give off gas, this gas can escape. I clean up the corks and airlocks and give the airlocks a fresh charge of sulfite sterilizing solution. Then I put the carboys in the cellar and pretty much forget about them for a while, until I'm ready to bottle the wine.

You could bottle the wine now, but I don't recommend it. The wine will be only about six months old at this point. It may taste fairly decent, but it'll get better if it has any aging potential at all. A light red wine or fresh white, drunk as a nouveau, could be bottled now, but even these will benefit from another three or four months in storage.

The wine will probably be a bit cloudy—not much, but less than perfectly clear. Nothing makes homemade wine more suspicious-looking than a cast or cloudiness. The cloudiness is most likely caused by particles of spent yeast, and if bottled will add off flavors to the wine as the dead cells slowly disintegrate. The cloudiness will settle by itself or be removed in the step that comes just before bottling—a step called *fining,* which we'll discuss later.

How Much Aging?

How long to age the wine before bottling? It's up to you, really, but here are the considerations that will lead to a rational decision:

Full-bodied reds. I'd say let them age in 5-gallon carboys for at least a year, preferably two, before bottling. Drinking them too young is like eating the cookie dough before you bake it into cookies. The dough may be irresistible to the young, but the wiser person knows that there's no comparison with the baked cookies. During the storage time, the wine will settle down.

Flavors will mingle and meld. Harsh and bitter constituents will disappear. Off flavors and young tastes will age gracefully into smoothness. The cloudiness of the young wine may entirely settle out and you may not have to fine the wine at all. Right now I have 10 gallons of four-year-old Chancellor downstairs that's still not bottled. It's a crystal-clear ruby red, and still improving, although I think it won't improve much more. I guess I should go down there and bottle it. Four years is a bit long, I admit, but I get a perverse satisfaction out of not drinking all my wine young. The point is that aging in bulk makes a smoother wine than aging in the bottle. Wine, for some reason, ages faster in a small bottle than in a 5-gallon size—probably because the greater bulk in the carboys is less subject to temperature fluctuations than wine in small bottles. After the third racking, I'd give a big red wine *at least* a year in the carboys or the cask, if you're using an old one with little flavor to impart.

Light reds. A year would be nice, but six months will do. They'll be at their freshest and most drinkable at from one to two years old.

Full-flavored whites. I'm thinking primarily here of Chardonnay. From six months to a year after the third racking is minimum.

Light, fruity whites. From three to six months aging after the third racking is enough.

Racking Schedule

1. Within a month or two after the primary fermentation. *Typical time:* early November.
2. Two to three months later. *Typical time:* just before Christmas through January.
3. Three months later. *Typical time:* mid-March through April.

Storage Conditions for Aging

Storage conditions should be cool—from 50° to 60° F is

ideal. Nothing ages a wine more quickly than high temperatures, which, at 80° F, can age a wine twice as fast as at 50°. An
absence of molds and grungy conditions in general helps prevent
anything sneaking its way into the wine and spoiling it. The
storage room should be *dark.* Exposure to light, especially to
sunlight, reduces wine quality quickly. This will give you reason
to remember to turn off the cellar light. Wine bottles are smoky
or dark to keep light from the wine. Try to provide the same
conditions in your storage cellar. Finally, find a storage area
where there are no vibrations to jostle the wine and where the
temperature doesn't fluctuate over short periods. I won't say not
to talk too loud, but a quiet place away from hustle and bustle
makes for better aging. Wine is delicate stuff. We've heard about
wine that's "travel sick." Bouncing around in train, car, or plane
upsets wine. I always let wine that's traveled sit in my cellar for
a month before opening it.

The perfect place for storage is a root cellar or part of an
underground cellar insulated from the temperature swings and
activities of the rest of the room. At least keep the aging wine
in a cool, dark place.

WINE DISORDERS

Wine disorders do happen, but the only ones I've had
experience with are acetobacter and hydrogen sulfide. If you
keep air away from your wine and keep your containers topped
up, you should not experience the awful, slow vinegarization of
what otherwise was a promising wine. Acetobacter, by the way,
has a hard time establishing itself in wines over 12 percent
alcohol, although severe air contact will eventually allow it to
grow. That's one good reason for adding sugar to low-sugar
musts.

The rotten-egg smell of hydrogen sulfide gas in your wine,
or the chemically related smells of garlic or asparagus, means
disaster has struck. I've read of many ways to rid a wine of H_2S,
but they all involve adding poisonous substances like copper

sulfate. I wouldn't serve a wine containing such compounds. If a racking with good aeration—that is, allowing the stream of wine to splash down into the filling bottle, bubbling air into itself —doesn't solve the problem, discard the wine.

There are other wine disorders, but if your air security is good, you shouldn't see them. One disease, called ropiness, or oiliness, which turns the wine into a thick, ropy mass, is caused by a lactic bacterium that doesn't need air to thrive. It also spells the end of the wine. It's never happened to me or anyone I know who makes wine, so don't worry about it. If it develops, think of yourself as one in a million, and pour out the wine.

It can happen that, after bottling, anaerobic bacteria turn an odd bottle. This "bottle sickness" will probably be confined to that bottle, and the rest of your wine will most likely be all right.

FILTERING

Filtering, by the way, can be done in the home winery. It takes the place of *fining* the wine—clearing it by adding a fining agent. It also removes substances that will deposit out in the bottle. And it can remove quality right along with all these things. I'm not an advocate of filtering wines, but if you're interested, small-scale filtering equipment, hoses, and pumps can be purchased. Wine & The People in Berkeley, California, specializes in systems for the home winemaker.

FINING

Given the carboy storage times I've recommended, most well-made red wine will fall brilliantly clear and can be bottled with no fining. Occasionally, however, a wine—especially a white—will have a slight haze or cloudiness that refuses to settle out. If one must clear a wine, fining does less harm to the wine than filtering.

Many agents are used to clear wine—ox blood was once common and is still used in Burgundy, France. Gelatin and isinglass are still used occasionally. Bentonite from Wyoming—a very fine, pure clay—is most commonly used in North America to clear white wines of a haze. While the clay works well, it leaves a large fluffy lees, and you can lose an awful lot of wine in the fining process.

Egg white fining is used to reduce tannins in red wine. The procedure is very simple. Carefully separate one fresh egg white, with *no* trace of yellow. Beat the white gently. One egg white is enough for about 10 gallons of wine. Pour half the beaten white into the 5-gallon carboy and stir it in gently and thoroughly with a *clean* rod or stick. Try not to incorporate too much air into the wine. Replace the cork and airlock. Within ten days the wine should fall clear. If it hasn't, your wine will remain cloudy. If it tastes good, throw a big party and make wine punch. If it doesn't taste good, it's probably a candidate for the drainpipe. As soon as the wine clears, rack off the lees, and bottle it.

Since fining reduces tannins and can remove the subtle highlights from a wine, I never do it unless a wine has an objectionable haze. I'd estimate that 95 percent of the wines I've made have fallen perfectly clear of their own accord.

BLENDING

After a sufficient storage period and fining, if necessary, bottle the wine. The only additional operation may be blending. Most often the home winemaker will bottle examples of 100 percent varietals, but blending two or more wines can be the last fine tuning in your quest for a truly fine wine.

Fine Bordeaux wines are usually blends of Cabernet Sauvignon, Merlot, Cabernet Franc, Malbec, and occasionally Petit Verdot. Varying proportions of these wines are blended to achieve stunning balances among the wine's components. In California, more and more winemakers are blending Merlot with Cabernet Sauvignon to soften the wines. In the East, vintners have found that a fifty-fifty mixture of Maréchal Foch and Cascade makes a good wine. Commercial blending experts always set a goal for blending. So should the home winemaker. If you have no clear goal in mind, don't blend.

To that I'd add another rule: Unless the blend is better than any component in it, don't blend. And finally, blend similar wines: robust reds with robust reds, light whites with light whites, and so on.

Some of the goals achievable by blending:

Color correction. Since my Chancellor grapes sometimes lack color, I've planted several Colobel vines among them. These are teinturier grapes, rich in color, that add depth to the color of the Chancellor. Alicante Bouschet is a variety used similarly for color in California. Only a small percentage of one of these is needed in the blend to enrich a poorly colored wine.

Acidity. It's possible to reduce the acidity of an over-acid wine by blending in a neutral, low-acid wine of similar type. You may not have these available from the home vineyard, however. If the wine is severely acidic, consider diluting it with a similar California jug wine just to make it drinkable.

Tannins. Winemakers use Merlot to soften Cabernets because Merlot is low in tannins and Cabernets are high. Too much tannin can pucker the mouth and render a wine undrinkable until age dismantles the tannins in the bottle. This is what happens when big, tannic Bordeaux age into soft maturity. Heavily tannic wines can be made drinkable earlier by the addition of some low-tannin wine of otherwise similar characteristics.

Oak. You may, despite your best efforts, over-oak a wine. By adding a similar wine that's not over-oaked, or not oaked at all, you can reduce the oakiness to the proper level.

Body. I'm not sure improving body is a reasonable goal. *Body* refers to the fullness of flavors and feel in the mouth. Trying to improve a wine with low body by adding one of high body will probably produce a mediocre wine of medium body. In most cases I'd think the full-bodied wine should be kept as a treasure and not blended. In rare cases, the blend could be better than either, and blending would be a good idea. Chambourcin adds body to a blend, for instance, while by itself it may be of inferior quality.

Unless you have one of these clear-cut goals in mind, blending probably won't improve the wines involved.

Blend small batches at a time, and gather some friends or family knowledgeable about wine to help you. In blending, several opinions can guide you in making the final decision whether to blend, and, if so, in what proportions. It's really trial and error until you feel that the blend is an improvement upon all of the individual wines used in it. If you decide to blend, use a clean carboy and siphon the appropriate proportions into it from the containers of the pure varietals. Be careful not to bubble too much air into the wine: keep the end of the siphon hose beneath the surface of the filling bottle. I'd plan to bottle the wine immediately after blending to avoid further aeration in the future.

FINAL MEASUREMENTS BEFORE BOTTLING

At bottling, it's a good idea to take the following final measurements for your records, or for the label if you choose: pH, titratable acidity, residual sugar, and alcohol. The pH and TA don't *have* to be done again, but aging, fining, racking, and other handling can change these figures to some degree. Kits are available from The Wine Lab to measure final SO_2, but you may want to simply list the total of all sulfite additions you've made.

Alcohol Content of Finished Wine

At the end of the primary, the Brix was down to somewhere around 8. This remaining sugar was slowly fermented to alcohol during the secondary. When the fresh-crushed must was all sugar and no alcohol, its specific gravity was about 1.080. As alcohol started forming and sugar began disappearing, the specific gravity started dropping.

Pure ethyl alcohol has a specific gravity of less than 1.000. Pure water has a specific gravity of 1.000 and is the standard on which the scale is based. Water with dissolved sugar has a specific gravity higher than 1.000. At the end of the primary, the specific gravity gets down to 1.030 or thereabouts. During the secondary, it drops to 1.000, and then keeps dropping. Finished wine has a specific gravity of less than 1.000, with the actual number depending on the alcohol content.

"Complete dryness" means that all the sugar has been converted to alcohol. Figure the alcohol content of your finished wine from Table 13, page 115.

Testing Residual Sugar

An accurate way to determine if your wine has any residual sugar after it has completely finished fermenting is to use a urine glucose measurement kit, such as those used by diabetics. They can be purchased in any drugstore and go by trade names such as Dextrocheck and Clinitest. They will show residual sugar up to a few percent very accurately. Less than 1 percent residual sugar usually adds a little softness to a wine and is desirable. Amounts in the order of 2 or 3 percent will make a wine taste sweet, and could be due to sugar left after alcohol content rose high enough to kill off the yeast, or to a fermentation that stuck toward the end. Most wine yeast are killed off at about 15–16 percent alcohol by volume. Therefore, if you've got a wine with 11 or 12 percent alcohol and 3 percent residual sugar, the fermentation stuck. You should try to restart it (see directions on page 156). If your wine shows 16 percent alcohol and 3 percent sugar, you undoubtedly started with grapes of high Brix, and your wine will remain sweet. Some extraordinary wines—port, sauternes, Ausleses—are made with residual sugar left. Such sweet wines make excellent after-dinner or dessert wines.

Your label could then contain all of the following:

—Brix   —Res. Sugar
—pH   —Total SO_2
—TA   —Percent Alcohol

More than this even the most dedicated oenophile won't ask.

BOTTLING

There are wine bottles, and then there are wine bottles. Here are the most common types:

I use Bordeaux bottles for reds and Burgundy bottles for whites. The tall German white wine bottles are hard to stack on their sides. Never use screw cap bottles or odd shapes that may take odd-sized corks. Bottles definitely run in grades of quality. The highest grade has an extra heft from the additional glass used. Both high-quality Bordeaux and Burgundy bottles have an indentation called the punt on the bottom that is ostensibly used

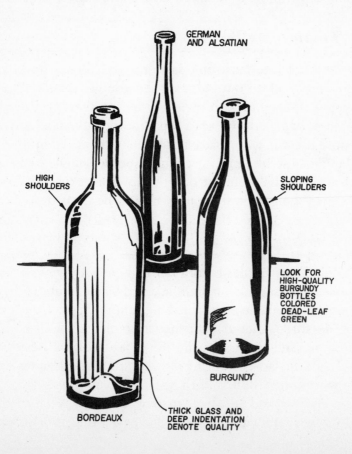

GERMAN AND ALSATIAN

HIGH SHOULDERS

SLOPING SHOULDERS

LOOK FOR HIGH-QUALITY BURGUNDY BOTTLES COLORED DEAD-LEAF GREEN

BURGUNDY

BORDEAUX

THICK GLASS AND DEEP INDENTATION DENOTE QUALITY

to hold sediment when the wine is being decanted, but I've never noticed that it works very well for that purpose. I have found that bottles with indentations on the bottom are usually of higher quality than those without. All bottles should be dark shades of green. The best Burgundy bottles are "dead leaf green," which is a more brownish yellow-green than others. This bottle color is beginning to be used in the United States and is more available to home winemakers.

One can, of course, buy wine bottles. I never do. I save nice bottles that I buy from the store and I have a deal going with several restaurants that I patronize. The restaurant owners are amenable to putting aside good-quality bottles for me to pick up. Now if I only could wangle the owners into getting the dishwashers to rinse them for me, I could save myself some work.

Pre-cleaning Bottles

Probably the most time-saving thing you can do in all of winemaking is clean out bottles when you get them and never let bottles sit around with wine residues in them. I plug them with pieces of paper towels to keep airborne dust and debris out, and store them in a dry place until I need them. Then they will need minimal scrubbing. Very cruddy bottles can be cleaned up and used, but they're a lot of work to clean. Any bottles that don't yield their deposits quickly should be discarded.

Cleaning Again at Bottling

I wash my bottles before filling them with wine, whether they're clean or not, in an ammonia-and-water solution, using a bottle brush available at winemaking supply shops. Then I rinse the bottles three times to make sure all ammonia is gone and they smell sweet and fresh. Usually the labels soak off—especially European wine labels—during the washing. American labels are made with sterner stuff, and I've soaked some American bottles for a half hour and still had to scrub them off. One of those copper wire scrubby pads for pots and pans works well on labels.

After the final rinse, I set the bottles on a table, then cover them with a towel or cloth. Figure five bottles for each gallon of wine—so if you are bottling one 5-gallon carboy, have at least twenty-five bottles on hand.

Filling the Bottles

It helps to have a couple of people bottling, but it can be done alone. I place a clean towel or newspapers on the floor and set five bottles on them. Using the siphon hose from a carboy on the table above, I get the siphon going and fill the bottles to a point in the neck that will be about a half inch below the bottom of the cork when it's inserted. A little practice will make you expert in this.

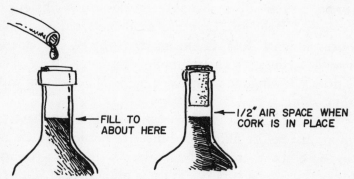

Some winemaking supply shops sell a stainless steel device that fits on the end of the siphon hose and dispenses wine when it's pressed on the rim of the bottle, then closes when the hand pressure is released. This keeps wine from dribbling all over when you are filling the bottles, but a deft hand with a kink in the siphon hose accomplishes the same thing. When filling, I try to be very careful not to froth and overaerate the wine. I run it relatively slowly down the inside of the bottle, adjusting the rate of flow by how hard I'm kinking the siphon hose. I check to make sure the level is correct in the neck, then when five bottles are filled, put them under the towel. I take out five more and fill them, return them under the towel, and so on until the carboy is finished. I don't say *emptied* because most often there will be a deposit in the bottom of the carboy. Take care not to suck up any deposits into the wine. Ordinarily, you'll lose a little wine in the very bottom that gets stirred up with the deposits, but that's better than bottling muck.

Now you have a couple dozen bottles under the towel ready for corking.

CORKING

Corks should be of excellent quality. Don't pinch pennies. Look for long, straight corks. I use #9 corks, a little larger than the #8s used by many winemakers. The longer the corks and the fewer dark pits in them, the higher the quality. They should never be tapered—always straight. Synthetic polyethylene corks trade-named Bouchon Tage are available from Mack-Wayne Closures in Santa Rosa, California, but why go synthetic when real corks do the job? The synthetics don't breathe the way real cork does, allowing the wine inside minimal interaction with the world outside.

The dry corks will be larger than the hole you have to put them in. Just before filling your first five bottles, bring a pot of water to a boil and drop in about thirty or so corks—twenty-five plus extras in case a cork doesn't seat properly and you have to recork. Cover with a top so the corks are steamed. Some say the heat makes corks crumbly and reduces their life, but I've never noticed that. Mine have lasted for six years with no problems. The alternative is to soak them for several hours in a 1 percent solution of sulfite in cold water. Soaking corks isn't as easy as it sounds, since corks obstinately float. Put them in a jar, fill to the top with solution, keeping the corks under the water with one hand, then clamp on the top and turn it upside down. After soaking or boiling for about five to ten minutes, the corks will be ready to use, having absorbed some water and become pliable.

You can't pound the corks in the bottles with a mallet. Believe me; I've tried, early on in my winemaking career. What's needed is a nifty piece of equipment called a hand corker.

I have one made by Sanbri, a French firm, and it continues to serve me through the years. It has a chamber into which you place the cork. A piston is adjusted so that the top of the inserted cork is flush with the rim of the bottle's neck. The chamber is closed by bringing the handles together, and the cork is squeezed by hand pressure. Holding the handles closed with

TOP OF CORK
FLUSH WITH RIM
OF BOTTLE

one hand and positioning the corker over the bottle, the other hand works a lever that drives the piston forward, driving the cork into the neck of the bottle. Practice on some empty bottles until you get the hang of it. It takes a little practice to get a feel for doing it correctly every time, but it's nothing you won't learn quickly. If you seat a cork poorly, pull it with a corkscrew or cork puller and reinsert a new one.

I take the bottles out from under the towel one by one and immediately cork them. When all are corked, I rinse them under cool water in the sink. They should be taken to the cellar at once and laid on their sides. Occasionally a cork will leak, but this usually stops within a day, and only a few drops are lost. If a cork continues to leak, take the bottle upstairs and recork it.

If you've got the energy, repeat this scenario for the next 5-gallon jug. I find that 10 gallons—fifty bottles—a day is about my limit. If I have one hundred bottles to do, I save the second fifty for another day.

Laying the bottles on their sides allows the corks to touch wine. The cork cells will swell, making a perfect closure.

When you're sure that all your corks are secure and the bottles have dried off, you can bring them up for labeling and capsuling.

LABELING

I used to make all my labels by hand—cutting out the paper, using India ink and brush and pen, doing a little drawing on each one. They looked fine, but it was a lot of work. Over the years, I've decided to use pressure-sensitive labels (white, 4 × 1.5 inches), easily obtainable at any office supply house. On these go the measurements we discussed before: pH, Brix, residual sugar, alcohol, total SO_2, plus the variety of grape, the year, and "Jeff and Marilyn Cox." They are unceremoniously written out and slapped on the bottles, from which they peel easily before the next washing.

I've grown to like the no-nonsense look of these labels for my everyday wine. If I'm going to make a bottle into a gift, then I get fancy just for that one bottle. I find a quality paper, usually buff or cream-colored (any color will do as long as it harmonizes with the bottle color). Then I carefully draw a picture of my conception of a beautiful wine label, including a sketch and data about the wine. If it's a special occasion, or for a special person, I'll refer to it on the label.

I've done dozens—each different—for friends. They make beautiful, personalized gifts. Many home winemakers who type better than they draw type up labels and have them run off on a small press or even on a copying machine (although you're limited to the paper color the copier will accept).

On page 193 are an example of a label for an anniversary and an example that Earle Presten showed me.

By the way, that wine was excellent, although it didn't stint on the oak flavors—obviously.

Attaching the Labels

The easiest way to attach a label to a bottle of wine is with a glue stick. These are sold in most stationery stores. They're like a tube of lipstick, except that they contain a white pasty glue instead of lip gloss. Run a strip of this down the side edges of the label, lay the label on the bottle at the center of the label, then smooth down first one edge, then another, keeping a gentle tension so the label doesn't buckle. For very fancy gift bottles, I'll put the year or a special greeting on a small label that flies

JEFF AND MARILYN'S

1987

Chancellor

BRIX : 21
TA : .90
pH : 3.2
Alc. : 11 %

FOR JUDY AND BARRY ON YOUR 10TH ANNIVERSARY. TRUE LOVE AND FINE WINE GET BETTER WITH AGE.

1980
CABERNET SAUVIGNON
This wine is dedicated to a cast of thousands:
Liz Cooper, Brian Feltovich, Christy Gianelli, Paul Hessenger, Ray Wilson, Jim Wilson, et al.
The grapes were picked at Webster Ranch, coming in at an unbelievable 23.3% sugar. The wine was fermented dry at a local Napa Valley winery and brought to maturity in the cellar of Spring Creek Vineyards. It was aged in an American oak barrel for one year and another three months in a French oak barrel.
Bottled Dec. 10 & 11, 1981
Special thanks to Earle and Valerie for the use of their cellar.

above the large one. I even made a tiny booklet once to describe the way we made a particularly interesting wine, and hung it by a gold thread around the neck. That one was for a wedding.

Label-making can go too far. Two San Franciscans were arrested not long ago for faking labels of 1975 Château Mouton-Rothschild, attaching them to Bordeaux bottles full of ordinary California red, and trying to sell them at the "bargain" rate of $250 a case to liquor dealers. Their "special consignment" of Mouton led to special confinement after the federal agents got hold of them. Perhaps it was fitting that they chose the 1975 Mouton to fake: it carried a reproduction of a purple, orange, and green work by Andy Warhol.

Faking appearances in the wine world is not limited to the illegitimate. I once purchased a bottle of 1963 J. W. Burmester Vintage Port at the Sherry-Lehmann wine store in New York City. I asked the salesman not to wipe off the bottle, for it was a crusty, dusty old bottle that appealed to me as much for its cobwebby-looking outside as for the rich port I knew was inside. The salesman said not to worry. "It won't come off. They spray it with something. People seem to like the bottles looking like that," he assured me.

FOIL CAPSULE

Foil Capsules

Foil capsules on the top don't add a thing to the quality of the wine in reality, but, psychologically, I'd guess they're good for several quality points. They dress up the bottles immensely, and I always use them on gift bottles. Red foil for reds; gold foil for whites. Most winemakers' supply shops sell them. To put them on, I run three stripes of glue stick from the lip of the rim as far down the neck as the capsule will go, spaced evenly around the neck. Drop the capsule over the neck and twist it on tight with a wringing motion. With all the bells and whistles attached, my fanciest gift bottles look like the one shown on page 194. Of course, the wine inside the bottle should be at least as good and fancy as the gussied-up outside, or the bottle will promise more than the wine can deliver.

CELLARING THE WINE

Wine will age in the bottle. Whites tend to peak within two or three years, then start a decline in quality. Light, fruity reds are usually good for a couple of years, but their freshness and fruit decline after that. Big reds can go for years, but it's the rare one that will keep improving after five to eight years. All of which means that you're going to have to have a place to store carboys and bottles of many vintages. If you make just a hundred bottles (20 gallons) of wine a year, you'll soon have hundreds of bottles of varying ages. We've discussed storage before, but let me give you a little more detail about what you'll need for the long haul.

Cellar Temperature

Of all the storage factors that adversely affect wine, high temperature is the most damaging. Storage at temperatures in the high seventies will dramatically shorten the life of wine, turning whites an ugly brownish color and reducing taste. This is called *maderization* and is synonymous with a wine over the hill. Reds that age prematurely turn pale and flat, and their ruby red color changes to a brownish plum. Besides high temperatures, constantly fluctuating temperatures will also prematurely age the wine. Fluctuations also cause what's called the *bellows effect.* As the temperature changes, the wine inside the bottle expands and contracts, pumping air through the cork and causing oxidation.

The ideal temperature is a constant 58° F, which allows wine to age slowly and gracefully to perfection. Although you may not be able to arrange for a constant 58° (cooling units are not worth the cost for wine storage), remember that the limits are 50° minimum and 65° maximum, average yearly temperature. The normal seasonal rise and fall is slow enough (10° annually 6 feet below ground; only 1° 20 feet down) that the wine rides along with it without damage. Below 50°, maturation is delayed; above 65° it is hastened to the point of damage. The maturation of wine cannot be hurried without harming the quality. The best things take time.

An Insulated Storage Area

You can achieve temperatures like these in an ordinary cellar if you build an enclosure for a wine storage area that's insulated to R-50. Choose a corner of your basement farthest from the furnace or heat source. Because you'll probably be storing fine commercially made wine as well as your own, and because wine bottles have a way of filling whatever storage space is available, figure you'll need bins to hold about 800 bottles of wine (as long as you're going to do this, make it worthwhile). A bin 14 inches wide by 11 inches tall by 8 inches deep will hold twelve Bordeaux or Burgundy bottles, laid on their sides on top of one another.

The bins should be placed along the two stone, block, or brick walls of the cellar, rather than on the insulated walls, if you have enough room to accommodate the seventy or so bins that the 800-plus bottles require. If each wall has thirty-six bins, for example (built six bins across by six bins high), that'll give you seventy-two bins on the two walls, enough for 864 bottles. If you need extra room, you can use the insulated walls. This enclosed area will not only be excellent for wine, it will be just as good for storage of root crops like potatoes, and fruits like apples and pears. Because it's entirely enclosed, a fresh air source is a good idea; if you have a casement window, open it the merest crack. Otherwise, 2-inch tubes, one in each insulated wall near the floor, will suffice for air exchange. It's comforting to have a room full of garden produce and wine snugged away in the basement, believe me. We grow Belgian endive roots in the summer, then put them in our root cellar to sprout, giving us icy-fresh, light green, crisp and creamy Belgian endive heads in January and February, which we down with a dry white like a Seyval Blanc. Naturally, lemon juice replaces the vinegar in the salad dressing.

Here's how a root cellar/wine cellar might look.

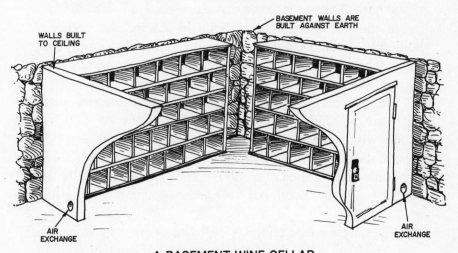

A BASEMENT WINE CELLAR

Walls are built of 2 × 4 studs and braces. Stud walls are insulated to R-50. The ceiling is also insulated to R-50. Walls of stone, brick, or concrete touch outside earth and keep temperatures cool and constant in the wine cellar.

WINE ACCOUTERMENTS

Tasting the wine through all its developmental stages is the prerogative—nay, the duty—of the vintner. But actually *drinking* the wine, with no more cares about its production, comes only after bottle aging in the cellar. Then it ceases to mean anything but what wine always means to the consumer: a delectable drink, preferably taken with food.

Corkscrews

Which brings us to corkscrews. There are hundreds of devices on the market to get a cork out of a bottle, and most are worthless. Forget all the types with levers and gears. Your arm is all the lever and gearing you need. Find a corkscrew that is made from a round wire, not a square or flat one with edges to cut the cork. The point of the corkscrew should follow the helix line of the turns, rather than point in toward the middle. It should have at least six, if not eight, turns around an empty space in the center. The popular Screwpull is such a corkscrew and does the job admirably.

My preference is for a cork puller. These have two prongs which are worked down on either side of the cork. With a pulling twist, the cork comes right out and is held by the prongs. Because the prongs don't pierce the cork but only grasp its sides, they don't destroy the cork, and it can be reinserted all the way into the bottle and taken out over and over again without damage.

Despite the best efforts, we all lose a cork once in a while. Some break off in the middle, leaving the bottom half plugging the neck. In such a case, I try to reinsert the corkscrew very gently, which usually doesn't work. If that fails, push the remainder of the cork into the bottle, use a nice lacquered chopstick to hold it away from the wine, and decant.

Or, a cork may simply shred. The screw will pull out with a lot of crumbles, but most of the cork will remain seated around the edges. Just try to dig out as much as you can. If some cork goes into the bottle, oh well. Or, the whole cork may suddenly slide into the bottle under the pressure of trying to insert the corkscrew or puller. In such a case, reach for the chopstick and

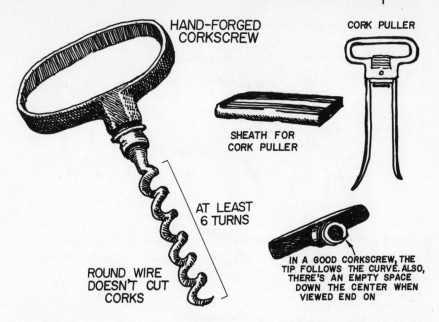

HAND-FORGED
CORKSCREW

CORK PULLER

SHEATH FOR
CORK PULLER

AT LEAST
6 TURNS

ROUND WIRE
DOESN'T CUT
CORKS

IN A GOOD CORKSCREW, THE
TIP FOLLOWS THE CURVE. ALSO,
THERE'S AN EMPTY SPACE
DOWN THE CENTER WHEN
VIEWED END ON

decant. Any pieces of cork floating in the wine that's poured can also be fished out with the chopstick.

Wineglasses

Drinking Lafite—or your own good wine—from a jelly glass is abominable. Get some real wineglasses. They are designed to give you the greatest possible sensory experience of the wine. For reds, get a tulip-shaped glass, at least 8 ounces, with a rim that curves inward.

For whites, a similar—if squatter, but just as generous—glass will do, especially one with a balloon shape. For champagne, flutes are the real thing, with a slightly inward-curving rim and the shape that gives the most beautiful bubbles. Champagne in other glasses tends to go flat quickly.

Fill the still wineglasses with only an ounce or two of wine. Swirl and turn it, developing the bouquet and looking closely at the color. Baccarat makes the best—and most expensive—wineglasses.

INWARD-CURVING TOPS HOLD AROMAS IN THE GLASS

Fill only to here so you can swirl and smell the wine before drinking

AT LEAST 8-OUNCE CAPACITY

WHITE WINE GLASS
JUST A BIT SHALLOWER THAN A RED WINE GLASS

RED WINE GLASS
NEVER USE COLORED WINEGLASSES

CHAMPAGNE FLUTE
THE SHAPE KEEPS THE BUBBLES COMING

SENSORY EVALUATION OF WINE

The sensory evaluation of wine happens first with the *eyes,* then the *nose,* and then the senses of taste and feel in the *mouth.* Let's look at them in that order, even though the odor of wine is the most subtle and important sensory constituent, taste is of less importance, and the look of the wine is least important.

Clarity and Color

After pouring a couple of ounces of a wine into an 8- to 10-ounce glass, I first look for clarity. Any tartrate crystals will also be seen now. Anything but a brilliantly clear wine makes me feel uneasy, even though a slight haze may mean nothing more than that the wine wasn't reduced in quality by fining. Then I look at the color. Some may be looking for a standard of excellence in wine color, but I just look at the color, simply drinking it in with my eyes. With no preconceptions, I know right away whether the color is pleasing or not. Muddy, brown, or purple colors just aren't as pretty as a deep ruby red or a strawy gold white with a hint of green. The purity of the reds achieved in fine wines is astonishing. If you're fond of deep rubies and garnets in gemstones, as I am, a glass of fine red wine will have you practically ecstatic.

Looking at the Rim

Then, with reds, I evaluate the rim. I tilt the glass, causing the wine to thin out as it approaches the rim, allowing more light to pass. At the rim, the wine is very thin, and colors change. Then, I hold the glass above a white tablecloth or piece of paper to check the rim color. A red that simply thins out to a lighter tone but doesn't change color (hue) indicates a young wine.

If the rim shows bluish or purplish colors, that could be due to the variety or it could mean that the grapes were not quite ripe when picked. If the red color thins out to a deep golden orange color, that means the wine is well aged and peaking. A brownish orange or brown plum rim means that the wine is declining, and has passed its peak.

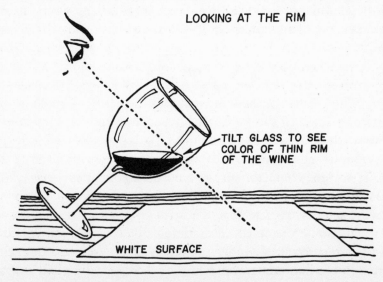

LOOKING AT THE RIM

TILT GLASS TO SEE
COLOR OF THIN RIM
OF THE WINE

WHITE SURFACE

LEGS

Legs

Then I swirl the wine in the glass to get a look at its legs. For many years I had read that the legs of wine—the rivulets that form on the sides of the glass after the wine is swirled—were caused by the glycerin in the wine. I've since discovered that in reality they are formed because of the lower surface tension that alcohol causes. "Which is why you can get impressive legs with a glass of vodka," says Henry Finder of Loudonville, New York, who has investigated the phenomenon. A friend recently gave me a bottle of Saint Regis, "America's First Non-Alcoholic Wine." It's a sweetish, less-than-ordinary jug white from California from which the alcohol has been removed by gentle heat. Because it contains no alcohol, it also has no legs.

The "Nose" of the Wine

The "nose" of the wine includes the *aroma*—which is the particular smell of the grape variety, such as the Welch's grape juice smell of Concord, or the hints of bell pepper in a Cabernet Sauvignon—and vinous smells, which are winey without any particular varietal characteristic. The nose also includes the *bouquet,* the odor produced by fermentation, such as yeasty smells and flowery smells that arise during bottle aging. The nose may show *off smells.* Some of the common defects in the nose are volatile acidity—the smell of vinegar in small amounts; acetaldehyde, which smells like a nutty sherry; sulfur dioxide, which smells like the sulfurous odor of a burning kitchen match; mercaptan, which smells like a skunk; hydrogen sulfide, which smells like rotten eggs; sauerkraut odor, usually from a malolactic that proceeded in the bottle; and any other smell you choose not to like.

Oak will be another constituent of the nose. If excessive, it can detract from the sensory experience. When a wine—especially a red—is oaked just right, the nose gets a faint whiff of vanilla, rather than of a heavy wood.

When varietal aromas, a flowery bouquet, and a hint of vanilla oak mingle in harmony, the result is a great wine with enormous evocative power. We know that the sense of smell is linked closely with memory. A certain smell can bring back a moment sharper and clearer in our minds than any other stimulus. You'll find that a great wine with a balanced nose is as sensual and pleasing an experience as you could ever expect from something to drink.

Retronasal Aroma

The direct aroma comes through the nose, but a richer aroma comes through the back of the nose when the wine is tasted. The wine is sipped and the sip chewed in order to coat the mouth with it, and especially to work up aromas that will seep up the back of the nose and flood the olfactory organs. As Emile Peynaud said, "There are two types of aromas in wine, which are due to the same substances. There is the direct aroma, which comes through the nostrils, and the indirect aroma, or retronasal, when the wine is in the mouth.

"One can judge the quality of a wine by the intensity and persistence of the retronasal aroma," Peynaud said.

When people speak of a wine's long or short finish, they are talking about the persistence of the retronasal aroma. A great wine will continue to unfold both aromas and flavors in the mouth for quite a long time, presenting facet after facet and nuance after nuance of both. The taster can find some new aspect of the flavor or a new aroma even after the sip has been swallowed, the lips smacked, and the sigh heaved.

Educating the Nose

If you are serious about being able to identify the smells in great wine by their proper terms, you can learn the skill at home with one of the new kits available. "Le Nez du Vin," for instance, contains fifty-four vials of pure essences of scents found in wine, packed in a folio-sized box with accompanying reference cards. They include tar, mercaptan, apricots, mushrooms, and fifty other smells. It's an expensive kit. To order one, write to Francis Mollet, 68 Lockwood Road, Riverside, Conn. 06978.

A less expensive kit is the Component Collection, Box 750, Madison Square Station, New York, N.Y. 10159, at a third of the cost of Le Nez du Vin, containing thirty vials of pure wine component essences. Another is the Winealyzer, available at many stores, but a beginner's kit that won't show much to those who have tasted their way through a dozen good bottles of wine.

The Taste of Wine

Further sensory components are the four tastes: sweet, bitter, sour, and salty. If you run into salty, something terrible has happened—or you've broken into the cooking sherry. Residual sweetness, perhaps a slight bitterness or astringency from tannins, and a light acidity are all parts of a balanced wine. Any of them in excess, or missing, detracts from wine quality. For greatness, a wine needs all three in barely detectable amounts.

Table 17 **OPTIMUM SERVING TEMPERATURES**

TYPE OF WINE	DEGREES FAHRENHEIT
Robust red wines	60–65
Light red wines	55–60
Robust white wines	55–60
Light white wines	50–55

These temperatures are "room temperatures," as *room* refers to the cellar in which they're kept. The only reason to chill a wine below 50° would be to kill the taste or mask the lack of one. The exception is champagne, which is good served at 40°–45°. The lower temperature keeps the fizzing from proceeding too fast, and the wine will warm a bit as you drink it, so that the cold doesn't mask the taste.

Body

A final component of wine in the mouth is its body, fullness, or mouthfeel—call it what you will. No one really understands what causes the body of a great wine, but one knows it when it's there. Lesser wines feel thin, watery, unidimensional by contrast. A wine with good body fills the mouth with almost an oily characteristic, but not unpleasant the way oil would be. It tastes round, rather than flat, meaning that it has depth of body.

I have before me a piece of paper on which I made notes the night I drank a fifty-seven-year-old Bordeaux. It carried such an intense aroma and bouquet that it approached the smell of myrrh. I also found "almonds, beefsteak, frankincense, honey, and nuts." The taste was "velvety-smooth, concentrated, with a huge, elongated finish that yields new flavors all the way." The rim was a wide golden orange and the color shone with rubies and garnets. My comments end with this question, "Will you be as young at fifty-seven as this wine?"

I'd like to make a wine as good as that. Wouldn't you? Let's do it.

ON CONSUMPTION OF WINE

Three bowls only do I serve for the temperate: one for health, which they empty first; the second for love and pleasure, and the third for sleep. When this bowl is drunk up, wise guests go home. The fourth bowl is ours no longer, but belongs to violence; the fifth to uproar, the sixth to drunken revel, the seventh to black eyes, the eighth is the policeman's, the ninth belongs to biliousness, and the tenth to madness and hurling the furniture.   —Eubulus (ca. 375 B.C.)

THE HOME WINEMAKER'S RECORD BOOK

The following information is helpful to have as reference when making wine in subsequent years. Copy these pages.

Year _____ Variety _____

Bud burst _____

Full bloom _____

Véraison _____

Harvest date _____

Sprays	
Material	Date
_____	_____ Number of vines _____
_____	_____ Pounds of grapes _____
_____	_____ Gallons of juice _____
_____	_____ Gallons of wine _____
	_____ (After all rackings) _____

Brix at harvest _____ Sugar corrected: _____ (pounds/5 gallons) (Adjusted Brix) _____

pH at harvest _____ Acid corrected: _____ (grams acid blend/5 gallons) _____

TA at harvest _____

SO_2 _____ (ppm) _____ (Adjusted acid) _____ (Adjusted pH) _____

Crush _____ (Date) _____

(Time) _____ (Date) _____

Press whites _____

(Time) _____ (Date) _____

Primary fermentation _____ From (date) _____ To (date) _____

Press reds _____
(Time)

Malolactic culture added _____
(Date)   (Type of culture)

Racked to carboys _____
(Date)   (Date)

Further rackings   SO$_2$ added
(Dates)   (ppm)

_____
_____
_____

Bottling _____
(Date)

Days on skins _____

Wine finishes working _____
(Date)

Cold stabilization _____
From (Date)   To (Date)

Fining _____
(Fining agent)   (Date)

Oaking _____
In cask from (Date)   To (Date)

Type of wood in cask _____

Chips _____
(grams/5 gallons)

Total SO$_2$ at end
of primary _____

REMARKS

Total SO$_2$ at bottling _____

pH at bottling _____

TA at bottling _____

Residual sugar at bottling _____

Alcohol by volume at bottling _____ %

APPENDIX 2

FOR MORE INFORMATION

Societies

The American Wine Society
3006 Latta Road
Rochester, N.Y. 14612
The society publishes many pamphlets covering all aspects of grape growing, vine selection, and winemaking. It also has hundreds of regional chapters that hold regular tastings. Among its publications are bibliographies of the major wine reference works, books on specialized aspects of wine or grapes, and a journal.

Regional Grape Growers' Associations

Many states have a grape growers' association. Check with your USDA agricultural extension agent to find the name of the association that covers your area. These groups sometimes publish information, and are a good way to find sources of vines and supplies.

Tax Information

For tax rules applicable to vineyards, write to Forbes & Company, Certified Public Accountants, 4 Embarcadero Center, San Francisco, Calif. 94111, and ask for "Special Federal Income Tax Aspects of Vineyard Operations" by Cropsey and Peters. At this writing, the cost is $5.

Selected Periodicals

Eastern Grape Grower & Winery News
103 Third Street
Watkins Glen, N.Y. 14891
This bimonthly magazine publishes an annual Directory of the Eastern Wine and Grape Industry, which lists every commercial winery in the East, plus sources of grapestock, grape-growing supplies, and winemaking equipment. The magazine itself is always full of good information on viticulture and winemaking. Write for current subscription price.

Wines & Vines
1800 Lincoln Avenue
San Rafael, Calif. 94901
The monthly magazine of the wine industry, with a primary but by no means exclusive focus on California. There's not a lot for the home winemaker specifically, but if you like to dream about commercial production, *Wines & Vines* shows you dreams coming true, dreams failing, and dreams dashed. It also publishes an annual *Buyer's Guide* that is quite complete, listing every commercial winery in North America, plus all vineyard industry suppliers.

The Wine Spectator
Tasco Publishing Corp.
305 E. 53rd Street
New York, N.Y. 10022
This semimonthly newspaper is consumer oriented, and always full of great tips on what's good at the best prices.

Wine East
620 N. Pine Street
Lancaster, Pa. 17603
A bimonthly magazine that puts the emphasis on eastern wines, wineries, and the wine trade.

California and Western States Grape Grower
Munford Publications, Inc.
3636 N. First Street, Suite 150
Fresno, Calif. 93726
A bimonthly magazine focusing on the western states' grape industry.

Practical Winery
15 Grande Paseo
San Rafael, California 94903
A monthly magazine that is growing into an excellent publication for the serious winemaker. It's full of good how-to, and will serve as continuing education for readers of this book.

There are, of course, many other magazines, newsletters, and scientific journals devoted to all aspects of winemaking, grape growing, marketing, wine appreciation, and so forth. The ones listed above are solid sources for general information.

Selected Bibliography

GENERAL REFERENCE

Lichine, Alexis. *Alexis Lichine's New Encyclopedia of Wines & Spirits.* 3d ed. New York: Alfred A. Knopf, 1982.
A very thorough encyclopedic work brought up-to-date regularly by its editors, written for the wine buyer and those interested in the subject generally.

VITICULTURE

Wagner, Philip M. *A Wine-Grower's Guide.* Rev. ed. New York: Alfred A. Knopf, 1965.
An excellent book on grape growing for the amateur, with a focus on French-American hybrids.

Winkler, Cook, Kliewer, and Lider. *General Viticulture.* Berkeley: University of California Press, 1974.
This is the premier viticultural textbook, but is getting a bit dated. Its primary focus is on growing grapes in California, although other climates are covered.

Weaver, Robert J. *Grape Growing.* New York: John Wiley & Sons, 1976.
Weaver covers the same material as Winkler, but in a more concise and understandable way for the home grower. The book is designed as a freshman text for college courses in viticulture.

WINEMAKING

Wagner, Philip M. *Grapes Into Wine.* New York: Alfred A. Knopf, 1976.
A paperback companion volume to Wagner's viticultural work.

Lundy, Desmond. *Leisure Winemaking.* Calgary, Alta.: Detselig Enterprises Ltd., 1978.
A delightful book full of information on the chemistry involved in winemaking, written for the serious home winemaker. It was recommended to me by a commercial winemaker who uses it to produce award-winning Napa Valley Cabernet Sauvignon.

Amerine, M. A. and M. A. Joslyn. *Table Wines.* 2d ed. Berkeley: University of California Press, 1970.

A monumental work for commercial wineries and graduate students in enology. Everything you'd ever want to know about the technology of winemaking, plus a lot more.

Amerine, M. A., et al. *Technology of Winemaking*. Westport, Conn.: AVI Publishing Co., 1980.
Even more detail on winemaking technology than *Table Wines*. Only for big producers or interested amateurs.

WINE TASTING AND SENSORY EVALUATION

Amerine, M. A. and E. B. Roessler. *Wines, Their Sensory Evaluation*. San Francisco: W. H. Freeman & Co., 1976.
An excellent, no-nonsense approach to wine tasting and techniques for judging wine quality.

APPENDIX 3

SOURCES OF SUPPLIES

If there is no winemakers' supply shop near you, and no local source for vineyard hardware, I'd recommend writing to the following places for their catalogs.

Wine & The People
907 University Avenue
Berkeley, Calif. 94710

Specializes in equipment for the home winemaker, including hard-to-find items and home-scale filtering systems. Also ships frozen vinifera grapes grown in California's North Coast climate.

The Compleat Winemaker
1219 Main Street
St. Helena, Calif. 94574

Besides winemaking equipment, they also carry vineyard supplies, and this is a one-stop source for most of what you'll need.

SACO Supply
New Park, Pa. 17352

A complete supplier of vineyard equipment, from Wirevise and Wirelink fasteners to pruning shears.

Winebuys
166 East 61 Street
New York, N.Y. 10021

Equipment for the home winemaker in the New York area.

Presque Isle Wine Cellars
9440 Buffalo Road
North East, Pa. 16428

Almost everything for the grower and home winemaker, and they ship.

Winemakers, Ltd.
999 Main Road
Box C-406
Westport, Mass. 02740
A good catalog for northeastern winemakers.

I'd also recommend writing for one or the other of these publications, if you're going to be mail-order shopping for your home vineyard and wine operation. They give a yearly update of growers, suppliers, and equipment available. The ads are full of information on the specific products advertised and are a great place to window-shop.

Current Buyer's Guide Issue
Wines & Vines
1800 Lincoln Avenue
San Rafael, Calif. 94901

Current Directory of the Eastern Wine and Grape Industry
Eastern Grape Grower and Winery News
103 Third Street
Watkins Glen, N.Y. 14891

For yeasts and malolactic cultures, check the following places:

The Wine Lab
1200 Oak Avenue
St. Helena, Calif. 94574

Western winemakers should order the ML-34 strain of malolactic culture from The Wine Lab. This strain is suited to California musts. The Wine Lab catalog makes recommendations of specific yeasts for specific varieties, including French-American hybrids, which is very helpful.

Eastern winemakers should use the low pH-tolerant PSU-1 malolactic starter, available—along with yeasts—from:

Tri-Bio Labs
1400 Fox Hill Road
State College, Pa. 16801

Although most winemaking shops and mail-order houses carry barrels, it may be cheaper to order from the manufacturer.

Blue Grass Cooperage Inc.
Box 37210
Louisville, Ky.

They sell new, American white oak 52-gallon barrels.

Independent Stave Co.
Box 104
Lebanon, Mo. 65536

They also make American white oak barrels.

Mutual Stamping and Mfg. Co.
Box 656
Fairfield, Conn.

Mutual makes and sells stainless steel drums in a variety of sizes. As primary fermentation tanks, these are unsurpassed.

For French Nevers or Limousin oak barrels, as well as American oak, try:

Robert L. Stollenwerk Co.
Box 282
Egg Harbor City, N.J. 08215

Barrel Builders
1085 Lodi Lane
St. Helena, Calif. 94574

Custom Cooperage
1194 Maple Lane
Calistoga, Calif. 94515

Mel Knox Barrel Broker
1229 Third Avenue
San Francisco, Calif. 94122

While wine-analysis equipment is available from most mail-order winemaking suppliers listed above, good pH meters may be harder to find. A new line of easy-to-use pH meters has been developed by

Corning Science Products
Box 1150
Elmira, N.Y. 14902

The folks at Corning can tell you where their new Delta-shape pH meters can be purchased through the mail.

APPENDIX 4

SOURCES FOR GRAPEVINES

There are thousands of retail outlets for grapevines in the United States. The following is a representative sample of mail-order suppliers from coast to coast.

The codes show whether they carry vinifera varieties (V), French-American hybrids (FH), or American varieties (A).

Alpine Nursery (A,FH,V)
Route 1, Box 9
Altus, Ark. 72821

Barboursville Vineyards (V)
Box F
Barboursville, Va. 22923

Big Streat Nurseries (A,FH,V)
Route 14
Dundee, N.Y. 14837

Boordy Nursery (FH)
7812 Buxwood Road
Riderwood, Md. 21139

Bountiful Ridge Nurseries
(A,FH)
Princess Anne, Md. 21853

Bully Hill Nursery (FH,V)
Taylor Memorial Drive
Hammondsport, N.Y. 14840

Butler's Nursery (FH,V)
460 Gower Road
Nazareth, Pa. 18064

Chicama Vineyards (V)
Stoney Hill Road
West Tisbury, Mass. 02575

Congdon & Weller Nursery
(A,FH)
North Collins, N.Y. 14111

Dean Foster Nurseries (A,FH)
Box 310
Hartford, Mich. 49057

Elk Run Vineyards and Nursery
(V)
15113 Liberty Road
Mt. Airy, Md. 21771

Foster Nursery Co., Inc.
(A,FH,V)
69 Orchard Street
Fredonia, N.Y. 14063

Grafted Grape Vine Nursery
(A,FH,V)
R.D. #2
Clifton Springs, N.Y. 14432

Grapevines (FH)
Route 4, Box 101
Mountain Grove, Mo. 65711

Juergen Loenholdt (FH,V)
R.D. #1, Box 199
Himrod, N.Y. 14842

Linda Vista Grapevines, Inc. (V)
4401 Linda Vista Avenue
Napa, Calif. 94558

Long Island Vinifera Nurseries
(V)
Main Road, Box 213
Jamesport, N.Y. 11947

Mirassou Vineyards (V)
Route 1, Box A
Soledad, Calif. 93960

Omega Virginia Nursery (V)
Box 646
Madison, Va. 22727

Ponderosa Nurseries, Inc. (V)
1662 East Prosperity Avenue
Tulare, Calif. 93274

Prudence Island Vineyards (V)
Sunset Hill Farm
Prudence Island, R.I. 02872

Riverdale Farms, Inc. (V)
Box 1229
Stockton, Calif. 95201

Schloss Tucker Vineyards
(A,FH,V)
R.D. #1, Box 125B
Waterford, Va. 22190

Sonoma Grapevines, Inc. (V)
1919 Dennis Lane
Santa Rosa, Calif. 95401

Spring Ledge Farms (V)
Route 14
Dundee, N.Y. 14837

Sun Ridge Nursery (V)
Route 5, Box 534M
Bakersfield, Calif. 93307

Hermann J. Wiemer Vineyard
(V)
Box 4, Route 14
Dundee, N.Y. 14837

APPENDIX 5

GRAPE PESTS AND THEIR CONTROLS

If you see leaf damage

SYMPTOMS

At first, a scattering of small whitish spots on the leaves. Then yellow and whitish blotches on severely damaged leaves. Eventually the leaves turn brown and fall off.

CAUSE

Grape Leaf Hopper. A ubiquitous pest in California, the adults are about an eighth-inch long, slender, and light yellow with red and brown marks. The white leaf spots are from feeding episodes by adults. With a severe infestation, leaves are destroyed. Such defoliation badly damages grape quality.

TREATMENT

A parasitic wasp, *Anagrus epos,* is a grower's best friend, as it keeps the hopper populations down to acceptable levels. Populations of young leaf hoppers up to ten per leaf are considered acceptable. Allow refuges of wild blackberries to grow nearby, as the parasitic wasp overwinters in them. French prune orchards also harbor the Anagrus wasp. The parasites can be purchased for release in the vineyard. Leaf hoppers can do considerable feeding before the damage is worth taking action against. Releases of lacewings can help. Sprays of pyrethrum and soap, or soap and nicotine sulfate, or soap and sulfur are all effective.

SYMPTOMS

One side of a leaf is rolled up, and there's frass (larval excrement) and, usually, a worm inside.

CAUSE

Leaf Roller. The worms are green. They attach wet lines of silk from the leaf edge to points near the center. When these dry, they roll the

217

leaf right up. No treatment is necessary unless damage is defoliating vines. Usually parasites keep this pest within bounds. If the pest's populations increase, the parasites will soon follow.

TREATMENT

Bacillus thuringiensis gives excellent control. Make sure your spray reaches inside the rolled leaves by spraying from all sides.

SYMPTOMS

Larvae about a half-inch long, straw-colored—or sometimes greenish, gray, or smoky-colored—are seen in or on swollen buds, developing leaves, or shoot tips, then on leaves which are webbed together, and later in the clusters, where their webs are found. Fruit is punctured and decays, then shrivels.

CAUSE

Orange Tortrix. The adult moth is brown or beige, with a darker saddle of color across folded wings. It's found in the vineyard through most of the year in California. Another sign of this pest is oval, flat, cream-colored eggs deposited in overlapping layers.

TREATMENT

Bacillus thuringiensis gives positive control if vines are sprayed thoroughly from bud burst, and resprayed after each rain for two months.

SYMPTOMS

In early to mid-summer, the leaves of red and black grape varieties begin to turn red, especially between the largest veins. This red color advances until only the main veins and a little tissue alongside is green.

CAUSE

Pacific Mite. It has a yellow to amber body and black spots on its back. It's barely visible to the naked eye. Prefers hot, dry positions on the vines.

TREATMENT

Predatory mites and ladybird beetles will keep the mites in check, but if the mites affect more than eight leaves per vine, release *Metaseiulus occidentalis,* the predatory mite proven capable of controlling Pacific mite. Lime-sulfur or flowable sulfur sprays used for fungus control will help control this West Coast pest.

SYMPTOMS

Leaves shrivel shortly after opening. The lower and earliest leaf may turn black and die before it's half grown. Lower leaves are misshapen and mottled with a bronze-glazed appearance.

CAUSE

Willamette Mite. Barely visible, it appears pale yellow with very small black dots on its body. Prefers shaded, moist positions on the vines.

TREATMENT

The same predatory mite that controls Pacific mite uses Willamette mite as an alternative prey. Sulfur dust will also control this mite.

SYMPTOMS

Leaves are stunted and start to curl. Older leaves turn a bronzy green. Little red mites are seen on leaves, canes, and trunk.

CAUSE

European Red Mite. This familiar red mite attacks more and more American grapes in the East. It prefers high, central positions on older wood.

TREATMENT

Ladybird beetles and predatory mites, especially the black ladybird beetle, *Stethorus punctus,* offer the best control. If the mites are found more than three to a leaf, they'll need further treatment with sulfur dust, flowable sulfur, or lime-sulfur. If little spraying is done with insecticides, mites will seldom be seen.

SYMPTOMS

Leaf tissue is eaten away, except for the veins and, in the early stages, the upper epidermis of the leaves.

CAUSE

Western Grapeleaf Skeletonizer. A yellow caterpillar with purple and black bands across its body.

TREATMENT

A parasitic wasp, *Apanteles harrisinae;* a parasitic fly, *Sturmia harrisinae;* a viral disease, and *Bacillus thuringiensis* have all been used to control this pest. A sex pheromone has been isolated from female skeletonizers that's being used to confuse males.

CAUSE

Japanese Beetle. Metallic bronze and green beetles, a quarter to a third of an inch long.

TREATMENT

Use Bag-A-Bug pheromone traps that lure males by a sex scent and food odor. This gives excellent long-term protection. Handpick until populations are reduced to acceptable levels by the traps. These beetles break out in regular four- or five-year cycles.

SYMPTOMS

Large leaf areas and even whole vines come under attack by large (2–4 inch) caterpillars with a conspicous horn—later replaced by an eye-spot—on the next to last segment of their bodies.

CAUSE

Sphinx (or Hawk) Moth Larvae. The color of these large worms is light green when young, with a dull red to black horn. Later they are yellow-green to red-brown marked with yellow, and lose the horn in favor of an eye-spot.

TREATMENT

Bacillus thuringiensis.

SYMPTOMS

Leaves and young shoots are eaten. You see lots of grasshoppers.

CAUSE

Grasshoppers. These voracious insects are hard to kill, as they are so mobile.

TREATMENT

Poison grasshopper bait is available from agricultural outlets. One grower in Nebraska had success using a spray made from a half-quart of grasshoppers ground in a blender with water, then strained and diluted into the spray tank.

SYMPTOMS

Buckshot size, bristly green galls on the undersides of grape leaves and on young shoots.

CAUSE

Phylloxera. This root louse has an aerial stage during which it produces characteristic galls on the leaves. Nick a gall apart with a fingernail and there's a darker orange area with a tiny whitish larva, louse, or eggs inside.

TREATMENT

Pinch off any galls you see with the fingers and squash them. If there are too many, releases of green lacewing can help. Endolsulfan, the recommended chemical control, damages Baco Noir, Chancellor, Colobel, and Cascade. Dusting with rotenone from pre-bloom to four weeks later should also help.

VARIETAL SUSCEPTIBILITY TO LEAF-DAMAGING PHYLLOXERA

MOST SUSCEPTIBLE	MODERATELY SUSCEPTIBLE	LEAST SUSCEPTIBLE
Seyval Blanc	Delaware	Niagara
Aurora	Ravat 51	Florental
Rayon d'Or	Leon Millot	Catawba
Cascade	Vidal 256	Maréchal Foch
Villard Blanc	Baco Noir	Steuben
Chancellor	Chelois	Cabernet Sauvignon
	Dutchess	Chardonnay
		Riesling

If you see damage to buds or young shoots

SYMPTOMS

Buds are eaten out and young shoots are cut off and fall over.

CAUSE

Cutworms. Colors vary according to species, but the damage will be done at night. The worms are one to one and a half inches long, and are smooth-bodied.

TREATMENT

Rotenone dust worked into the soil around the base of the trunk will help, as that's where the worm goes during the day. Handpick any you see.

SYMPTOMS

Swollen or just-breaking buds in the spring are eaten out, with a conspicuous hole in the center. Later, small larvae eat the emerging leaves, so they are misshapen. Emerging fruit clusters may be eaten.

CAUSE

Grape Flea Beetle. A small, metallic blue or purple beetle that can jump like its namesake. Larvae that grow from eggs deposited in the buds grow to a third of an inch, and are yellowish brown with black markings.

CAUSE

Grape Bud Beetle. Found primarily in the central valleys of California. Similar to flea beetle, except that it is gray.

TREATMENT

Rotenone dust effectively controls emerging larvae. Keep plants dusted from the swollen bud stage until shoots are 6 inches long. Adult beetles may survive rotenone, and if the infestation is bad, you may want to use pyrethroids. Sticky traps made from gallon jugs (see page 106) also help keep populations down.

SYMPTOMS

Dwarfing and stunting of new shoots for first five or six nodes. The growing tip of the shoot may be killed, causing a profusion of laterals that give a witch's broom effect.

CAUSE

Grape Bud Mite. They live in the buds and are carried out the shoot as it elongates. Found mostly in California.

TREATMENT

There's no known chemical treatment, but a healthy vineyard ecology, with predatory mites and ladybird beetles, should help keep populations to a minimum. As a last resort, cut off infested shoots and burn them in a regular sanitation program.

SYMPTOMS

Masses of brownish aphids are seen on young tips, leaves, shoots, and occasionally clusters. Usually accompanied by ants.

CAUSE

Brown Grape Aphid. The ants lap up honeydew excreted by the aphids, and protect them from predators. Usually the aphid damage isn't worrisome, but if an outbreak is severe, some shoot tips and fruit may be lost.

TREATMENT

A jet spray of soapy water (a half-cup of Ivory Liquid in a gallon of water) directed right on the aphids will rid the vines of most of them very efficiently. Aphids, by the way, really attract beneficial insects, so don't bother them unless damage is heavy.

If you see damage to grape flowers or fruit

SYMPTOMS

When the young shoots are 10 to 15 inches long, flower clusters, young leaves, and young fruit are eaten.

CAUSE

Hoplia Beetles. The beetles are found feeding in groups. They're broad, a quarter to a third of an inch long, and grayish to reddish brown in mottles on the backs with silvery, shiny undersides. When disturbed, the beetles drop to the ground. Found mainly in the West.

TREATMENT

First try rotenone-ryania-pyrethrum dust. If the problem persists, try pyrethroids.

SYMPTOMS

Grape clusters look sooty and sticky, and there are cottony, waxy masses down in the clusters.

CAUSE

Grape Mealybug. These are fine food for predators, and an outbreak usually means ants are keeping the mealybugs' natural enemies at bay.

TREATMENT
Ant traps. Pour boiling water down any anthills nearby. Pesticides are not recommended for control, as they kill natural controls.

SYMPTOMS
Silvering, bleaching, or russeting of berries, stems, and leaves. "Halo spot" of berries where an insect's eggs were deposited. Later, scarred and scabby patches appear on the berries.

CAUSE
Thrips. Thrips are small—one-fiftieth to one twenty-fifth of an inch in length. They are winged insects, elongated, narrow-bodied, and can fly, run quickly, and hop.

TREATMENT
Much the same as for leaf hoppers.

SYMPTOMS
Berries are punctured, and juice exudes to form a brown, sticky, ugly mess. Occurs just before harvest. Berries soon shrivel and rot.

CAUSE
Consperse Stinkbug. Look for large (three-eighths inch by one-quarter inch in breadth), shield-shaped stinkbugs, brown on their backs and pale green underneath. Their amber legs have small black spots.

TREATMENT
This is a hard one, since damage occurs just before harvest and sprays of any kind aren't possible. Remove weedy, grassy patches near affected areas of the vineyard, if they exist, to destroy the bugs' habitat. If your vineyard is small enough, handpick and drop them into a can with kerosene in the bottom.

SYMPTOMS
Flower clusters are eaten, blossoms first, then young fruit and leaves.

CAUSE

Rose Chafer. These insects are ubiquitous in the Midwest at grape blossoming time, and sometimes show up in large numbers. They also damage ornamental bushes. The beetle is about a quarter to a third of an inch, light brown, and covered with light hairs. Its long, spiny legs give it a clumsy motion.

TREATMENT

If sandy areas near the vineyard are grassy with perennial weeds, cultivate them, because that's where the rose chafers pupate. Rotenone or other botanical dusts can be used on severe infestations.

SYMPTOMS

Small whitish maggots are feeding on flower parts in vineyards along Lake Erie.

CAUSE

Grape-Blossom Midge. Mostly a minor pest, it can sometimes cause unacceptable damage in the Lake Erie area.

TREATMENT

Rotenone dusted on flowers, if the crop is threatened.

SYMPTOMS

Blossoms and small berries are eaten and webby. Later in the season, berries show a purplish ringed spot with a hole in the center. Splitting the berry open reveals a larva. Damaged berries then decay in humid weather, or dry out in hot and dry weather.

CAUSE

Grape Berry Moth. This pest—found throughout the eastern states from Maine to the Gulf and west to the Rockies—is a dark green to dark purple larva with a light brown head and black spots on the chest when seen on flower clusters and young leaves. It will cut a piece of leaf on three sides and fold it into a tent to construct a cocoon in.

TREATMENT

Don't cultivate soil after August 1, so that the cocoons remain exposed after they fall to the ground. Cultivate in spring to bury remaining cocoons 3 inches deep and don't disturb soil until two weeks after bloom. If you spot the larva on flowers or leaves, *Bacillus thuringiensis* provides excellent control without harming beneficials.

SYMPTOMS

Small squat beetles, about a tenth of an inch long and similarly wide, appear on the leaves at about the time the grapes bloom. They leave short, curved groups of lines on the upper surface of the leaves. White grubs with no legs are discovered inside the berries in late July, and the beetles reappear to feed in the fall.

CAUSE

Grape Curculio. Their presence is best detected by the curved feeding marks they leave on the leaves. Check berries for worms later in the season.

TREATMENT

Rotenone dust on infested vines should curb them. Clean cultivation, as with the grape berry moth, will also help.

If you see damage to the arms, canes, or trunk

SYMPTOMS

In California and Oregon, shoots droop, wilt, or break off when 6–10 inches long. An inspection of the crotch of the spur from which the shoot arose reveals brown or black beetles, cylindrical, about a half-inch long, feeding in a burrow.

CAUSE

Branch and Twig Borer. As these beetles eat their way through the wood, they plug the holes behind them with grass and chewed wood. They can cause extensive damage.

TREATMENT

Prune off the weakened shoots and the burrowed wood. Burn it and all other prunings that may be left around. As a preventive, burn spring prunings. Spraying usually doesn't help control this insect, but good vineyard sanitation does.

SYMPTOMS

Canes are bored into by small beetles, although none are found in crotches near the base of the shoot and spur, in areas east of the Rockies.

CAUSE
Grape Cane Borer. Most common in states bordering the Mississippi.

TREATMENT
Its control is the same as for branch and twig borer.

SYMPTOMS
Sticky masses of dirty white or brownish spots appear on one- and two-year-old wood and sometimes older wood. A hand lens reveals masses of tiny insects, usually hemispheric in shape.

CAUSE
Scale insects. These tiny insects live in colonies and exude a sweet and sticky honeydew. They make excellent food for ladybird beetles. There are many types of scale.

TREATMENT
Dormant oil spray.

If you see stunted, dying vines

SYMPTOMS
The symptoms are indefinite, but the vine looks weak and sick, and is stunted in its growth. Pulling up some roots, you see roughened, knotted areas as if something is eating or colonizing the roots.

CAUSE
Phylloxera. These root lice are very destructive. Once infested, the vine is best pulled.

TREATMENT
Planting vines on phylloxera-resistant rootstock is the only realistic control. Own-rooted susceptible vines are possible in sandy soils where the insect doesn't do well, and possibly in other kinds of soils that aren't in established vineyard areas. American vine roots resist the phylloxera because the insects don't chew far enough into the root to reach the cambium. In vinifera, the cambium is closer to the root

surface and the root lice eventually reach it and kill the roots. Own-rooted vinifera yield well for about five years, then suddenly crash when the phylloxera damage reaches the root cambiums. A phylloxera saliva constituent also stunts and kills grapevines.

CAUSE

Nematodes. These small soil worms may cause root knots or other types of galls on grape roots.

TREATMENT

Ordinary marigolds planted under the vines offer a degree of protection against nematodes. Turn them under in the fall and replant after frost danger is over. If the infestation is very bad, replanting on nematode-resistant rootstocks may be indicated. This pest is most frequently found in sandy soils. Maintain a ground cover that's as free of broad-leaf weeds as possible (stick to grasses), as these are thought to be an alternate host for some nematodes.

SYMPTOMS

Foliage discolors and wilts. Vigor decreases, production falls off, and eventually the vine dies. Occurs primarily in the southern Midwest and southeastern United States and affects all grapes, including muscadines. Inspection of the roots shows damage or insects feeding. The larvae penetrate the root bark, then eat an irregular furrow that may spiral around the root or run with the grain. The passageway is packed behind the insect with reddish brown frass.

CAUSE

Grape Root Borer. In the destructive, larval stage, the borers are about an inch and three-quarters long. They're whitish, with brown heads, and are sparsely covered with stiff hairs.

TREATMENT

Female moths—which resemble large wasps, except that the rear pair of wings are clear and vibrate more slowly—are often found around the base of vines, laying eggs, in August and September, and can be killed by hand easily. The most effective control is to mound about 8 inches of dirt around the base of the vine around July 1, making it impossible for emerging moths to reach the soil surface. The dirt can be removed safely after August 21.

GRAPE DISEASES

Powdery Mildew

Also called *oidium,* it's the only fungus found in California vineyards. In the rest of the country, it's often joined by other types. Powdery mildew likes cool weather for germination, and temperatures from 70° to 90° F for rapid development. Although it grows best on leaves in the shade, it isn't dependent on moisture the way most other grape leaf and berry fungi are, which is why it's found in the dry California climate and the others aren't.

Powdery mildew attacks both leaves and fruit, but you'll notice it first on leaves, where it appears as whitish patches of cobweblike growth on the upper surface. It will also attack flowers, which fail to set and fall off, and small berries, which will take on irregular shapes, crack, and dry. Ripe or ripening berries aren't affected. Later, the whitish patches turn gray as spore stalks are formed. The leaves eventually turn brown, then black. A badly infected vine smells like mildew.

Treatment involves several mechanisms. First, be aware that a temperature of 100° F or more will effectively stop powdery mildew, and sulfur sprays will harm the heated leaves, so don't spray if it's that hot. Second, good sanitation under the vines—that is, cleaning up twigs, dead leaves, and fallen or dried berries in the fall and/or spring, then cultivating—is essential. Third, elemental sulfur dust is an excellent preventive. A pump-action duster will work well in a small vineyard. Keep a fine dust of sulfur on shoots, flowers or fruit, and leaves, making sure you get the leaves that are shaded.

Dust when the shoots are 6 inches long. This is most important, for that is the time when temperatures are right for spore germination. Dust when shoots reach 12, 18, and 24 inches, and every two weeks thereafter until mid-August. Also, reapply the dust right after every rain—don't put it off. Check leaves after mid-August. Even after the fruit is harvested, leaves are building the vine's food reserves and strength, so spraying protects them if powdery mildew shows up.

A lot of commercial growers are using Bayleton fungicide, because it protects against both powdery mildew and black rot. It's a systemic fungicide, working in the vascular tissues of the vine. I believe that if it's flowing around in the sap, it will flow into the grapes as well, and I don't want Bayleton in my wine.

Sulfur dust only *prevents* powdery mildew. Once it starts on the plants, the dust is no longer effective. Then turn to liquid lime-sulfur spray, available in most garden shops, or wettable sulfur powder. Apply them at the rates recommended on the labels after every rain, and at least every two weeks through July.

Vinifera are all susceptible to powdery mildew in varying degrees. The most susceptible are Carignane, Muscat of Alexandria, and Sylvaner. American grapes are less susceptible, but under cool, wet conditions conducive to the fungus's growth, Concord can be badly damaged. Concord is reputed to be damaged by sulfur sprays or dusts, especially in hot weather, but growers I've talked to said they had no problems with rates on the order of 1.5 pounds of wettable sulfur to 100 gallons of water.

Downy Mildew

When it's raining and the vines are covered with a light film of water, downy mildew spores germinate, moving about by means of a flagellum—a whiplike tail as seen on spermatozoa. Early in the year it infects leaves, tendrils, berry clusters when they're pea-sized, petioles, and succulent shoots. Lower leaves are often infected when rain splashes soil containing the free-swimming spores onto their surfaces. I tried an experiment once at a large vineyard near Harrisburg, Pennsylvania. We selected a few rows of susceptible vines, and put reflective mulch under one row of vines just before bloom, leaving it there for a month. The reflective material was aluminum foil on cardboard, laid under the vines with the shiny side up. Not only did the mulch prevent soil from splashing up onto leaves, but it bounced sunlight up under the leaves, helping to keep them dry. We noticed no mildew on the mulched vines. I'm not necessarily recommending this as a treatment, as such a mulch is expensive, but rather to point to the etiology of the disease. It's found everywhere east of the Rockies, but has not been found in California.

Look for downy mildew early in the morning about the time the grapes are blooming, especially after a wet or humid night. Later in the day, when the vineyard dries out, it's much harder to spot in its early forms. You'll see oily-looking spots on the upper surface of the leaves, and a swollen, water-logged appearance of the shoot tips, tendrils, and petioles if the fungus is present. The translucent oily spots on the leaves will, if left unchecked, produce a fuzzy whitish growth on the underside of the leaves, appearing a few days after the spots show up.

All varieties of vinifera are susceptible to downy mildew.

French-American hybrids vary in their tolerance. Most American varieties aren't very susceptible.

The very susceptible varieties are Catawba, Chancellor, Chardonnay, Ives, and Riesling. Concord, Seyval Blanc, and de Chaunac are susceptible. Of all these, Chancellor is the most susceptible. Since this variety is so suited to the eastern climate and makes such fine wine, it's important for growers of this cultivar to follow the spray schedule. Chancellor may become systemically infected—that is, the fungus penetrates to inner tissues and spreads through the plants' vascular system. In such cases, your choices are to tear out the vines or use a systemic fungicide like Maneb.

The spores overwinter in dead grape leaves on the ground. Good sanitation is important. That means all leaves should be raked up and burned, then the soil should be cultivated under the vines before bud break, and kept cultivated in the top two inches.

Bordeaux mixture is the most effective treatment for downy mildew. Sulfur alone isn't nearly as effective. Sometimes Bordeaux mixture is found in garden shops ready-mixed. The old French formula is 2 kg. of copper sulfate, 0.75 kg. of slaked lime, and 2 kg. of salt per 100 liters of water. Both the copper and the salt can harm leaf tissue at those rates, so I've adapted the formula to a lower—yet still effective—level.

LIGHT BORDEAUX MIXTURE

Copper sulfate	7 ounces
Table salt	9 ounces
Slaked lime	2 ounces
Water	25 gallons

Some vines don't tolerate Bordeaux mixture well, and you may have to substitute captan or Maneb, which are not as phytotoxic, if you have trouble.

Apply Bordeaux mixture just before bloom, seven days later, two weeks after that, and three weeks after that. Captain is applied in a similar schedule. It would be wise to spray routinely for downy mildew in humid areas if you're growing the above-named susceptible and very susceptible varieties. With other varieties keep a close eye on the vines, but don't spray unless you have to.

Black Rot

Black rot is probably the worst disease of grapes east of the Rockies. Californians can be thankful it doesn't affect vines there. I lost four successive crops of grapes to black rot before I finally said, "Let us spray." The fungus germinates in warm, humid weather, such as found east of the Mississippi in June. It attacks leaves, forming small, reddish brown, irregularly shaped spots that soon show black fruiting bodies. On the shoots, tendrils, and young stems, it makes small, dark, elliptical cankers. Berries show its effects between the time they're half grown and *véraison.* At first, the berry has a little blanched area, which soon turns whitish with a brown ring around the edges. This grows quickly and becomes sunken. Within two days, the black fruiting bodies appear, and the whole spot turns reddish brown to black. The berries soon after shrivel to mummies firmly attached to the clusters.

These mummies contain the spores for the next infection, so vineyard sanitation is essential. The mummies must be removed and burned, and the soil under the vines should be raked and well cultivated.

Bordeaux mixture is effective. On vines that show toxic effects from Bordeaux mixture, captan and Ferbam are often used by commercial and home growers. It's important to spray at the right time—when the shoots are 18 and 24 inches long, just before bloom, just after bloom, and about two weeks after that. The sprays at blooming are the most important.

Anthracnose

Although common in the East where summer rains are frequent, anthracnose is not found in California. It attacks all new parts of the vine, producing grayish brown cankers with raised edges and a sunken center. These cankers will destroy the wood or tissue under them. On leaves, the spots are pale gray with reddish brown or purple borders, and they may accumulate and fall away, leaving holes in the leaves. They resemble black rot on the berries, except that there is a red or purple ring. These berries also shrivel into mummies full of spores, and they must be removed and burned. If you find anthracnose in your vineyard, prunings should also be burned. Good sanitation and cultivation are imperative.

American grapes range from moderately tolerant to moderately susceptible. French-American hybrids are usually more susceptible, and almost all vinifera varieties are highly susceptible. Muscadines are resistant.

For control, spray the vines during the dormant season with a liquid lime-sulfur mix, diluted one part in eight parts of water. Garlic oil in a 200-part-per-million solution pre- and post-bloom also works against this disease. Bordeaux mixture is commonly used during the growing season, applied when the shoots are 7 inches long, just before bloom, just after bloom, ten days after that, and when the berries are about half grown. Captan is also effective. Repeat a spray if heavy rains come just after you've sprayed.

Botrytis Cinerea (Noble Rot)

This fungus disease is only noble if you *want* it to develop in order to make the rare Sauternes-type wine. The rot develops late in the season on ripe grapes, usually right after a September rain. The grape skins crack or shrivel into a brownish, soft, moist mass of grapes with low acid and very high sugar—up to 40 percent sugar. The mold absorbs water from inside the grapes, but doesn't harm the sugars or spoil the taste of the resultant wines, which are enormously rich and sweet. Some botrytized wines are made in California, mostly by wetting the grapes at the right time and purposely infecting them with Botrytis. Such wines are also beginning to be made in the East, especially with varieties like Ravat 51 in the Finger Lakes region.

Botrytis is usually *not* wanted. It appears in warm, dry spells after cool, wet weather late in the season. It grows best between 65° and 75°, needing only fifteen hours of wetness for spore germination. Round, faint clear spots are seen on the berries at first. If pressed with the thumb, the skin cracks, and if rubbed, the skin slips away from the pulp underneath. After a few more days, large masses of gray- to buff-colored spores protrude through cracks in the skin, and the bunches look rotten.

Botrytis overwinters on decaying vegetation and in mummies, so good sanitation is important. Mummies and prunings from infected vines should be cleaned up and burned. Make sure the vine growth is open and airy. As far as I know, none of the less toxic fungicides work very well against Botrytis. Even captan only protects 60 percent of berries in the bunches. This should be applied just before bloom, and every two weeks thereafter until August. Or work with it and start making botrytized wine.

Dead-arm (Eutypa Dieback)

Other fungus diseases include dead-arm disease in California, called Eutypa dieback in the East and in Canada. In California it's a problem in the cool, foggy coastal regions. In the East, it's a growing problem in the Finger Lakes. Badly affected buds will be dead in the spring, and spots will develop on both sides of leaves about three weeks after a rain. These spots are light green with brown to black pinpoint centers and yellow borders. Similar spots develop on the shoots, which eventually can split the stems and form blackened areas. During the winter, the affected parts of the canes turn whitish, with small black points. All types of grapes are susceptible to this disease.

Prune off all diseased parts as soon after leaf fall as you can and burn them. Cultivate thoroughly under the vines during the growing season. Try lime-sulfur or Bordeaux mixture when the shoots are just an inch long and again at 7–8 inches. Growers in California often spray routinely with captan when the shoots are an inch long, and that seems to give good control. New research shows that infection risk is greatest in winter when pruning creates open wounds. One good recommendation is to leave 1- to 2-inch stubs when pruning trunks or canes, then go back after growth starts and the weather is warm and prune off the stubs. Infection is unlikely at this time, and any winter infection is cut off with the stubs. Burn the stubs.

Black-mold Rot

Black-mold rot is a problem in some areas where tight-clustered varieties are grown. Sometimes the berries squeeze each other to the point that some rupture, spilling sugary juice over themselves and nearby berries. The black to purplish sooty mold soon develops and ruins the berries for winemaking. There is no known control for black-mold rot. Make sure the clusters are well separated. In very tight-clustered varieties, thinning of berries from the clusters would help, but this is enormously time-consuming. Some growers use gibberellic acid, a plant hormone, to cause the clusters to grow more loosely. Rhizopus rot is similar to black-mold rot, and berry-thinning the clusters with gibberellic acid is also the remedy.

Crown Gall

Any puncture in the vine trunk, such as from freezing, can be invaded by a bacterium, *Agrobacterium tumefaciens,* that causes crown gall. It's a problem in many temperate wine-growing areas of the world, such as in plantings of vinifera in the East. The galls are seen in cracks in the trunk, creamy to green in color in the spring. As they grow, they

SCHEDULE FOR CONTROLLING FUNGUS DISEASES

POWDERY MILDEW (PREVENTIVE)
Dust with sulfur when shoots are 6, 12, and 18 inches, and every two weeks thereafter until August. Reapply after every rain.

POWDERY MILDEW (CONTROL)
Apply wettable sulfur or lime-sulfur when shoots are 6 inches, then every two weeks until August.

DOWNY MILDEW
Apply Bordeaux mixture or captan just before bloom, just after bloom, then seven days later, two weeks after that, and three weeks after that.

BLACK ROT
Apply Bordeaux mixture or captan when shoots are 18 and 24 inches, just before bloom, just after bloom, and two weeks after that.

ANTHRACNOSE
Apply lime-sulfur when vines are dormant. Apply Bordeaux mixture when vines are 7 inches, just before bloom, just after bloom, ten days after that, and when berries are half grown.

BOTRYTIS (BUNCH ROT)
Apply captan just before bloom, then every two weeks until August. Often the spray at bloom will be enough.

DEAD-ARM OR EUTYPA DIEBACK
Apply lime-sulfur, Bordeaux mixture, or captan when shoots are an inch long, and when they reach 7 to 8 inches.

Spraying for one of these with Bordeaux mixture, lime-sulfur, or captan will control most of the other diseases simultaneously. While it's never wise to spray unless there's a problem, fine wine grapes in the East will become infected with one or another disease and preventive sprays in that region are necessary.

turn dark and rough. Often the galls will disappear after a few years, but a bad infection will stunt and kill the trunk. There's no commercial product registered in the United States for crown gall, and it's not much of a problem in California, so it doesn't get much attention there. Here's where some experimentation could pay off.

Since crown gall is caused by bacteria, prevent further infection by not cutting through galls when pruning. Sterilize your blade by dipping in alcohol after each cut on a badly infected vine. If there's very serious damage to the trunk, bring up a new trunk and plan to bring them up regularly over the years, as the gall will most likely stay with you. Keep the area under the vines cultivated, and possibly covered with paper (if you use plastic, cover it with something opaque or the sun will bake the soil) to keep the organisms from splashing up onto the trunk during rains.

Good soil care under the vines and trunk renewal can be supplemented with your attempts to rid the vines of the bacteria by experimenting. Garlic has natural antibiotic properties, and Agrobacterium probably wouldn't like it any more than your friends do after you've eaten a garlicky salad. Garlic oil at only 200 parts per million kills pathogenic fungi, including anthracnose. I'd make a garlic solution by whizzing cloves in the blender, then drenching the root area with it. You could plaster the galls with rich compost and wrap it on with tape as a kind of bandage—possibly replacing the monopoly of Agrobacterium with a panoply of soil organisms. After a season, unwrap, wash, and take a look. This has worked with blight cankers on American chestnut.

I haven't tried those things because I've never had to deal with crown gall on my grapes. I'm just suggesting the kind of homemade gee-whiz tactics you can use.

There's an old saying that a farmer's footsteps are the best fertilizer. While he's making those footsteps, he's observing, thinking, and mapping out his next move. And so do we all have to get smart when confronted with intractable problems. I know one farmer who got so smart he realized the question wasn't "What do I do next?" but "What don't I do next?" Now he hardly makes a move, but gets some of the best rice yields in Japan.

Pierce's Disease

Originally thought to be a virus, this disease is now known to be caused by a rickettsia-like organism. Nevertheless, its symptoms are virus-like. It first appears as a scalding and burning of the leaves in late summer along the margins and tips of the large veins. The scalded area turns brown. If the whole leaf is involved, it will drop away, leaving the petiole attached to the shoot. It starts with one shoot, then gets progressively worse. The fruit may be poorly formed and wither, or ripen prematurely and turn soft, then wither. In the following year, growth is slow and the first leaves are deformed and mottled. Scalding will show up on the later leaves, and the canes will fail to mature properly—some green patches will remain among the matured cane's normal brown.

Diseased vines should be uprooted and replaced with varieties resistant to Pierce's disease, or with certified disease-free stock. In the latter case, be prepared to replant again, for the disease will probably return. It's sometimes a problem in California, except in the hottest regions, but doesn't usually take whole vineyards. In the past, however, it has done just that. The disease is native to the Gulf Coast, where resistant varieties of wild and cultivated grapes are found.

Viruses

Many viruses affect grapevines. Rather than name them all, be aware that they all mottle or yellow the leaves, or cause them to be badly misshapen. One virus causes the leaves to roll downward at the margins. They can be spread by insects and by soil nematodes, but most often they are the result of planting infected wood.

Dr. Joseph Foster of the Animal and Plant Health Inspection Service, the USDA agency that quarantines plants before release, says that Europe is a reservoir of grape virus, and cautions all of us not to bring home cuttings from our friends' chateaux in Bordeaux. "Europe has a yellows virus that isn't found here," he told me. "The North American leaf hopper is the vector in Europe. If the disease got over here, it would undoubtedly be spread by leaf hoppers." He said that many European varieties are infected with stem pitting, corky bark, leaf roll, and other viruses—and so grape plants and cuttings are prohibited from entering this country. But they do enter Canada. Some Canadian nurseries sell grapes grafted with European scion wood to U.S. buyers, and Dr. Foster says there's a good chance that these vines are infected with one or more of the virus diseases.

The recommendation, therefore, is to make sure you're buying certified virus-free stock from a vineyard in the United States. If a virus even then shows up in your plants, replant with certified stock from some other source.

Soil-borne viruses that are transmitted by nematodes may be controlled by plantings of marigolds under the vines as a preventive measure. In some areas, commercial growers fumigate the soil.

There are other conditions that can mimic disease. Spring frost injury to young leaves can look at first like a mottling virus, but subsequent leaves are healthy. Soil nutrient deficiencies, which we covered under fertilization, can cause yellowing and poor performance, which could be mistaken for a virus. In areas where air pollution is heavy, such as southern California, or near the New York area, small brown to black stippled spots on the leaves may be ozone damage rather than disease.

Large Vineyard Pests

Deer are a very serious pest in the vineyard, nibbling tender parts, setting back the vines, delaying maturity, and reducing yields. The last thing I read about deer was that the only thing a grower can do is fence in the vineyard. But take heart. I know other remedies that may preclude that enormous expense.

Illinois orchardist Ray Grammer has found a deer remedy he claims is "99 and 44/100ths percent effective." He hangs bars of soap from his trees. He's tried several brands, including deodorant soaps, and found they all worked the same—better than any repellent he's used in the past. You could sprinkle soap shavings along the tops of some leaves so they melt down over the lower areas, or hang bars near the top wire every 8–10 feet. Just make sure the soap doesn't drip onto the grapes or your wine may be "bubbly" in the wrong way. Probably the smell, so perfumedly human, as well as a soapy taste on the leaves, repels the deer. Also, you can ask your barber for a day's worth of hair clippings. Bag these in old nylon stockings or any netting that lets air through. Hang them every 10 feet or so all around the vineyard's perimeter. Men's hair is more repellent simply because it's not usually coated with hair setting or holding chemicals and has a more human smell.

Birds can be an even worse pest than deer. Commercial bird netting can be thrown over the vines when the grapes are almost ripe and gives excellent control. There is a compound called Mesurol that makes the grapes taste hot, and after one peck, that bird won't bother your vines any more. However, there is a danger that residual Mesurol could make your wines hot. If the directions are followed, however, Mesurol can protect without harming the wines.

In Glenora, New York, Roger and Sayre Fulkerson erected a Klapotetz in their vineyard and found it effective in keeping birds away. This device is a windmill that causes wooden flaps to revolve and hit a striker, making a clapping sound. A similar device is used to keep moles from gardens and lawns. The ancestor of the Klapotetz was introduced into Lower Styria (Austria) by Roman legionnaires about 100 B.C. to help keep birds out of their vineyards.

What about windless days? "Perhaps the Klapotetz simply stares down would-be raiders. After all, who's going to question two thousand years of active duty in Austria?" commented an eastern wine writer.

Bees, yellowjackets, and sugar-loving wasps attack ripening and ripe fruit. They are trouble, and I've been stung several times on the hand reaching to pick bunches, and once above the eye by what must have been a lookout bee. They seldom if ever puncture the fruit themselves, but come in after birds have slashed open the berries to suck up the sugary innards, or after berries crack or split for other reasons. Some growers spray Sevin, a toxic chemical. To be of any use, it has to be sprayed too close to harvest, so I'd never use it. The home vineyardist can erect a trap for these insects—one per row, spaced toward alternate ends of the rows. A fish carcass or piece of meat is hung from the bottom trellis wire 4 to 6 inches above a pan of water with some oil floating on its surface. The wasps will prefer this to the grapes, gorge themselves, then try to take off. Just like overloaded planes, they'll fall into the water and be killed by the oily water. One grower reported reducing the bee and wasp problem in his vineyard 90 percent using these traps. They'll only be needed just before harvest.

In a few areas of the country, woodchucks, porcupines, mice, and voles can be a problem. Woodchucks and porcupines have been successfully kept out of vineyards by electric fence wire suspended about 2 to 3 inches above the ground around the vineyard. Make sure no grass grows to touch the wire by weighting down newspapers under the wire. A .22 rifle is another effective weapon. Mice and voles are best baited, or you can march some of your lazy cats to the vineyard and tell them to get to work.

A very effective way to produce quality grapes and protect them from birds, bees, and many diseases and fungi is to bag the bunches.

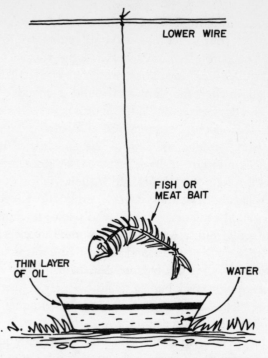

This is very time-consuming, but it's sure and effective if you've got a small-enough vineyard to do it. The best bags are number 35 waterproof white parchment bags from the Carpenter Paper Company, 0–110 SW 7th Street, Box 568, Des Moines, Iowa 50302. They sell a minimum 1,000 bags. The bags are placed over the developing clusters when the berries are about half grown, or even earlier if you want to ward off fungus diseases. Cut off the lower corners to allow moisture to drip out, and attach them as shown below.

Regular paper bags will work, but tend to become watersoaked and can even disintegrate if the paper quality is poor.

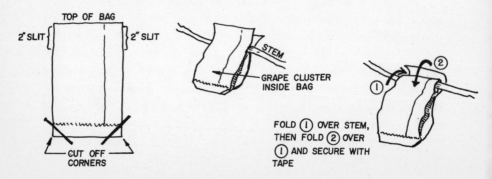

INDEX

Page numbers in italic refer to illustrations.

accouterments for wine, 197–99
corkscrews, 198–99, *199*
wineglasses, 199, *200*
see also equipment
acetobacter, 181
acid in grape juice
adjusting, 145–49
and sugar, ratio of, 112–13, *113,*
120
testing for, 116–18
acidity of wine, 145
and pH, 147–49
reducing, by blending, 184
aging wine, 179–81
air, and wine
in bottling, 189
contact avoided, during processing,
161–62, 163, 181
in must, during primary
fermentation, 157
in racking, 179
air drainage, in vineyard, 17
airlock, 163–65, *164–65*
for aging wine, 179
vacuum in, 166
aisles in vineyard, 60, *61*
management of, 62–63
alcohol content of wine
of finished wine, 185–86
ratio of, to Brix, 142
allelopathic effect, 42
Alley, C. J., 92
American Wine Society, 208
Amerine, Maynard, 6
animals, as pests, 45, 237–39
anthracnose, 231–32
aphids, 222
appreciation of wine, 8–11

appreciation of wine *(cont.)*
courses on, 11
sensory, 200–205
aroma of wine
education in, 204
"nose" of the wine, 202–3
retronasal, 203
see also odors from processing wine
art of winemaking, 2, 157
Assmanshausen wine yeast, 154
associations and societies, 208

Bacillus thuringiensis, 105
Bailey, L. H., 7
balanced pruning, 78–79, *table,* 81
Balling (or Brix), 113–16, *114,*
tables, 115–16
and adding sugar to must, 143–44,
table, 144
and alcohol content of wine, 142
and pH, 121
and TA (ratio of), 120
bare-rooted stock, 56
trimming, 56, 57
barrel(s), 169–78
bungs for, 173, *173,* 174
frame for, 171, *172*
leaking, 173
new, preparation of, 173, *173,*
174, 176–77
oak, 170–71
for secondary fermentation, 162
old, 172
reusing, 174–75
siphoning to and from, 171, *172,*
174
sizes of, 171
sources of *(list),* 214

barrel(s) *(cont.)*
  storage of, 177
  topping up, 171, 174–75
  whiskey, as vats, 135
basket press, 150, *151*
Baumé hydrometer, 113
bees, as pests, 238, 239
Beaulieu Vineyard, Napa Valley,
  Calif., 170–71
bellows effect, 196
bentonite, as fining agent, 183
biblical references to wine, 7
bilateral 3-wire training, *102*
birds, as pests, 238, 239
bitartrate, 169
black-mold rot, 233
black rot, 231
"bleeding" of pruned canes, 87
blending, 130, 183–85
body of wine, 205
  improvement of, by blending,
    184–85
borers, 225–26, 227
botrytized grapes
  harvesting, 121–22
  sulfite added to must of, 141
"bottle sickness," 182
bottles
  corking, 190–92, *191*
  filling, 189, *189,* 190
  indentation in, 187, *187,* 188
  labeling, 193–94
  types of, 187, *187,* 188
bottling wine, 187–90
bouquet, 202
boxes, for harvested grapes, 126–27
branch and twig borers, 225–26
Brix (degrees Balling), 113–16, *114,*
  tables, 115–16
  and adding sugar to must, 143–44,
    table, 144
  and alcohol content of wine, 142
  and pH, 121
  and TA (ratio of), 120
browning of juice and wine, 130,
  133
bud beetles and mites, 222

buds
  fruitfulness of, 75–77, *76*
  leaving on vine, 73, *73*
  winterkilled, 74
bunch rot, 93
bung, for barrel, 173
  position of, *173,* 174
  removal of, 174
Bureau of Alcohol, Tobacco and
  Firearms (BATF), 15–16
Byloff, Robert, 148

Cabernet Sauvignon, varieties of, 9
California, viticulture in, 14
  heat summations for, *table,* 24–25
  spacing of vines in, 33–34
  varieties for, *tables,* 26–27
California Champagne wine yeast,
  154
California red wines, vs. French reds,
  10–11
Campden tablets, 140, *table,* 141
cap, punching down, 156–57
carboy(s), glass, 135
  cleaning, 166
  extra, 168
  filling, *164, 165*
  for secondary fermentation,
    161–63
    airlocks for, 163–66, *164–65*
    oaking in, 175, 178
    siphoning to and from, *167,*
      189–90
cellaring wine, 195–97
  temperature for, 195–96
champagne
  glass for, 199, *200*
  serving temperature for, 205
Chancellor (French-American) hybrid,
  17
chaptalizing, 142
Chardonnay
  oaking, 170
  varieties of, 9
citric acid, 145
clarity of wine, 200
  lack of, 179, 200

clarity of wine *(cont.)*
fining and, 182–83
clay soil, 40, 44
cleanliness
of barrels, 174, 176
of bottles, 188–89
of carboys, 166
in winemaking, 133–34
climate, and selection of grape
variety, 11, 12–15, 17, 74
cloudiness in wine, 179, 200
fining for, 182–83
cluster thinning, 91–94, *94,* 104
benefits of, 91–92, 93–94, 104
timing of, 92–93
cold stabilization, 146–47, 168–69
cold weather
multiple trunking and, 72
protection against, 74
see also frost and freezing
color of wine, 200–201
browning, oxidative, 130
pH and, 148–49
from skins of grapes, 132, 157
storage temperature and, 195
Component Collection (wine-scent
kit), 204
compost, 108
making, 109, 111
controlled appellation, 15
cooling grapes, after picking, 127
cordon cane system of training, 79,
86–87, 97
cork(s)
lost in bottle, during opening,
198–99
soaking, 190
types of, 190
corker, hand, 190–91
corking bottles, 190–92, *191*
cork puller, 198, *199*
corkscrews, 198–99, *199*
Cottrell, Tom, 126, 128, 139,
157–58, 159, 160
courses on wine appreciation, 11
cover crops in vineyard, 60, 62, 91
crock, as fermentation vat, 134, *136*

crown gall, 235–36
crushing grapes
with feet, hands, or pestle, 131
speed of, after picking, 127–28
cultivating soil beds in vineyard,
62
curculios, 225
cuttings from vines
burning, 90–91
weight of
fertilizing and, 109
Geneva double curtain and, 90
ratio of, to buds retained, 79
cutworms, 221

dead-arm (grape disease), 233
deer, as pests, 45, 237–38
degrees Balling (Brix), 113–16, *114,
tables,* 115–16
and adding sugar to must, 143–44,
table, 144
and alcohol content of wine, 142
and pH, 121
and TA (ratio of), 120
delayed pruning, 88, 93
deposits
from aging wine, 190
from secondary fermentation, 162
see also lees
de-stemming grapes, 131–33
d-glucose, 142, 143
Dipel (biological pest control), 105
diseases of grape vines, 228–40
burning cane cuttings to avoid,
90–91
genetic engineering and, 14–15
disorders of wine, 181–82
dormant oil spray (for insects), 106–7
double pruning, 88, 90
double trunking, 72, *72*
drainage, in vineyard, 40, 42, 44–45
and slope, 44
drip irrigation, 64
Drosophila melanogaster, 127
drought, 64–65
drum, stainless steel (as vat), 134
dryness of wine, "complete," 186

earth anchor (for trellis), *52, 53*
Eastern U.S.
  balanced pruning in, *table,* 81
  cane-length pruning
    recommendations for, *map,* 80,
    table, 80
  multiple trunking in, 72, *72*
  viticulture in, 12–13
education
  of nose, 204
  of palate, 8–11
egg white fining, 183
equipment
  hydrometer, 113–16, *114*
  refractometer, 115
  sources of *(list),* 212–14
  stemmer-crusher, 131–32
  sterilizing, 133, 134
Espernay 2 (wine yeast), 154
"experts" on wine, 9, 11

fermentation, malolactic, 139,
  149
  spontaneous, 160–61, 179
fermentation, primary, 156–62
  duration of, 157, 158–60
  end of, 161
  temperature of, 156, 157–58
  vats for, 134–36, *136*
fermentation, secondary, 162–69
  in barrels, 169–78
  temperature of, 165
fermentation, spontaneous, 160–61,
  179
fermentation, stuck, 155–56,
  186
fertilizers and fertilizing, 108–11
filling vessels
  barrels, 171, *172,* 174
  bottles, 189, *189,* 190
  carboys, *164, 165*
  see also siphoning
filtering wine, 182
Finder, Henry, 202
fining, 179, 182–83
flea beetles, 106, 221–22
Flor Sherry wine yeast, 154

flowers
  buds of
    fruitfulness of, 75–77, *76*
    leaving on vine, 73, *73*
    winterkilled, 74
  cluster thinning of, 91–94, *94,* 104
  nicking off, 60, 72, 111
Foch (Maréchal) wine, 160
foil capsules, on bottles, 194, *194,*
  195
forest site for vineyard, 45
Forni, Peter, 126
Foster, Joseph, 236–37
Frank, Konstantin, 43
Freas, Susan, 132
free-run juice, 150–51
French-American hybrid varieties, 5,
  11–12
  Chancellor, 17
  cluster thinning of, 93–94
  training systems for, 69
French viticulture
  soil types for, *table,* 39
  spacing of vines in, 34
French wines
  controlled appellation of, 15
  red, vs. California reds, 10–11
frost and freezing
  and cluster thinning, 93
  damage to vines from, 72, 73–74
  delayed pruning and, 88, 90
  overhead sprinkler and, 64
fruit flies, 127–28, 136
fruit yield, vs. vegetative growth,
  72–73, 78–79
fungus diseases, 234
funnel, 151, 162

garbage can, plastic (as vat), 135
genetic engineering, 14–15
Geneva double curtain trellis (GDC),
  49, *49,* 50, 51, *100*
  and cane cuttings (weight of), 90
gift, homemade wine as, 192–95
glass carboy(s), 135
  cleaning, 166
  extra, 168

glass carboy(s) *(cont.)*
  filling, *164, 165*
  for secondary fermentation,
      161–63
    airlocks for, 163–66, *164–65*
    oaking in, 175, 178
  siphoning to and from, *167,*
      189–90
glasses, for wine, 199, *200*
goblet (head-trained vine), 46–47,
    47, 95
grafted vines
  planting, 57, *58*
  watering, 59
Grammer, Ray, 237
grape juice
  acidity of
    adjusting, 145–49
    and sugar, ratio of, 112–13, *113,*
        120
    testing for, 116–18
  Brix (sugar content) of, 113–16,
      114, tables, 115–16
  browning of, 130
  "first-run," 133
  pH of, 119
    and acid level, 147–49
    and Brix, 121
    and sulfite, 139–40, *table,* 141
  pressing of (white), 150–52
  TA (acid content) of, 117–18
  see also must
grape leaf hopper, 217
grapes
  bagging, to protect from pests,
      239, *239,* 240
  crushing, speed of (after picking),
      127–28
  de-stemming, 132, 133
  growth and development of,
      111–12
  harvesting, 123
    timing of, 112–21, 122–23
  juice of, *see* grape juice
  overripe, 141
  red, *see* red wine
  research on, 15

grapes *(cont.)*
  ripeness of (determining), 112–21
  shipped east to winemakers, 127
  skins of
    and bacteria, molds, 156
    and color of wine, 132, 157
    contact time of, 158–60, 161
    ratio of, per pound, 93
    soaking on (white), 132
  soil and, 38–39
  sugar in
    and acid, ratio of, 112–13, *113,*
        120
    sunlight and, 36–37
  storage of, in boxes, 126–27
  varieties of
    for California, *tables,* 26–27
    climate and, 11, 12–15, 17, 74
    processed singly, 130
    regional recommendations for,
        table, 20–23
    selection of, 1–17, *tables,* 18–27
    tasting *(list),* 9
  water and, 13
  yield of, vs. vegetative growth,
      72–73, 78–79
grappa, 152
grasses, annual
  in aisles of vineyard, *61, 62*–63
  in vine beds, 60
grasshoppers, 220
great wine
  elements of, 3–4
  recipes and, 126
Grgich, Mike, 78, 153
growing season (number of days),
    table, 48
growth stages of vine, 65, *66,* 67
Gypsy moths, 106

hardpan, 41
harvesting grapes, 123
  timing of (determining), 112–21
  weather and, 122–23
haziness of wine, 179, 200
  fining for, 182–83
head-trained vines, 46–47, *47, 95*

heat summations, for California, *table,* 24–25
heeling in grapestock, 56
herbaceousness of wine, 131
herbicides, 62
hilling vines, 74
history of wine grapes, 5–7
hoplia beetles, 223
Hudson River umbrella training system, 99
hydrogen sulfide gas, 137, 153, 157, 181–82
hydrometer (for Brix), 113–16, *114, tables,* 115–16
  and adding sugar to must, 143

injury to vines, 73–74, 123
insecticides
  botanical, 107
  chemical, 107–8
iron deficiency, *table,* 110
irrigation of vineyard, 64–65

Japanese beetles, 106, 219–20
juice, grape
  acidity of
    adjusting, 145–49
    and sugar, ratio of, 112–13, *113,* 120
    testing for, 116–18
  Brix (sugar content) of, 113–16, *114, tables,* 115–16
  browning of, 130
  "first-run," 133
  pH of, 119
    and acid level, 147–49
    and Brix, 121
    and sulfite, 139–40, *table,* 141
  pressing of (white), 150–52
  TA (acid content) of, 117–18
  see also must

Keuka high-renewal training, modified, *103*
Knapp, Doug, 4
Kniffen training system
  four-arm, *98*

Kniffen training system *(cont.)*
  pruning for, *88–89*
  umbrella, *101*

label on wine bottle
  American regulation of, 16
  French regulation of, 15
  for homemade wine, 126, 185, 186, 192–95, *193*
labrusca, 5
lateral branches (on vine), 67, *67*
leaf roller, 217–18
leaking
  of barrel, 173
  of corked bottles, 191
leaves of grape vines
  deficiency symptoms in, *table,* 110
  and sunlight, 112
lees, 168, 169
  compact, 137–38, 153
legs of wine, 202, *202*
leuconostoc, 160

McGrew, John, 61, 75, 153, 158
maderization, 195
magnesium deficiency, *table,* 110
mail-order purchase of vines, 55
  sources for (list), 215–16
malolactic fermentation, 139, 149
  natural (spontaneous), 160–61, 179
manganese deficiency, *table,* 110
marc, 152
mashing grapes
  with feet, hands, or pestle, 131
  speed of, after picking, 127–28
mass-produced wine, 9–10
mealybugs, 223
Meredith, Carole, 15
midges, 224
Midwestern U.S., viticulture in, 14
mildew, 123
  downy, 229–30
  powdery, 228–29
Mitchell, Jim, 3
mites, 106, 218–19
Montrachet wine yeast, 153, 154
Morton, Lucie, 15

moths, 220, 225
mulching, 60–62
  with stones, 63, *63*
multiple trunking, 72, *72*
muscadine grapes
  pruning vines of, 79, 87
  yeast added to must of, 155
must
  acidity adjusted in, 145–49
  making, 130–33
  pressing juice from, 150
  sugar added to, 142–44, *table,* 144
  sulfite added to, 136–41, *table,* 141
  temperature of (in primary
    fermentation), 156, 157–58
  vats for, 134–36

neem tree seeds, 105
nematodes, 227
new wine, 161, 163
"Nez du Vin, Le," 204
nitrogen
  deficiency of, in muscadine must,
    155
  excess of, 91, 109
Northeastern U.S.
  balanced pruning in, *table,* 81
  cane-length pruning
    recommendations for, *map,* 80,
    table, 80
  multiple trunking in, 72, *72*
  viticulture in, 12–13
"nose" of the wine, 202–3

oak barrel(s), 170–71
  for secondary fermentation, 162
oaking wine
  in barrel, 169–71
  with chips, 175, 178
  correcting, by blending, 184
  importance of, 178
  scent of, in wine, 203
odors from processing wine, 202–3
  hydrogen sulfide gas, 137
  from oversulfuring, 139
Office of International Vines and
    Wines, 14–15

Ohio River valley (viticultural area),
    16–17
oiliness of wine, 182
one-wire trellis, 48, *49,* 51
orange tortrix, 218
overcropping
  fertilizing and, 109
  pruning and, 77, 78–79
  and winter injury to vines, 74
overfertilizing, 109, 111
over-oaking, 184
overoxidation, 135
overripe grapes, sulfite and, 141
oversulfuring wine, 138
oxidation
  from bellows effect (in storage),
    196
  sulfite vs., 136
  of white vs. red wine, 128, 130

palate, education of, 8–11
Pasteur Champagne wine yeast, 153,
    154
percolation test, 42
periodicals, 208–9
pest control, 104–8, 217–27
  biological, 105
  botanical, 107
  chemical, 107–8
  dormant sprays, 106–7
  feeding repellents, 105–6
  homemade, 105, 106, 239, *239*
  of large animals, 237–39
Peynaud, Emile, 4, 203
philology of winemaking, 5, 6–7
pH level
  of grape juice, 119
    and acid level, 147–49
    and Brix, 121
    and sulfite, 139–40, *table,* 141
  scale of, 147
  in soil, 39
phylloxera, 220–21, 226–27
picking grapes, 123
Pierce's disease, 13–14, 236
pink wine
  making (summary), 129

pink wine *(cont.)*
  processing, 130, 132–33
Pinot Noir, varieties of, 9
planting vines, 56–57, *58*
  depth of, 57, *58*
  soil preparation for, 43–45
plastic vats for wine, 135
pomace, 150, 152
potassium
  deficiency of, *table,* 110
  high level of, and pH of grape
      juice, 119
potassium metabisulfite
  added to must, 136–41
    amount to use, 139, 140, *table,*
      141
  added to wine, at first racking,
      167–68
  in airlock, 165, *165*
  as sterilizing solution, 133, 134,
      174, 176
press, grape, 150, *151*
pressing grapes
  red, 162
  white, 150–52
Presten, Earle, 174, 192
primary fermentation, 156–62
  duration of, 157, 158–60
  end of, 161
  temperature of, 156, 157–58
  vats for, 134–36, *136*
pruning vines, 65–79, *map,* 80, *tables,*
      80–81, *82–89*
  balanced, 78–79, *table,* 81
  cane-length for, *map,* 80, *table,* 80
  cuttings from
    burning, 90–91
    fertilizing and, 109
    Geneva double curtain and, 90
    ratio of, to buds retained, 79
  delayed, 88, 93
  double, 88, 90
  in first year, *68, 69, 70*
  light, 91–93, *100*
  muscadines, 79, 87
  and overcropping, 77
  selection of best canes for, 75–77, *76*

pruning vines *(cont.)*
  in summer, 91
  timing of, 75
  trellis and, 96
punching down cap, 156–57
pyrethroids, 107

quality in wine
  and color of wine, 148
  elements of, 3–4
  and imitation, 8
  recipes and, 126
  recognizing, 8–11
  sunlight and, 181
  and timing of crushing grapes,
      127
quantity of wine to make, 30
  number of vines needed for, 32

racking
  early, 158–59
  first, after secondary fermentation,
      166, 167–68
  later, 178–79
  schedule of, 180
  second, 169
  for stuck fermentation, 155
  see also siphoning
rain, and grape harvest, 122
Ramey, Bern, 7
Ravat 51, 122
record-keeping, 185
  sample form for, 206–7
red wine
  aging of, 10–11
    duration of, 179–80
  bottles for, 187
  color of, 132, 201
  glass for, 199, *200*
  oaking, 170
  oxidation of, 128
  pH of, 149
  processes in making (summary),
      129
    on first day, 130–32
  skin contact times for, 158–59, 161
  stems in, 131

red wine *(cont.)*
TA of, 145
temperature of must of, 157–58, 159
refractometer, hand, 115
renewal spur, 75, 77–78
retronasal aroma, 203
Riesling, varieties of, 9
rim color, examination of, 201, *201*
ripeness of grapes (determining), 112–21
root lice (phylloxera), 220–21, 226–27
roots of vines, 31
allelopathic effect of, 42
depth of, 40, 41
trimming (before planting), 56, 57
rootstocks
bare-rooted, 56
trimming, 56, *57*
ordering, 55
sources for *(list),* 215–16
for problem soils, 42–43
ropiness of wine, 182
rose chafers, 224
Rosenbrand, Theo, 153

scale insects, 106
scent of wine
education in, 204
"nose" of the wine, 202–3
retronasal, 203
see also odors from processing wine
secondary fermentation, 162–69
in barrels, 169–78
temperature of, 165
sediment(s)
from aging wine, 190
from secondary fermentation, 162
see also lees
sensory evaluation of wine, 200–205
serving temperature of wine, 204 and *table,* 205
single-stake trellis, 46–47, *47, 51*
siphoning wine, *167*
in barrels, 171, *172, 174*
into bottles, 189, *189,* 190

siphoning wine *(cont.)*
finished, 178–79
from vat to carboys, 162
see also racking
site selection, for vineyard, 30, 34–45
soil considerations for, 38–45
skin(s) of grapes
and bacteria, molds, 156
and color of wine, 132, 157
contact time of, 158–60, 161
ratio of, per pound of grapes, 93
soaking on (white), 132
slope of vineyard, 35–36, *36*
and drainage, 44
smell of wine, *see* scent of wine; odors from processing wine
societies and associations, 208
sodium metabisulfite, 133, 134, 139
soil, 38–45
depth of, 41–42
percolation test of, 42
pH of, 39–40
preparation of, 43–45
problems in, 40–41
rootstocks for, 42–43
temperature of, 41, 42
types of, 38
determining, 40
in France, *table,* 39
solar radiation
and bud formation, 77
and quality of wine, 181
and ripening of grapes, 112
and vines, 36–37, *table,* 37
Southern U.S., viticulture in, 13–14
Southwestern U.S., viticulture in, 14
spacing of vines, 33–34, *table,* 35
and solar radiation, 36–37
sphinx (or hawk) moth larvae, 220
spontaneous fermentation, 160–61, 179
stakes for trellis, 51, 53
stemmer-crusher, 131–32
stems of grapes, left in must, 131–32
sterilizing solution, 133, 134
for barrels, 174, 176
stinkbugs, 224

stones in vineyard, 41
  as mulch, 63, *63*
storage conditions
  for aging wine, 180–81
  for bottled wine, 191–92
    in cellar, 195–97
    insulated area, 196–97, *197*
stuck fermentation, 155–56, 186
suckers, 67
sucrose, added to must, 142–43
sugar
  in grape juice
    added, 116, 142–44, *table,* 144
    Brix as measure of, 113–16,
      114, tables, 115–16
  in grapes
    and acid, ratio of, 112–13, *113,*
      120
    sunlight and, 36–37
  in wine (testing), 186
sulfite solution
  added to must, 136–41, *table,* 141
  added to wine, at first racking,
    167–68
  in airlock, 165, *165*
  as sterilizing solution, 133, 134,
    174
sulfur dioxide, 137, 140
summer pruning, 91
sunlight
  and bud formation, 77
  and quality of wine, 181
  and ripening of grapes, 112
  and vines, 36–37, *table,* 37

TA, *see* titratable acidity
tannin in wine
  destroyed by SO$_2$, 139
  from grape stems, 131
  reduced
    by blending, 184
    by fining, 183
tartaric acid, 116–18, 145, 147–48
taste of wine, 204–5; *see also* palate,
    education of
tax considerations, 208
teinturier grapes, 130

temperature
  for aging wine, 180–81
  for cellaring wine, 195–96
  for fermentation
    for cold stabilization, 169
    primary, 156, 157–58, 159
    secondary, 165
  of grape juice, and oxidative
    browning, 133
  of grapes, stored after picking, 127
  for serving wine, 204 and *table,*
    205
  of soil in vineyard, 41, 42
thinning flower clusters, 91–94, *94,*
    104
  benefits of, 91–92, 93–94, 104
  timing of, 92–93
three-wire trellis, 49, *49,* 51
  bilateral training on, *102*
thrips, 223
Thuricide (biological pest control),
    105
titratable acidity (TA), 117–18
  adjusting, 145–47
  and Brix (ratio of), 120
  and pH, 147–48
topping up vessels
  barrel, 171, 174–75
  carboy, *165*
trace elements, deficiency of, *table,*
    110
training systems for vines
  changing, to manage vine vigor, 91
  and pruning methods, 69
  trellises for, 46–50, *47, 49, table,*
    51, *95–103*
traps for pests, 106, 238, *239*
"travel sickness" of wine, 181
treading grapes, 131
trellises, 45–55
  construction of, *52*
    materials for, 50–53
    method for, 54–55
    tools for, 54
  systems of, 46–50, *47, 49, table,*
    51, *95–103*
trench for planting vines, 44

trunks, multiple, 72, *72*
T-trellis (Geneva double curtain
    trellis), 49, *49,* 50, 51, *100*
    and cane cuttings (weight of), 90
Tudal, Arnold, 47, 64, 153, 159
Turkington, Ross, 90
two-wire trellis, 48–49, *49, 51, 52*
tying canes to wires, 71, *71*

umbrella training systems
    Hudson River, *99*
    Kniffen, *101*

vacuum in carboy, and airlock, 165,
    166
varieties of grapes/vines
    for California, *tables,* 26–27
    climate and, 11, 12–15, 17, 74
    processed singly, 130
    regional recommendations for,
        table, 20–23
    selection of, 1–17, *tables,* 18–27
    tasting *(list),* 9
vats, for primary fermentation,
    134–36, *136,* 151
vegetative growth, vs. fruit
    production, 72–73, 78–79
véraison, 65, 112
vertical-cordon training, single stake
    for, 46, 47, *47, 95*
vibrations, and aging wine, 181
vine(s)
    "bleeding" of, 87
    diseases of, 228–40
        burning cane cuttings to avoid,
            90–91
        genetic engineering and, 14–15
    growing-process of, 65–67, *66–67*
    injury to, 73, 74, 123
    lateral shoots on, 67, *67*
    number needed for *x* gallons of
        wine, 32
    ordering, 55
        sources for (list), 215–16
    parts of, *31*
    pests and, 104–8, 217–27, 237–39
    planting, 56–57, *58*

vine(s) *(cont.)*
    planting *(cont.)*
        depth of, 57, *58*
        soil preparation for, 43–45
    pruning, 65–79, *map,* 80, *tables,*
        80–81, *82–89*
        balanced, 78–79, *table,* 81
        cane-length, *map,* 80, *table,* 80
        cuttings from, 79, 90–91, 109
        delayed, 88, 93
        double, 88, 90
        in first year, *68, 69, 70*
        light, 91–93, *100*
        muscadines, 79, 87
        and overcropping, 77
        selection of best canes for,
            75–77, *76*
        in summer, 91
        timing of, 75
        trellis and, 96
    roots of, 31
        allelopathic effect of, 42
        depth of, 40, 41
        trimming (before planting), 56,
            57
    selection of, 1–17, *tables,* 18–27
    spacing of, 33–34, *table,* 35
        and solar radiation, 36–37
    sunlight and, 36–37, *table,* 37
    training systems for
        changing, to manage vine vigor,
            91
        and pruning methods, 69
        trellises for, 46–50, *47, 49, table,*
            51, *95–103*
    trellises for, 45–55
        construction of, 50–55, *52*
        systems of, 46–50, *47, 49, table,*
            51, *95–103*
    trench for, 44
    tying to wires, 71, *71*
    varieties of, 5–7
        in California, *tables,* 26–27
        climate and, 11, 12–15, 17, 74
        regional recommendations for,
            table, 20–23
    vigor of (managing), 91, 92

vine(s) *(cont.)*
water and, 13
watering, 59, 64–65
vinegar, threat of, 161
vineyard
cultivating, 62
drainage in, 40, 42, 44–45
managing rows and aisles of,
60–65, *61*
planting, 56–57, *58*
depth of, 57, *58*
soil preparation for, 43–45
site selection for, 30, 34–45
size of (calculating), 32–33
slope of, 35–36, *36*
soil of, 38–45
spacing of vines in, 33–34, *table,* 35
and solar radiation, 36–37
tax rules on, 208
trellises for, 45–55
construction of, 50–55, *52*
systems of, 46–50, *47, 49, table,*
51, *95–103*
watering, 59, 64–65
weeds in, 61, 62, 91
wind and, 45, 74
vinifera, 5–6
on Eastern seaboard, 12–13
genetic engineering and, 14–15
multiple trunking of, *72*
training systems for, 69
varieties of *(list),* 9
in California, *table,* 26–27
vin nouveau, 163, 179
vintage, chart of, 10
viruses, and grapevines, 236–37
viticultural areas (BATF-designated),
16–17
list of, 18–19
viticulture, *see* California, viticulture
in; Eastern U.S., viticulture in;
French viticulture; Midwestern
U.S., viticulture in; Southern
U.S., viticulture in;
Southwestern U.S., viticulture
in; West coast of U.S.,
viticulture in

Vitis labrusca, 5
Vitis vinifera, see vinifera

Wagner, Bill, 3
Walthari method, 138
washing soda, for cleaning barrel,
176
water
surplus of, 91
and vine-growing, 13
and winter injury to vines, 74
watering vines
irrigation, 64–65
newly planted vines, 59
weather, and harvesting grapes,
122–23
Weaver, Robert, 3–4
weeds in vineyard, 61, 62, 91
weight of cane cuttings
and buds retained, 79
fertilizing and, 109
and Geneva double curtain, 90
West coast of U.S., viticulture in, 14;
see also California, viticulture
in
western grapeleaf skeletonizer, 219
whiskey barrels, as vats, 135
white flies, 106
white wine
aging, 180
bottles for, 187
crushing grapes for, 132–33
de-stemming grapes for, 132, 133
glass for, 199, *200*
oxidation of, 128
pH of, 149
pressing, 150–52
primary fermentation ends for, 161
processes in making (summary),
129
soaking on the skins, 132
sulfite added to, 140
TA of, 145
temperature of must of, 157–58
transferred from vat to carboy, 162
wildflowers, in aisles of vineyard, 62
wild grapes, 13

wild yeasts, 136–37, 153
wind, 45
 and winter injury to vines, 74
wine
 color of, 200–201
  browning, oxidative, 130
  pH and, 148–49
  from skins of grapes, 132, 157
  storage temperature and, 195
 disorders of, 181–82
 education in, 8–11, 204
 oxidation of
  from bellows effect (in storage), 196
  sulfite vs., 136
  of white vs. red wine, 128, 130
 quality of, 3–4, 126
 quantity to make, 30
  number of vines needed for, 32
 sensory evaluation of, 200–205
Winealyzer, 204
Wine & The People, Berkeley, Calif., 127
wine bottles
 corking, 190–92, *191*
 filling, 189, *189*, 190
 indentation in, 187, *187*, 188
 labeling, 193–94
 types of, 187, *187*, 188

wineglasses, 199, *200*
winemaking, *table*, xxv–xxviii, 129
 as art, 2, 157
 bibliography of, 210–11
 cleanliness in, 133–34
 first day's procedures, 130–33
  summary of, 149
 philology of, 5, 6–7
 quantity of, 30
 recipes for, 126
winterkill, 73, 74, 123
 double pruning and, 90
wire for trellis, 53
 tying canes to, 71, *71*
Wirevise tensioners, *52, 53*
Wu, Gary, 170–71

yeast(s), wild, 136–37, 153
yeast(s), for wine
 added to grape juice, 152–53
 and alcohol concentration, 137
 sources of *(list)*, 213–14
 and stuck fermentation, 155–56
 and sugar, 143
 types of, 153–55
yield of fruit, vs. vegetative growth, 72–73, 78–79
young wine (drinking), 179, 180
Yquem, Château d', 4